P₁
THE ULT

I was unable to put this book down. It is so beautiful and sensitively written. The stories are incredible, and I was impressed by the courage and generosity of the contributors. It brought tears to my eyes. The book gives so much hope without having to spell out God, or trying to convert anyone.

Alamail P. France, Yoga Teacher

In these inspirational tales of de-addiction, the author uses true stories of people she has encountered to narrate the 'highs' and lows of addiction. The book is an account of people who had hit a dead end, and turned towards spirituality to bail them out of the mess their personal lives were in. In a world ruled by technology and materialism, the book deals with belief and faith, which act as a guiding light for those groping in the dark for answers to life's problems. Most of the people featured are Westerners, who came to Indian shores to find answers in 'Eastern spirituality'. Jenny is a devotee of Sathya Sai Baba, and has drawn inspiration from her spiritual master.

Deccan Herald, India May 2004

The book is fantastic! It's not just that the stories are heart-rending and inspirational, but you have managed to convey the work involved and the relationship with the Power necessary.

Orange Trevillion UK, Reflexologist, Reiki Master and Hotelier

I have been in General Practice for twenty-five years. All who have tried to help people recover from addiction will know that this is a tremendously difficult and demanding task. This book shows us another way to achieve our aims. Providing we keep an open mind, all roads that lead to the destination should be explored. There are lessons for us all to learn, and much on which to reflect in this book. I commend reading it to all involved in traditional allopathic medicine, as a stimulating, thought provoking experience.

Dr Adam Price FRCGP, UK, General Physician

Mine is one of the stories in this book. I was addicted to cocaine and meth amphetamine, going to jail when I was twenty. That's where I received two chapters of *The Ultimate High* which Mom found on the Internet and printed out. It affected me a lot. I found that others had the same problems or worse, and they got help with a Higher Power. I realised that there is hope, and I don't use drugs now.

Vikram, Los Angeles

Thank you! We loved the book - a really valuable tool for those people in need.

F.D., Melbourne, Australia, Counsellor

THE ULTIMATE HIGH

Journeys from
Addiction to Recovery
with Sai Baba

Jenny Gaze

Published by Jennifer Gaze

Copyright © Jennifer Gaze 2013

www.jennygaze.com

All rights reserved. No part of this publication may be reproduced, stored in a retrieval system or transmitted in any form or by any means electronic, mechanical, photocopying, recording or otherwise, without the prior written permission of the author.

First published 2003 in India (Sai Towers Publishing)
2nd Edition 2005
3rd edition, 2013

ISBN: 978-1484194966

Cover painting 'The Light' by Kim Wedell
Author cover photo: Roberto Piccini
Cover and Book Design: Candescent Press

Also by Jenny Gaze

Begging for Change . . . An Uplifting Story of Love in Action
(2007)

And the sequel

The Power of Love . . . Changes Everything
(2012)

www.jennygaze.com

Dedication

To all whose lives are touched by addiction,

And to those beautiful souls who courageously and honestly opened their hearts and shared their stories.

And to Sathya Sai Baba,

Who guided these and countless others out of the chaos of addiction, and sent these eighteen people to cross my path at exactly the right time for the evolution of this book.

Contents

Foreword	i
Preface	v
Introduction: How This Book Came About	1
1. Michael D's Story: THE ULTIMATE HIGH	11
2. Vimansa's Story: PIERCING THE VEIL	31
3. Dave's Story: SUPERMAN	43
4. Grace's Story: 'WHAT'S IT LIKE IN HEAVEN?'	55
5. Hilary's Story: THE PERILS OF NIGHT DUTY	71
6. Rajesh's Story: CULTURE SHOCK	75
7. Kay's Story: IN THE PINK	93
8. Carl's Story: 'ROLLERCOASTER'	113
9. Ruth's Story: 'GO TO AA OR DIE'	129
10. Eddie's Story: SWITCHING OFF	145
11. Mui's Story: A MOMENT OF CONSCIENCE	149
12. Cherie's Story: NOWHERE TO HIDE	167
13: Marcel's Story: CEILING ON DESIRES	177
14: Carols' Story: HUNGRY FOR LOVE	191
15: Manou's Story: 'I NEED TO DECIDE'	205
16. Jim's Story: DREAM ON	221
17. Jenny's Story: BEAM ME UP	239
18: Vikram's Story: ROCK BOTTOM?	261
Epilogue: The Road to Recovery	273

Foreword

The Ultimate High shows the power of the spiritual journey in healing destructive addictive behaviour. Each story reflects the anguish and pain of addiction and the unending complexity such damaging behaviour creates. Each person is healed by a common link in the form of Sathya Sai Baba – a guru residing in India. Prior to meeting with him most had no interest in spirituality. In fact, most were defiant about anything involving religion of any sort. His love and power touched each person, acting as the primary conduit for their healing. Many were involved in therapeutic modalities, AA and the like, depending on the form of addiction. Some had managed to temporarily cure their addiction only to be drawn back time and again.

The struggle each experienced is described so openly and truthfully that we cannot help but feel the suffering of addiction. As their journey unfolds toward healing, we are shown the tremendous power of devotion and prayer, and the unthinkable miracles that can occur even when there is no initial faith! We see how people who would not ordinarily be drawn toward anything vaguely spiritual are inevitably pulled toward opening their heart, and following "higher order" thinking and behaving. Their lives are transformed forever.

How can we measure this type of situation, this type of spiritual relationship, in terms of therapeutic efficacy? Jenny shows how the ineffable guru-disciple relationship has produced the power to nullify the addictive impulse. This book is eye-opening and inspiring. It begs the question in terms of what we do and don't know about psychological and behavioural healing, for herein is proven that healing can occur outside the normal bounds of our Western, rational thinking.

Penny Fenner *Psychologist, Leadership Coach, Author*
Essential Wisdom Teachings – The Way to Inner Peace*,*
and Director, Skilful Action, Melbourne, Australia

www.skilfulaction.com

*'Thinking about sense objects will attach you to sense objects,
Grow attached and you become addicted
Thwart your addiction and it turns to anger,
Be angry and you confuse your mind,
Confuse your mind and you forget the lesson of experience,
Forget experience and you lose discrimination,
Lose discrimination and you lose life's only purpose.'*

Bhagavad Gita Ch 2 Vs 62, 63

Preface

Most stories in this book date from around 2003. Soon after publication of *The Ultimate High* several of us who feature in these pages organised a meeting on addiction in Puttaparthi, a small town in India, home of the ashram of Sathya Sai Baba. Eighteen people attended. One was Carl, who had stopped injecting cocaine only days before, and his story was added to the book in 2005. Following that meeting, an **Alcoholics Anonymous** group was started in the town. People have been surprised to find it there, and relieved to be able to talk freely about their problems in a place where they thought everyone was too holy or spiritual to have been down that road! Of course that is another delusion. In 2013 *the group continues*, and welcomes people with *any* addiction.

Also I met Vikram from the US, and added his story of addiction to crystal meth in 2005. He had just come out of prison when we met, and I respect him and his family for having the courage to talk so openly. Drug abuse is not uncommon in the Indian community in Western countries, but is considered deeply shameful and is well hidden, which only helps it to continue.

There have been many heart-warming responses to *The Ultimate High* but I will share just one. In March 2004, while in India, I heard an inner voice which said, "*This book must go to Russia.*" I thought maybe it was my imagination, but I knew I must be vigilant. I knew no Russians, let alone translators or publishers. Nothing happened, and I returned home to the UK. A few months later I was giving a talk on the book in England. Afterwards, a woman with a strong accent said, "Thank you so much, *this book must go to Russia.*" I went cold. It turned out that she was involved in publishing and translating books in Russia. I met her and the publisher in November 2004 in India. They have now published this book in Russian. Consciousness arranges things perfectly; we just have to be alert and follow the leads.

Now in 2013, *ten years later*, I contacted as many as I could of the contributors, some by email and some I ran into with much synchronicity going on. Some inevitably I have lost touch with. It has been good to re-connect with them after all this time, and fourteen brief updates have been added on their current lives, so you will find out if they are still clean and sober. Recovery and healing is a great blessing, and I pray that these stories may be of help, and inspirational to those affected by addiction.

God bless you!
With love, Jenny Gaze, January 2013

Introduction

How This Book Came About

A man having a book in his hands reads one page and turns it over, goes to the next page, reads that, turns and so on. It is the book that is being turned over, the pages that are revolving, not he. He is where he is always; even so with regard to the Soul. The whole of nature is that book which the Soul is reading. Each life is one page of that book; and that read it is turned over until the whole of the book is finished, and the Soul becomes perfect, having got all the experiences of nature. Yet at the same time it never moved, nor came nor went; it was only gathering experiences.

- Swami Vivekananda

The experience of addiction is written in the pages of the lives of many on the planet at this time. The author is one of them. My drugs were cannabis and tobacco. Like the others in this book, I was fortunate to escape from the coils of compulsion, and start to rebuild my life. Many are not so blessed. They never escape and may suffer from physical/mental illness, broken family, imprisonment, and even death as a direct consequence. In 1999 the son of a close friend died from a heroin overdose. He was twenty-four, and had become schizophrenic due to drug use. I had known him since he was a child. It inspired in me an intense prayer for all those caught in the trap of addiction, especially young people, and offering my help if there was *anything* I could do. It seemed to me that drugs were destroying part of a generation. Maybe that's how this book came about.

Each chapter tells the story of a person who has overcome addiction and changed their life. Whether it was heroin, cannabis, food or prescription drugs, the effects were devastating. The common factor in these stories is that a turnaround came when they reached a point that the only place to turn was to a 'Higher Power' . . . though not all believed in God at the time. Some names have been changed, some are real, and like all personal dramas, they are on-going. The healing process can be long, but once it is turned over to a Higher Consciousness, not simply done through our own will power, then miracles and changes happen, as you will read.

It doesn't matter in what form you see your Higher Power. Turn to that source in any form, or as Consciousness, or Light, and help will come. Healing of addictions is possible through prayer to 'God' to use a commonly used term. It's a word a lot of addicts are uncomfortable with . . . *I know I was* . . . even though they may be drawn to spirituality. Now I see it as synonymous with the consciousness of pure love. Deep down is that not what we are all looking for? Maybe addiction is a spiritual disease. If so it requires spiritual medicine.

There are many paths to the divine, and to enlightenment. *I am definitely not saying there is only one way.* As mine is with my teacher, Sathya Sai Baba, these stories happen to involve his help, grace and intervention. And his medicine is strong! So I will give a brief account of his life. Although Sai Baba left his body in April 2011, his consciousness is still here to answer prayers, and miracles still happen all the time. Like Jesus, Buddha, Krishna and many others, he is not restricted to a mortal body.

He was born in 1926 in Puttaparthi, a remote village in South India. In childhood he performed miracles, and was revered and sometimes feared by other villagers, children and his teachers. At the age of fourteen, he announced that he was the reincarnation of Shirdi Sai Baba, a saint who died in 1918. He declared that he was ready to begin his mission. Since then millions from all over the world have come to have his *darshan* (sight of a holy being) and believe him to be an Avatar (divine incarnation) with the characteristics of omniscience, omnipotence and omnipresence. Daily he performed miracles as Jesus did, healing the sick, raising the dead and above all pouring out unlimited unconditional love, which can transmute us gradually from lead to gold. The transformation he creates in people's lives may be the greatest miracle.

He never stopped serving humanity, appearing before huge crowds almost to the end of his life, giving *darshan* twice a day for most of his eighty-five years. He built free hospitals, schools and universities, and provided clean drinking water to thousands of villages and towns, including Chennai (Madras). He expounds the ancient Vedantic teachings of India with simplicity and clarity. Mostly Sai Baba lived in his ashram Prashanti Nilayam, Abode of Highest Peace. He did not seek publicity, or ask for money.

This is a thumbnail sketch. To me he is a magnet of pure love, and in his presence I am gradually being purified and refined, until the essence we all are will shine out unimpeded one day. He was a great being alive in our times. If one prays to Jesus, Allah, Mohammed, Buddha or any of the great ones, succour and relief will come. *Consciousness cannot be limited to one form. Baba says that we are all divine.* The only difference between him and us is that he was living consciously in that experience, and as yet we are not. We are gods . . . we just don't know it.

Over the years I heard many inspiring stories of how Sai Baba helped people overcome various addictions and changed their lives. The idea to collect them grew and finally became so strong that I wrote a letter to Sai Baba (Swami) asking him to take it if it was my job to write a book on this subject, and to ignore it if it was a mere fantasy of my ego. Then I carried it with me to *darshan,* amongst the crowds of tens of thousands, for six days. I was never able to get anywhere near him. So I began to think I should drop the idea. There was some relief, as I had got to the point where I didn't want him to take the letter, as it seemed such an overwhelming task.

So on the sixth night I looked at Baba's picture before I went to sleep, and told him that I would bring the letter for one more day. If he didn't take it, I would forget the whole thing. Next morning I found myself at the front, sitting in a place he was likely to come. Baba walked past on the *other* side of the aisle, seeming to avoid me. Then he swung round, making a beeline for me, looked deeply into my eyes, took the outstretched letter, and sweetly asked me where I come from. I was shocked. It was the first time he had spoken to me in seven years. He totally filled me with energy, and I shed tears of bliss. Immediately after *darshan*, I told a woman who witnessed this about the contents of the letter, and later that day she introduced me to a recovering heroin addict willing to talk about his experience. From then on the stories flowed in. Baba showed he had blessed the writing of this book.

It's my belief that addiction is so powerful, that it is almost impossible to overcome without spiritual intervention. Addictions are massively powerful entities. Each addictive substance, let's say alcohol, has its own massive thought-form in the ethers made up of every thought drinkers ever had about needing a drink. This forms a powerful negative entity, and when the person has the thought, *'I need a drink'*, he immediately taps into that thought-form and it exerts tremendous control over him. It is far stronger than he is. That is why addictions are so hard to overcome. They are extremely negative subtle energies, which are exerting increasing control over the population of the planet. To stand alone with one's will power against the might of such a force is too hard. We have to turn to a Higher Power in whatever way we conceive that word. Only the Divine can almost surgically remove those thoughts that tune us in to the wavelength of the addictive substance.

Addiction is deviously clever. Most of the addicts I have met have been highly sensitive people, with spiritual inclinations. I remember asking my fourteen-year-old son why he smoked marijuana. Quick as a flash he replied, "*To expand my consciousness.*" Marijuana can make you believe that, but maybe it's not that simple. Although medical cannabis, legal in the US, is proven beneficial in the treatment of diseases such as Glaucoma, AIDS, Cancer, Lyme Disease, chronic pain and nausea . . . especially the high CBD/low THC hybrid . . . for people who become psychologically dependent, it can be a destructive addiction. Children and young adults without full neo-cortical development are highly susceptible to its pitfalls. However, spiritual support can extricate us from the grip of this powerful substance. The most successful drug recovery programme is **The Twelve Steps**, which has been going strong since the 1930's. It works because it is based on spiritual principles, and is not about profit. It resonates with the teachings of all the great scriptures. Anything based on Truth will stand the test of time. There is no copyright or marketing needed on the Bible, the Bhagavad Gita, the Koran, or other holy books.

All these stories come from people living in Western culture, where alienation from the spirit within and loneliness are widespread. Greed and consumerism have replaced spirituality, and there is disillusionment with the Church. Television, money and sex seem to have become the gods. High divorce rates and family breakdown means traumatised children. Many people nowadays have never known a mother's love, or that of a father. This is as important for a healthy emotional life as mother's milk is to the physical. When one has received little love as a child it is hard to love oneself and others.

Only when there is lack of self-love does one subject body and mind to harmful substances, a form of self-destruction. Many people live in isolation with little or no family. The extended family is becoming a thing of the past in the Western countries. One of the worst epidemics in the West is loneliness. Another is drugs and alcohol. Anti-depressants and tranquilizers are big business, and popping pills, drinking or taking drugs is the only way that many know how to deal with their empty lives.

We often can't define it, but feel this emptiness. Drugs, alcohol, sex, food, TV and a host of other things are temporary ways to fill the void. It's a quick fix, but the longing doesn't go away. How many adults and children need their daily fix of television for several hours a day? How much brainwashing goes on? How many kids do their homework with this constant background babble? How much creativity is replaced by mindless fixation on the box? How many families still sit around the meal table and talk to each other?

The Following Statistics are from 2003:

From The National Council on Alcohol and Drug Dependence:

In the field, many workers believe that addiction is the number one health and social problem in the world today, and a major cause of most other societal problems.

An estimated 18 million Americans have alcohol problems. An estimated 6 million have drug problems.

This does not include allopathic and prescription drugs. On top of these figures it is estimated that 80% of the population, particularly women, regularly use mood-altering drugs such as Valium.

Alcohol and drug abuse costs the American economy an estimated $276 billion per year in lost productivity, health care expenditure, crime, motor crashes and other conditions.

Total cost of alcohol use by youth, including traffic crashes, violent crime, burns, drowning, suicide attempts, foetal alcohol syndrome, alcohol poisoning and treatment is more than $58 billion a year. Report for **US Department of Justice, Office of Juvenile Delinquent Prevention 1999.**

Untreated addiction is more expensive than heart disease, diabetes and cancer combined.

Side effects of pharmaceutical drugs kill more Americans every year than WW2 and the Vietnam War combined.

In the US a quarter of all emergency room admissions, one third of all suicides, and more than half of all homicides and incidents of domestic violence are alcohol related.

Smoking statistics taken from ASH… Action on Smoking and Health UK, 2003:

There are 4000 chemicals in cigarette smoke.

Smoking causes 50 different illnesses, 25 of which can be fatal.

More than 17,000 children under 5 in UK are hospitalized each year because of their parent's smoking.

Smoking causes 30% of all cancer deaths. It causes 90% of lung cancer deaths, 17% of deaths from heart disease, and 80% of deaths from bronchitis and emphysema.

100 million people died from smoking tobacco in the twentieth century.

That was ten years ago, and shocking. However, as more people are turning towards spirituality and seeking *'something'*, there is a positive change going on. A spiritual awareness is growing. Smoking is now banned in public places in many countries, and less people are smoking. Despite what appears in the media, UK statistics show that homicide, assault, burglary and other crime figures, many of them drug/alcohol related, are falling *significantly* in the last ten years. This is reflected in many countries, but is little reported. Public perception is that crime and addiction is getting worse, due to selective reporting of bad news in the media. This is not the truth.

Most of us are addicted to something, whether it is coffee, sugar, heroin or exercise. Many have multiple addictions. Every person has an interesting story . . . some dramatic, some painful, some "successful" in terms of wealth. We carry this history and tend to identify with it as who we are. The stories in this book are about addictions, but each person here is in the process of going *beyond* their story, to awareness of '*Who they really are*', the Nameless, beyond mind or words. The stories themselves are not important unless they can help others. What *is* important is seeing that we can go beyond them and escape, not into some fantasy world, but into true freedom. This is the spiritual path.

However fast you run you cannot catch it,
on plain or mountain,
The morning shadow moves in front of you.
Or the shadow may pursue you and you cannot escape from it.
This is the nature of desire.
You may pursue it, or it may pursue you,
But you cannot overcome it or catch it.
Desire is an insubstantial shadow.
But turn desire inward towards spiritual treasure,
Then it yields substantial results.

- Sathya Sai Baba

1

The Ultimate High

Man always tries to seek happiness by trying to satisfy his desires. If a desire is fulfilled he feels happy, and when it is not, he feels grief. But the trouble is desire is a bonfire that burns with great fury asking for more fuel. One desire leads to ten and man exhausts himself trying to satisfy the demands of his desire. He has to be turned back from the path of never ending desire to the path of inner contentment and joy.

- Sai Baba

I met Michael in 1998 when travelling alone, feeling lost in America. A friend gave me his number, so I plucked up courage to phone this man I'd seen in videos, talking in his motor mouth, over the top style. He was sweet and welcoming, offering to show me round Los Angeles. I was looking out for him at the bus station, and suddenly there he was, a vibrant man with long neat dreadlocks and a huge smile. He was the perfect host, a vital, creative, happy man. I remember his frequent utterance as we walked around LA, as if caught in deep appreciation of life, "*God is great!*" Michael is a storyteller by trade. He is a black American, born in 1950 in Chicago.

Michael D's story: In August 1978 I was twenty-seven years old, living in Chicago, and among other things I was a drug dealer. I remember it was one of those cases of being careful what you wish for, as you might get it. At the time I was wishing I could have a really intense kind of high. One day a friend came by and said, "I've got something you're going to love." At the time it was called freebase, long before it was called crack. So he cooked up some cocaine, and I remember taking that first hit. It was *fantastic*! Whoa, it was a very intense rush. It didn't last long, but it was orgasmic in nature. I thought, "*Wow this is great*!" He showed me how to make it, and I started doing it every now and then. But you're always chasing that first hit, and by December I was doing it on a regular basis, and it started to become more and more intense.

I was at school at the time, studying to be an electrical engineer, and I was also working as a technician. I had a girlfriend, and life was okay. But it soon got to the point where everything started deteriorating. I'd be driving at 70 mph on the expressway, steering the car with my knees, so my hands were free to hit the pipe as I was on my way to work. I remember virtually ignoring my girlfriend. The pipe became everything to me. I also stopped studying. One day at school we had a quiz, and when I went to think nothing happened. My mind was a total blank. I got up, walked out of the classroom, and never went to school again. Then I stopped showing up for work. All of these things were interfering with my getting high. It had become my sole reason for living.

I had flunked out of school and stopped working, but I was still dealing, so I had access to the drugs, and turned other friends of mine on. I always kept the equipment for the freebasing around, because someone would invariably need the chemicals at one in the morning, or any time of the night. I'd be waiting by my phone if I'd run out of cocaine. One of my friends would call, asking if I had the chemicals, and I'd wait for them to come by so I could smoke and smoke and smoke some more.

A couple of incidents come to mind that illustrate just how crazy I was. One time I'd gone by a friend of mine, and I was trying to turn him and his wife on to it. They didn't care for it and that was fine, as there was more for *me* to smoke. I remember smoking *so* much, and drinking a lot of ginseng tea. It was a cold Chicago day, and I was so hyped up and wired, that I couldn't keep still. I left my friends and couldn't sit still in my car. I was burning up, so I took off my jacket and sweater and was running around the car, so that my heart would slow down enough so I could sit inside. Finally I could get into the car, but I was still wired and had the windows rolled down. I set off and drove with my head hanging out of the car on the expressway. The temperature was thirty below zero. When I walked into my brother's place I remember pacing back and forth, my eyes bulging out of my head, wanting my heart to slow down . . . so I could take another hit from the pipe.

Another time a friend of mine came by and had cocaine of very poor quality. He wanted me to check it out. He left me half a gram. I was about to run out of my good stuff, so all I had left was this garbage. I knew it wouldn't cook up, so I went through this cocaine psychosis where everything white and speckled looks like cocaine. I badly wanted a hit, so I searched madly for any little particle, crawling around the floor, gathering all this stuff together, putting it with the rest and trying to make it cook up. It was no good. I was so mad at my friend that I wanted to kill him! Fortunately I didn't see him for several days.

This went on for a year becoming more and more intense, and I remember people panicking around me. You could see my heart pounding against my chest, and I'd pace back and forth tearing at my hair. For me it wasn't an issue of fearing I'd die, but of hoping my heart would slow down enough so I could take another hit *before* I died. That was how intense the addiction was.

One day I went to a head shop I knew to get the chemicals I needed to make freebase. The guy asked if I wanted to cook some stuff up. "Oh, yeah!" I said. He said, "Look, I've got a way to do it that will knock your socks off." I'm thinking, "WHAT? Knock *my* socks off?" At this point in time I was taking half a gram of good quality cocaine in one hit. After he closed the shop we went back to his place, and he cooked it up. I took a hit, and started rushing like I'd never rushed before. You're always chasing that first hit, but this time I caught up with it and it caught up with me. It was so intense, and I was rushing so fast, that for the first time I got scared and didn't even finish it. My heart was racing, my mind was racing, and I felt I was going to explode. I was afraid to move or blink, and sat on a stool for at least an hour, scared to move. The guy was in a state of mild panic, thinking that I was getting ready to die. I sat there till I was able to move, and *I didn't want it anymore.*

But he made me take some away with me. Even though I was scared, I had this reflex to do it again. But I could no longer hit the pipe with the same intensity. I tried a couple more times, but just couldn't do it anymore. Suddenly I realised all the things that had happened. My girlfriend and I had split up, I'd left school and my job, and for this whole year I'd been in a fog. I'd put aside savings bonds for my daughter and had smoked all that up, along with the rest of my savings. *I woke up.* When I finally came to, I was desperate and depressed, and didn't know what the heck I was going to do. But I was really very fortunate. A lot of my friends had got into much worse states than me, one guy losing over $100,000 in six months, going from a plush apartment to living on the streets.

I was now twenty-eight, and had been through the worst period of my life going through that madness. Prior to that I had smoked marijuana, and took cocaine, opium and LSD. Though I liked them, I wasn't really addicted to any of those things. I liked smoking herbs, but I wasn't going to *kill* anybody over it, or give up my last dime for a tab of LSD. With freebase, I learned what true addiction was.

I contemplated re-enlisting in the army, drove to the recruiting office, and had my hand on the door handle. Then something stopped me and I sat down on the kerb in front of the office. I thought, 'There must be something else.' I went home and began going through a major shift. All of a sudden I became a health nut. I started fasting, taking vitamins and herbs, and got into spiritual and metaphysical things. I had been raised a Catholic. Then in the late sixties, after some political involvement, I rejected religion altogether feeling it was all hypocrisy, and I was somewhere between an atheist and an agnostic. Now health and metaphysics became an obsession . . . and when I'm getting into things, I read. Not only was I reading everything I could about health issues, I went to school and studied Oriental Medicine. Interestingly enough, I became an acupuncturist whose specialty was detoxing people from drugs . . . and I was still a drug dealer at the time. I hadn't given up drugs totally, but stayed away from the pipe, and had no more interest in it. Occasionally I'd toot cocaine, but it wasn't interesting, in fact stimulants no longer had the same effect. Even coffee would make me go to sleep.

Looking back, I can see that there was a Divine hand looking after me. For example, I had an experience with angel dust a little before getting involved with the pipe. This is a stimulant and hallucinogenic based on elephant tranquillizer. My girlfriend and I were sitting around watching television, and I was smoking a joint with angel dust. Suddenly I was watching myself on TV, watching myself on TV in an infinite projection. For the next twelve hours I had this intense, horrific experience, where my eyes were open, but I didn't see this world. And in the midst of all that, there was a part of me that was totally unaffected, witnessing everything that was going on. Physically and mentally I was gone, like a blithering idiot. I couldn't sit up and could only slur a few words. But some part of me was just observing this, and when I got over the effect of the drug I never forgot that. Years later, when I had met Sai Baba and got into spiritual things, I was reading about witness consciousness, and I knew that's what I had experienced. I can look back at all these incidents in my life and see how there was an unseen hand that said, "Okay, that's enough of this," and guided me to end that insanity.

So now I was open to things in which I'd had no interest. I had a good friend who was into all kinds of spiritual stuff. One Saturday afternoon, she took me to see a psychic. There were about forty people in the meeting hall, listening to this man speaking about metaphysics. I was sitting there thinking that this was a bunch of nonsense, and what was I doing here? People were asking questions about past lives and

Atlantis, all stuff I'd never heard about before. I thought these people were nuts; but I sat and listened. I'd just had this intense year on the pipe, and had a lot of questions on my mind about the meaning of life, and what I needed to do. All of a sudden, I became aware that as this man was talking, he was answering my questions. He used words and phrases that dealt *directly* with the things that were on my mind. So in the midst of my scepticism I was somewhat intrigued.

After the meeting he asked people to come up for psychic healing. I was still thinking that this was too much nonsense, but my friend insisted that I go up. As I sat waiting for the healing, watching him say something to each person and move his hands around, I was thinking, 'Oh my God, they're going to come in here with a butterfly net and take us all away to a loony bin.' When he came to me he said, "*You are outside of your body and I'm going to bring you back.*" Then he mumbled something and moved his hands. All of a sudden there was a jolt, and I felt this surge of energy. I was jarred, as if someone had hit me in the back and thrust me mildly forward, and I felt energy surging through my body. I thought, 'Wow, what the hell was that?'

After this my friend and I went back to my place, talked a bit, then she left. I'd been tired, due to incorrect procedures during a fast I'd just finished. It was eight o'clock and I lay down and went to sleep. Some friends were having a party that evening, and I'd contemplated whether to go or not. But I was exhausted and didn't think I'd make it. Then I woke up at 10.30pm, full of energy. I wasn't even aware of it at first, but I started getting ready to go to the party. In the middle of brushing my teeth I realised I felt great. So off I went, and I was the *life* of the party. During the fast I hadn't been getting high, so when I started smoking herbs I was ripped out of my mind. I stayed till four in the morning. When I left the hostess gave me my jacket. As I passed it from my left hand to my right, it ended up on the floor. I picked it up and staggered out to the car. The woman was concerned about me driving in that state and called out for me to be careful.

I got into the car, sat down, and when the door closed my high was *gone*. My head was so clear I was shocked. The high was just . . . poof . . . it was gone. I wondered what the hell happened. And I had this surge of energy like I had before the party. I drove through the suburbs of Chicago, and when I got home felt so energised I wanted to go for a ride on my bicycle. I went out in the rain feeling great. I thought this must have something to do with this dude that I met yesterday.

In 1982 I was planning a trip around the world. I was an acupuncturist at the time, and was intending to take an acupuncture course in Sri Lanka. Then I was going to do some goofing off, and planned to be away for a year. So I went back to this psychic guy for a reading, to see if I was going to be able to pull this trip off. I went into his office and first he asked me what I did for a living. I was an acupuncturist, but it wasn't my *main* source of income; drug dealing was. I was trying to be coy about what I was doing, and every time I tried to do that, he'd ask me another question indicating that he knew. Finally I told him the truth.

He said, "Okay fine, I know, so don't bullshit me." He told me that yes, I was going to do this trip and have a phenomenal experience. He said that I would have an encounter that would give me a grip on the meaning of life and death. He told me not to worry about money because it would come to me. Right after that, money started falling from the skies. I was a dealer and was making money, but now I started *finding* money. I went through an old shirt and found $700 stuffed in the pocket, shook out a towel and money fell out. People would call me up and ask if they could loan me money. It was amazing. I went through this intense period of making money hand over fist, and the trip became a reality.

The main impetus for the trip was to take an acupuncture course in Sri Lanka. Another purpose was to visit some of the spiritual and degenerate places of the world, with a heavy emphasis on the latter. So in 1982 I travelled to Hawaii, Beijing, Hong Kong, Bali and Thailand; and as I was travelling little chinks were appearing in the armour I had built up against spirituality. It started to seep in. I read ***Autobiography of a Yogi*** by Yogananda, and found it was deep stuff. Previously, if God came up in any conversation, I would leave the room. If it happened in my apartment I would ask them to take it someplace else. Things were changing.

I took the acupuncture course in Sri Lanka, and met a Swedish woman there who was a devotee of Sathya Sai Baba, an Indian spiritual teacher. I went to her room one day and saw a picture of Sai Baba on her altar. My first thought was, 'What's up? Who is this brother, and why is she praying to him?' So I asked her and she told me some stories about him raising the dead and healing the sick. So I thought I might check him out when I went to India. I put the information in my notebook and didn't think much more about it, because I was into *other* things. I was going to India for decidedly *un*spiritual purposes, to smoke substances that are put in pipes and wrapped in paper. Little did I know I'd get the Ultimate High.

In August I flew to Madras in southern India, planning to go to Kerala. When I looked at the map I noticed that Bangalore was on the way, so I thought I'd stop off there first and visit this Baba guy. I had heard that he materialised things, but knew only what my Swedish friend had told me. So I took a train to Bangalore, and all of a sudden I had Baba on the brain. I couldn't stop thinking about him. I checked into a hotel in Bangalore and found a book on Sai Baba. Whoa! This was heavy stuff! Next day I was on the bus bound for his ashram in Puttaparthi, a small village a hundred miles north.

Now I had been looking for *something* on this trip. I'd told my friends that I wasn't coming back till I'd discovered whatever it was I hoped to find. When we arrived at an arch over the road, nearing the ashram, I saw the Sarva Dharma symbol displayed, showing symbols of the main religions of the world. *At that moment I knew I had found it.* I didn't yet know what it was, but I knew I was in the right place.

In the ashram I was directed to check into a room, and quickly made some friends. They told me about *darshan* where you sit on the ground and Baba comes round, and you get to see him. So I went along to the temple (*mandir*) not thinking about interviews or materialisations. I just wanted to make eye contact with this guy, to check him out and see if he was for real. I sat there with thousands of others, and felt the peace and stillness which is palpable when you are at Prashanti Nilayam. Sai Baba came out and glided over to where I was. He stood in front of me, leaned over and stared straight into my eyes. Right then, I knew that whoever he said he was . . . he *was!*

After this I went to the bookstore and got a pile of books. That day I was speed-reading, burning the letters off the page. The next morning, on the way to *darshan* I was talking to a man from New York. He said that if I get the chance, I should kiss Baba's feet. I thought, 'Well, I don't care if he's God Almighty. I've done some freaky things in my life, but kissing some dude's feet is not among them. Forget that!'

Anyway, Baba came to me again and said, "*Where do you come from?*" I replied "Chicago." He said, "*Go.*" I was told that means I should go for an interview. So I went to the interview room with the others, and he immediately started materialising things . . . rings, medallions, and hot food came out of his hand steaming. He talked to people, showing that he knew all about them. My eyes were popping out. So then he asked me, "*What do you want?*" I had just read that he said, "*People come to me for petty cures, tinsel and trash. Few come for what I have to give . . . Liberation.*" I didn't know anything, so I said, "Liberation." Then he materialised a medallion for me and I was taken in for a private interview. He closed the curtain, turned to me and said, "*Too much lust. Sometimes you want to be with Mary, and sometimes you want to be with all those other women.*" This was true. Then he started to talk to me about things I had never told *anybody*, stuff I wanted to forget about. He was naming names, and getting real particular. I was mortified but he said, *"Don't worry, I'll help you,"* and gave me a hug. I was happy. The only question I asked in that interview was, "Can I kiss your feet?"

Well, I was blown away. I had three interviews in six days. I figure I was an emergency case, and he had to get me in there often. He asked me about my profession and what was my success rate as an acupuncturist. It was a common question, and I had this magic figure I'd give. It *sounded* good. So I said to Baba, "70%." He started laughing, just about choking and I thought, 'What's so funny?' Suddenly he stopped and said, "*No, no, no! That's just your imagination.*" Needless to say, I didn't give that figure again.

He asked me again, "*What do you want?*"

"To be a good healer." I said.

"*Be good, see good, do good and you will be a good healer.*" He replied.

But I got the impression he wasn't satisfied with the answers I was giving.

In the third interview he asked me again, "*What do you want?*" This time I realised it was a deep question and I was thinking hard. "Love" I said.

"*Yes, yes, yes!*" he exclaimed.

At last I'd got it. If I never pass another test in my life, I passed that one, and it was good. He told me to leave the ashram, and said that my work was back at home. As the psychic had predicted, I had met Sai Baba and had this profound experience which helped me to understand the meaning of life and death. After these experiences I went to Bangalore, checked into a hotel, and wondered what I should do now. I was blown away. I felt as though I had talked with God, like Mohammed and Moses.

But part of me wanted to get back to the old Mike, and I started putting up a battle with this new God stuff. I had a tape I'd been carrying with me, because I like to boogie. It's by a reggae group Third World, and the song was called "***Try Jah Love***". I had boogied to this tape all over the planet, but had never paid much attention to the words. Now they hit me like a ton of bricks.

A lonely soul was I without direction
I didn't know which way I had to go
I sought the clues to life's unanswered questions
My mind's heart had to know
I heard Your call while wandering through the darkness
I'd walk a million miles to find that endless voice
That speaks to me when I am in temptation,
Echoing My choice
To those who will seek, they will find
I've been with you through all time,
If you're thirsty I will quench you with My love,
If you're hungry I will feed you with My words,
And all I ask is that you love as I do,
If you lose your way, I'll lead you to My love,
From a sinful life I'll cleanse you in My love,
For creation bears a witness of My love.

Whoa! Where did that come from? Those words weren't there before!

I was pacing back and forth in my room, back to the old hyper Mike. So I thought I'd smoke a joint to bring me down. I went out on the balcony and started to roll a joint. Baba had told me in the interview that he would come to me later, but I didn't know what that meant. As I was sitting on the hotel balcony in the middle of the noise of Bangalore, I looked up. There in the sky was an image of Baba, from the ground to beyond the clouds. I'm not talking about some *faint* image I might have imagined. There he was, with orange robe and humungous Afro, looking at me. I dropped the joint and thought, '*I don't think I need this.*' This image lasted about five minutes. I thought this should stop traffic, but everyone was going about business as usual. Then, in the clouds around Baba appeared images of Christ and other beings, all looking at him. These images lasted for three days, and were also on the walls and ceiling of the hotel room. Whenever I closed my eyes to meditate, there was a pinprick of light in the distance, and it would advance and brighten and grow. It would become so bright that I could not keep my eyes closed. Needless to say, this had rather a profound effect upon me.

I've been into a variety of things in my life and life has not been dull. Much of my adult life I was on the wrong side of the law. I was an acupuncturist whose specialty was detoxing people from drugs, and I was also a drug dealer. It was job security. I had been into a host of degenerate things, including women, orgies, and pornography. I had a load of pornographic magazines that I had been carrying for my perusal and to sell, as in this part of the world you get a lot of money for them. When I came off that balcony, I went to my bag, took out the magazines and tore them into little tiny pieces. Me, tearing up my smut! *That* was a miracle.

When I got back to the US, I was a different person. But change can be a difficult thing. Although I took no drugs and was celibate for a month, habits are hard to break. I was in the habit of making a lot of money as a dealer, and I realised that I couldn't give all this up alone. I remembered hearing about a man who wanted to stop drinking. Baba said to him, *"Drink. But every time you take a drink, dedicate it to me."* So every time I sold a package or smoked a joint, I dedicated it to him. And things gradually started falling away.

In 1983 I got the urge to go back to the ashram. There I had an experience with a substance very unlike those I had been used to. I had heard about *amrit*, Divine Nectar, which can materialise on sacred objects. To my delight, I was offered some by an elderly Australian woman. She poured a little into my hand. Even before I tasted it I could feel the vibration in my palm, then humming through my face. It was indescribable, but I could *feel* the sweet odour, and I could *see* the vibration permeating the air in the room, as well as the people and objects there. Then in a flash, there was no time, no space, no distance, and no otherness. It was pure S*at Chit Ananda* . . . awareness, consciousness, bliss. Time did not exist for me, but others told me I was in this state for about twenty minutes. I'm normally a hyper kind of guy, but when I came back to body consciousness I was so calm and laid back. I floated out of that room, blissed to the max. It was the *Ultimate High*.

Then Sai Baba called me in for an interview. Things were a little different to the first trip. Before he was the loving mother, now the stern father was in evidence. He was mad at me in a loving kind of way . . . but he was on my case. He didn't say anything directly about drugs, but what he said struck me right in the heart, and *I knew clearly that he wanted me to stop*. He asked me how I was, and I said, "Great Baba!" His reply was, *"NO. Not great. Your will power is weak."* I knew what he was talking about. I had to get out of the business. I was still involved with dealing drugs, and getting high on marijuana. As a drug dealer, you can make any amount of money, especially if you have control over your consumption. My drug business had developed to a point where I was getting ready to make a *lot* of money . . . if I didn't get busted or killed first.

When I came back from that trip I was resolved to get out of the business. But I still had this mind-set that first I'd get a bankroll together, save some money, *and then* I'll retire. Well, I started losing money for no logical reason. One day it hit me. It was an issue of faith. In January 1984 I decided I couldn't do it anymore. At the time I was several thousand dollars in debt, mostly to one guy. I called him up and said, "Look, I can't do this anymore and I don't know when I'll be able to pay you the money." He told me to forget about it, just like that! At last I walked away from the business. I knew then that I would stop smoking marijuana by the end of the year. On New Year's Eve 1985, on my way to a Sai Baba meeting in St Louis, I smoked my last joint. There have been no drugs since then.

In 1985 I moved to California, and in 1992 became a professional storyteller. I get paid to run my mouth and I love that. I do a lot of work with kids, telling stories and teaching the art of storytelling. Occasionally I work with people on drugs. I had studied in a Clinic in New York, using acupuncture to help get people off drugs. One day I rang the doctor who ran the clinic to tell him I was now a storyteller. He said that when I come to New York I should come and tell stories to the women's group at the Clinic. So when I was in the area I popped in. He had me go over to the group. In the room were fifty women who were de-toxing from heroin, crack, methadone and so on. They were hard-core addicts, many of them street women; and I was the only man in the room. They introduced me, "Michael McCarty is going to tell us a story." The women looked at me incredulously thinking, "He's gonna do WHAT? He's gonna tell *us* a story? We've got a story for *him*!"

So I got up in front of them. When I'm dealing with people about drugs, I don't preach or tell them what they should or shouldn't do. I don't have the right to do that, as I've smoked up continents. I just tell my story. First I told them about my association with the Clinic, and then I started to tell them about my experience with freebase. I described in detail about preparing the freebase, and the physical experience, and I did it with humour. I could see them looking, and saying to themselves and their friends, "He knows, he's been there." That opened them up. After that I started telling some of my other stories . . . folk tales, historical stories, and they were wide open to it. They loved it, and I got a standing ovation. They made such a hoopla, that the people who ran the clinic came running, thinking I was being lynched or beaten up. When they came into the room and saw all these women standing up and cheering, they asked me what on earth I'd done.

So I've been able to use that drug experience to reach people in a way that I could not have done without having had the experience. When these talks happen, it becomes wonderfully intense. A couple of years ago, I was in South Africa. Some Sai Baba Centres flew me over there to speak to them. I also spoke at a drug detoxification facility. Again I shared my experience, and people were able to relate. Hearing the story of another person's experience has a great power in helping people to understand their own. It gives people the hope and realisation that if this person survived it, then they can too.

After coming off the pipe, I gradually became aware of a life full of blessings, and that my life has always been guided and directed. Once I met Sai Baba I became fully conscious of that. One of the things Baba told me in 1983 was, *"You worry about money, you worry about health, you worry about your career. I will take care."* What I found is that as long as I don't worry, things fall into place. One of the things missing in my life was a meaningful relationship. I had decided I wouldn't worry and obsess about it, I'd enjoy where I was, even if that meant being single for the rest of my life. I let it go, and then met this wonderful woman Valerie; and we were married. It's extremely wonderful, downright divine. Life now is quite amazing.

If a person has a pure heart, and is living Swami's teachings, Swami's grace is automatic. No karma can prevent that.

- Sathya Sai Baba

Update from Michael D, January 2013

I've been drug free since 1984 (never did drink). And I have been joyfully married since August 1999. My wife isn't a Sai devotee. She's Methodist. We were married by Rev. Robert Pipes, who was a Baptist preacher and Sai devotee until he passed away in 2011. I'm still running my mouth for a living. The economy has had a dramatic impact on my work and my income, but I always have what I need when I need it! I recently told stories for Sai groups in Trinidad, Barbados and Jamaica, and also for High schools and Elementary schools in Trinidad.

www.havemouthwillrunit.com

2

Piercing the Veil

I have a vow; to lead all who stray from the straight path, again into goodness and save them.

- Sathya Sai Baba

Vimansa was born in Australia in 1965 and brought up in an isolated rural area. We met in 1994 when we shared a room in the ashram for two months. She was the perfect room-mate, and we remained friends and kept in touch. We shared our stories of our past druggy lifestyles, so there was a bond of understanding. She is a sweet, loving woman, loved by many. She worked with dedication to transform her inner pain and is now a shining jewel.

Vimansa's story: As a teenager I remember when preventative material was handed out at high school about the dangers of drug use. There was a before and after photo of a girl using drugs. It seemed quite haunting and foreign to me that she should look so different, and out of control. I wondered how she could have lost it so badly. Outwardly, I remember laughing with other students about the shock value of the material, and rationalizing that it was a fear campaign – too black and white to be taken seriously.

I went through periods of drinking alcohol at parties when I was at high school. But I always kept it together, and even stopped for a while, because I jogged regularly and didn't like hangovers. A lot changed for me though, in 1981. Sixteen was a big year. My parents split, and my mother moved us out of home while my father was away 'on business.' I didn't know what was going on between them, but Mum had been hospitalized for a mysterious illness (a breakdown?) and it was common knowledge in the small rural community where we lived, that Dad was having an affair with a married woman.

I felt isolated and confused. Both my older brothers had left home, and I was in the midst of this heavy separation energy. My mother was spending long periods in bed, and my father had sought me out to advise that Mum had gone mad. I didn't know what to believe. My eldest brother, whom I trusted, briefly returned to the family farm. He told me that my father was lying and was, in fact, the one who'd gone mad. I didn't know whether to be relieved or more confused. I didn't know *what* was going on.

Earlier that year I had applied to become an exchange student, and had been accepted to go to South America. I was pleased to be out of there, and leave behind the mudslinging, the impending court cases, the guilt of being on Mum's side, and the split in the family. So I went abroad and partied hard. I loved the freedom, my anonymity and the distance from my family and the conflict. While I began to experiment with marijuana, I was mainly indulging in alcohol – and lots of it. I remember joking that I was drunk more nights than I was sober that year.

On my return to Australia in 1983 I had to complete my final year of high school. It was a depressing year, returning to a small conservative town after the excitement of exotic travel. Now I had to deal with study pressures, the breakup with my on-off long-term boyfriend, and the onslaught of family dramas again. Dad was bad-mouthing Mum around town, and Mum had formed a new live-in relationship.

I couldn't wait to escape again, this time to university. I decided to live on-campus, and it wasn't long before I linked up with what I thought were the exciting or 'cool' people – the ones who had too much sex and drugs, and did too little study and sport. I started going out with one of the ringleaders, who was fascinated with everything about drugs . . . the paraphernalia, experimentation, the music and icons. We began to miss classes as we smoked marijuana every day, all day.

By the end of 1984, a number of us had been asked to leave our accommodation on-campus due to our disruptive drug influence. We moved into a nine bedroom quasi-derelict house in a grungy inner suburb. Our developing drug sub-culture flourished – lots of parties and gatherings, new contacts, and further experimentation. At nineteen, we thought it not only fun but also intelligent to experiment with drug use. We, like others before us (Timothy Leary, the Doors), were exploring the mind. We tried hallucinogens, collecting magic mushrooms on forest pilgrimages, and took LSD with quirky names. We were enthralled to discover altered states . . . perceptions, sound and colours, and found that all was not as it appeared to be. We tried amphetamines ('speed') which enabled us to stay up talking until sunrise, and cocaine, which made us feel confident and good about ourselves. We tried heroin, which was warm and able to block all pain. I liked the romantic and innocent excitement of these initial explorations.

But I started to become concerned when some of the hard drug use (heroin) was becoming habitual and out of control. My boyfriend, as one of the main instigators, agreed to stop. He lied. I remember waking up the next morning and seeing a series of buckets along the corridor, with vomit in them. All around it was not a pretty sight. Heroin had begun to experiment with us.

Our relationship continued, and he continued to lie. I began to have affairs, and lied as well. It was not a healthy dynamic! Throughout the 'experimentation', marijuana remained a constant within our household and friendship groups. It was part of our culture, how we joined. We smoked when we woke up, *before* we went to University, *at* Uni, *after* Uni, *before* study, *during* study, *before* bed, *in* bed. Marijuana was part of our lives. It was our friend, our normality. *I needed it.* When my thoughts and feelings became uncomfortable around low self-esteem, guilt and anxiety, I would have a smoke to distance them.

When non-smoking friends queried my drug use, I refuted that it had any effect on me, and dismissed them as straight or boring. I didn't question the mental/physical cravings for marijuana that accompanied regular use, the wretched vomiting after a particularly vicious bong (water pipe), the need to take speed to motivate me to study, or the stealing of rent money by my boyfriend to fund our drug-taking. I wasn't ready to admit there was a problem. Marijuana helped me to block those uncomfortable thoughts and feelings. I needed it to remain *un*aware.

My relationship with my boyfriend crashed after two years. Amidst our flat being searched twice for drugs, his charges for drug dealing, his lying about his continued heroin use and my lying about having affairs, my father committed suicide. We hadn't been close since he separated from my mother, and I had done my best to avoid him. He scared me. He'd verbally abused me at my part-time job, and I heard he'd been sleeping in his car, popping anti-depressants and seeing some seedy women. Things had got really dark for him, and I felt that he was capable of hurting one of us. As it was, he gassed himself in his car in a lonely country lane and left a note: '*Sorry it had to end this way.*' I coped by smoking more marijuana and further blocking my feelings.

In 1986, when I was twenty-one, I told my boyfriend that I needed space and was going to Central America alone to research a Sociology thesis. In fact, I left to go travelling with one of our male drug-taking friends with whom I had been having an affair. This man had a photo of Sai Baba above his desk. When I asked who it was, he replied that this was his brother's spiritual teacher. I remember thinking, 'Oh, what's a spiritual teacher?' and leaving it at that.

We survived a fear-filled six-month journey to Central America with muggings, strip searches and false arrests. Then I returned to set up a clothing business with my ex- and current boyfriends . . . all three of us. Again my personal boundaries were a mess, but as a business dynamic we were hugely successful. Our tie-dyes and cyber prints mainly appealed to the rave music and surf drug cultures. With material success came more 'friends', more parties and more business opportunities.

But amidst this, I became aware of feeling lost. I became aware that there was something that I didn't get. Many of our alternative friends had travelled to India, and were into Eastern spiritual mysticism. At gatherings, they would offer their drug taking to Shiva and I felt they were aware of another plane of existence that I was not. At these gatherings

I would often retreat by myself, and curl up into a ball. I felt like I hadn't been born, that I was unable to pierce the veil to 'get it', this spirituality. Mistakenly, I thought smoking more marijuana and taking more acid would help the process. But I just became more paranoid. *So I began to pray to God for help.* My boyfriend suggested I should go to India, and so I decided to visit Goa. I thought that maybe I would find God there at an acid-rave, or a Full-Moon party.

But before I left I had a dream in which Sai Baba appeared and told me to come to Bangalore first. It didn't seem incredibly consequential to me, so I decided to add a flight to Bangalore anyway. Arriving alone in Bombay in 1990, I felt overwhelmed by fear. What was I doing? Where was I going? A Hindu priest asked if I was okay, and helped me to work out the ticketing process. He asked me who I was going to visit and I felt embarrassed, and said 'a friend'. Arriving safely in Bangalore, I managed to find a bus to Puttaparthi. Fortuitously I met an Australian woman on the bus, and when we arrived after four bumpy hours she walked me through the ashram registration process.

I was allocated a small space in 'the shed', a Spartan warehouse-like building with a concrete floor and no furniture. I bought a lumpy mattress and settled in. Comfort was not the purpose of the visit it seemed. When I went to have *darshan* of Sai Baba in the temple, I often got to sit in the front line where he would come very close. But I had no idea what Sai Baba and the ashram were all about. I was pretty blown out by foreigners (as we non-Indians were called), touching his feet.

But I decided it was nice of him to let me rest at his place, and rest I did . . . sleeping a lot, and eating a little. Then I began to detoxify from drug use and felt a lot of emotional pain, especially about my father. I met some nice women from many different countries who offered healing in the form of Reiki, listening, hugs and encouragement. I also had to face my demons . . . literally. While I prided myself on my logic and rationality, I was absolutely amazed one night, after being there five days, to be woken by my own maniacal laughing, and the sight of two demons on me. I shouted "No!" . . . and they left.

While I felt comfortable and safe at the ashram, I still thought I should get to Goa. I repeatedly asked a taxi driver . . . in vain . . . to get me train tickets. Frustrated, I decided to go to Bangalore and get them myself. That same day, Swami left for his ashram near Bangalore. As I waited fruitlessly in my hotel for the taxi driver to return with the promised ticket, an Australian woman convinced me that as I still hadn't got it, I should go to the Bangalore ashram with her in the morning. We arrived there, and another woman suggested I should see if I could secure ashram accommodation. I was feeling overwhelmed and tired by not being able to organise the Goa trip so I thought, 'If I get in, I'll take it as a sign from this Baba that I'm meant to be here.' It didn't look likely. There were about twenty women crowding and pressuring the accommodation man for the two available places. Miraculously, he moved through the crowd and asked for *my* passport. I was in!

So I moved in with a group of Latin American women, and immediately became friendly with a girl my own age. After a few days we went to Whitefield village, and a young Indian man inquired if we'd like to join him for a smoke of *ganja*. I remember feeling apprehensive, but I rationalized that my friends back in Australia might be impressed by such an adventure. So we ended up in a room behind the ashram smoking super strong marijuana. Then there was a loud knock at the door. I heard the young man say, "It's the police!" I grabbed my friend in panic, and pushed past the man in the doorway. We kept going past the village and into some fields. I started to feel paranoid because I felt telepathic, and I told my friend I was returning to our room.

On entering the ashram I saw devotees wearing white, and I was thinking that they were angels. I felt ashamed. I went to my room and lay down on the bed, hoping that I could sleep it off before afternoon *darshan*. As I was lying there, disturbing images started to appear on my mind screen. I felt like I was in some astral lower world where humans had animal heads and animals had human heads. Their breathing was heavy, and they were trapped in this dark and derelict world. I tried to stop the images, I tried to open my eyes, I tried to change them, but nothing worked. They kept running like a film I felt I was being forced to watch, and I was scared that it would never stop, and I would never get out. I remember, amazingly, that someone briefly came in and said, "She's having a visit from Shiva."

After some time the intensity of the images did decrease, and finally finish. But I was still feeling freaked out and thought I would feel safer in *darshan*. I also had the fear that if I went Swami might kick me out, scold me, or give me dirty looks. I chose to go anyway. Swami walked past and subtly looked at me – incredibly, I thought, without judgement. I never did get to Goa. I stayed with Swami and he took my first letter, asking who I was and where I was going. I started to become aware that he knew me, and that we had a spiritual relationship. My prayers had been answered, and at last I felt I was starting to 'get it'.

On my return to Australia, my friends predicted that I would be too scared to ever smoke again. I didn't for a year. But then the fear subsided, the peer group remained and I began to smoke. But this time around it was different. I knew Swami, I had faith, and I had hope. I believed I could change. I began to pray for a new narrative, a new role in the play. Eighteen months after my initial visit, I felt drawn to see Sai Baba in India again. As soon as I walked through the gates of Prashanti Nilayam, I had this knowing that I would never take drugs again; and I haven't. *The urge, or addiction, had completely gone.*

Swami continued, however, to work on the emotional pain that I had tried to block with drug use. I went to live and detoxify at the ashram for three years. And so began the conscious journey of self-awareness . . . becoming aware of myself, listening to myself, trusting myself, loving myself. A number of modalities practiced by compassionate devotees assisted in my healing. Phyllis Krystal's 'Cutting the Ties that Bind' Homoeopathy and Reiki. I also studied Vipassana meditation in Sri Lanka with a Buddhist nun. This was a major turning point. I learnt about mindfulness, and the craving/clinging nature of the 'monkey mind'. I understood not to take thoughts so seriously; to let them go by like clouds passing through a clear sky

But first and foremost in this journey of self to Self-awareness has been Swami. By learning to love and trust him, I found I was learning to love and trust my Self. My priority from the outset was to develop my inner relationship with Swami, who is not different to my Self. At one stage I was concerned that due to this focus on our inner connection, I didn't have any big stories to tell people. So I decided in the next interview that I would speak to him. I tried many times but he would just ignore me, cut me off, turn his back, or move rooms. Finally he scolded, "*Shh, be quiet!*" I thought, 'Why is he scolding me when we have such a loving relationship?' As I completed this thought, Swami said, "*I will speak to you separately.*" People whispered that I would get a private interview, but I knew that he was confirming our inner connection. While Swami was talking privately with someone, I contentedly went and sat down at the back. When he came back into the room, he walked over to me and allowed me to touch his feet saying softly, "*Very happy.*"

Eventually I returned to Australia in 1995 when I was thirty years old. I went back to University to study Social Work, where I met my beautiful husband who is also now a devotee. We have created a healthy and supportive relationship, based on values that we have both learned from Swami, such as love, honesty, respect, and open communication. After working as a family counsellor for the past four years, I have recently started my own counselling/meditation practice, blending Eastern spiritual wisdom with my professional Western training.

In 2000, my beloved eldest brother killed himself. In the past I used drugs to block emotional pain. Now I share the difficult times with Swami, who is my centre, my core. At times I wish that I didn't have to go through many of my life experiences, but I trust that on this journey through pain and pleasure, that Swami is guiding me. This is not only a story of my addiction to marijuana, but also a story of a journey to God; to realizing Self.

Give the guru you mind as you would entrust gold to the goldsmith. The guru may need to melt, mould or beat your mind, but do not worry, as he will return to you a precious jewel. Do not say, 'Swami, give me peace, but don't give me pain' as Swami may need to inflict pain before the process of purification is complete.

- Sathya Sai Baba

Update from Vimansa, February 2013

Ten years on, and the addictive craving to take drugs has not returned. My purification and a loving relationship with Swami enabled a release from the heavy energies of addiction. I am not attracted to drugs any more to escape the mind and emotional pain. When faced with life issues, I am aware of Baba's presence, and the meditative place in which to centre. Happily, Swami has blessed us with the most beautiful daughter to love – so pure and sweet! We experienced difficulty conceiving for many years, and went to the ashram for an extended stay. We gave letters to Swami, and conceived straight after our visit to the ashram . . . on my birthday, a beautiful gift. Work-wise, we continue to run a successful consulting business Australia-wide, focusing on mediation and conflict resolution, with an emphasis on mindfulness. I am eternally grateful to Swami for his grace.

3

Superman

Keep away completely from intoxicating drink and drugs. By consuming such items all your sense organs will be paralyzed. Alcohol is not at all conducive to spiritual sadhana. In spiritual sadhana one has to attain ecstatic levels by a natural process, not by artificial methods like drugs and alcohol. All that is related to divinity comes by a natural process. We must drown in natural divine intoxication, not artificial intoxication induced by drugs and alcohol.

- Sai Baba 23rd July 2002

Dave was born in Wisconsin, USA in 1937. His motivation here was to help others with his story, not brag about his transformation. What struck me was his love for Baba. Every time he looked at Swami's picture as he was telling his story, tears of devotion poured down his face. It was hard to reconcile this soft, openhearted man with the hard drinking businessman he once was. This is his story of giving up alcohol and finding his Higher Power.

Dave's story: My name's Dave and I am an alcoholic. I was born into a wealthy, upper middle class family. My mother was proud that I had been born on Good Friday, and I was her golden boy, her darling. My parents belonged to the finest country clubs in the area, and I always looked on drinking as part of the social life in the business world. I started drinking when I was sixteen. My first drink made me feel like superman. I was senior president of the class, football captain, and ended up marrying the cheerleader. Everything was going perfectly, and I had a huge ego. My father had impressed upon me that I could do anything, or be anything I wanted to in life. But I was never enough for him. He never put his arm round me or said he loved me, and *whatever* I did he wasn't satisfied. I was confident and successful . . . but not happy.

I went to college in the fifties, the era of the Korean War. Veterans were coming home, and I was drinking with these men a few years older than me. I seemed to fit in. I was always the life of the party, and would get invited to other fraternities in order to make a good party. They were happy with me. Sometimes I woke up in *their* dorms, sometimes in my fraternity. It was normal for me to go to two or three parties a night. By the age of twenty I had a drinking habit, and started going into blackouts. I drank because it made me feel that there was *nothing* I couldn't do. It increased my self-confidence to the point of being absurd. It made me feel *so* good. In my family, from Thanksgiving through to New Year, that's how it was. I thought Christmas meant cocktail parties.

When I graduated I was sought after by a big steel corporation, and I had such a big ego that I would interview only with the Presidents of companies, no less. I joined the steel industry in the Mid-West, but things came too easy for me. I was athletic, good at sports, able to talk to people and please my employers; and I was the youngest to hold such a high position in the steel industry. One day I was called to the press office and scolded for not spending enough money entertaining the customers. So I showed them that I knew how to do it!

I stayed with them for seven years, until I got divorced. My wife had been trying to prove I was a bad alcoholic to get grounds for a divorce. One night we got drunk and she said, "Come on, let's get in the car and get some more booze." She drove me to the police station, and had the police arrest me because I was drunk. That's when I spent my first night in a prison cell. When we separated my drinking got much heavier, and the company suggested I take a leave of absence. I went into my first rehabilitation clinic outside Nashville, Tennessee when I was twenty-eight years old. But I went for all the wrong reasons. I wanted to learn how to *control* my drinking, and had no intention of giving up.

Then I joined another large corporation as the East Coast sales manager. What it amounted to was selling garbage trucks to the Mafia. I had the privilege to get on any airline I wanted on the East Coast. But the blackouts were getting worse, and I'd wake up some mornings and have to look in the phone book to find out which city I was in. One time in Cleveland, they had to take me off the plane on a stretcher. While they were carrying me I came out of the blackout, and heard someone saying that this man had a heart attack on the plane. I sat up and slurred, "Where's the guy that had the heart attack?" I ended up coming out of it in Cleveland jail, in my nice business suit and cashmere coat, with all the winos, druggies and bums staring at me.

So I went back into rehab in the Catskills, Upper New York State. I was making a lot of money for the company and they begged me to come out, but I said no as now I wanted to get hold of this. When I came out, I left that company and got married again. My second wife was a good woman. I married her as I needed someone to look after this sick alcoholic, and she was like a mother to me. The drinking and blackouts continued, and I remember sitting on the kerb in downtown New York, passing wine bottles back and forth with the winos.

One time I was driving to visit with my sister in Milwaukee. I went into a blackout, and next thing I knew I was standing on a bridge crossing the Mississippi River. I didn't have a clue where my car was, or why I was standing on this bridge. I didn't know how I got there, or if I was up there to jump. When I came out of it I was thirsty, and saw a beer sign on the side of the bridge; so I went and had another drink. In that same drunk I ended up on an inter-State four-lane highway going the wrong way, got arrested and thrown in jail again. But nothing serious ever came of these things. I must have kept God very busy protecting me. I never had a major accident, and that's a miracle.

After this I started to go to Alcoholics Anonymous (AA) meetings, still drinking, and thinking that I was going to be the first one to be able to continue drinking and control it. At that time they had a ninety-day pin. If you made it through ninety days you'd get this symbol that you'd stayed sober. I would go eighty-eight days and take a drink, so I didn't have to take one of those little pins . . . because that would *really* mean I was an alcoholic. When travelling, I would measure bottles at night in my motel room. I was trying to control my drinking, and only allowed myself *so* much. All this time, I didn't have a genuine desire to stop, but I read the AA literature. They talked about having a Higher Power, but I couldn't get it in my mind that *I* had one. I still had this ego problem that I was my own Higher Power.

By now I was getting bad blackouts. My wife got some AA people to take me back to the rehab in the Catskills. I was in there for a week and didn't even know it. They thought I had a wet brain. On the seventh day I was sitting at a table, and suddenly came to. I saw my wife sitting there, and two psychiatrists . . . I didn't know where I was. They were about to commit me to a mental institution with a wet brain. If they had put me in there I'm sure they would have stuck some more drugs into me, and maybe I never would have come out.

But this time I started taking my problem more seriously. The man who ran the rehab made me feel that I was complete garbage. He took me down to zero, breaking this ego I had going that I was the greatest. He wouldn't even speak to me at times. Then he'd tell me, "You're nothing. You're not as good as you think you are. Okay, these companies all want you, but you'll just go and get drunk again when you leave here." *I would have too.* But I stayed there for seven weeks, till he said I was ready to go out in the world again. He understood. He'd worked with people like me before. It was a very tough road for me, getting over my ego.

At the rehab we concentrated on finding my Higher Power. I wasn't brought up in any religion. My father thought that God was out on a golf course; that's where *he* was every Sunday morning. The family had no belief in anything. One morning I decided to take a walk in the beautiful woods around there, and sat under a tree. I don't know if I could call it praying, but I started asking, "What is a Higher Power? Please show me." All of a sudden I felt the wind on my face. It was new to me. I saw grass growing and leaves blowing and I said, "Something's gotta make this happen." So I thought, 'Okay, *that's* my Higher Power. Nature is gonna be what I call God.' From then on I was on a path to find God.

In 1970 we moved to Florida and I started a business with a couple of partners. We made concrete pipes for the construction industry. It was understood that I was an alcoholic, but that I was good at entertaining. We became highly successful, and I did a lot of entertaining with politicians and engineers. *But I never took a drink.* Sometimes you pick up another addiction after conquering one, and I now became a workaholic. I wasn't satisfied with just one corporation that made good money; I had to have four. All this time I was going to seven Alcoholics Anonymous meetings a week, and working with the Twelve Steps. And it kept me off the booze. Also I helped other alcoholics get into the programme, and found that giving to others helped me an awful lot. As well, I did a lot of speaking for AA throughout the country. Through this I truly lost the ego problem.

My second wife was a wonderful woman, but when I realized I'd married my mother it was hard to have a marriage relationship in all senses. My whole social life was in AA and did not include her. I was going to a meeting most evenings, and working all day. Then I met a woman in AA and fell in love with her. I told my wife, which was hard. I had bought my wife and child just about everything they could ever want. But I couldn't give her love. She had to put up with so much trouble from my drinking, and getting me out of jail. She was doing a thesis on Psychology. She said she should have done it on me! I didn't counter the divorce, but sold the business in the mid-eighties, and gave everything to her and our daughter. I gave her *all* my money. I didn't care about it because I knew I could make more.

My new partner Christl was also in AA, and we seemed compatible on every level there is. We decided to live together in 1988 to see if it would work. We are still together now in 2003, and very happy. We never got a piece of paper and got married, but she *is* my wife.

At that time I was searching, going to every religion I could think of. I had tried Unity, Judaism, Methodism, Lutheranism and the Metaphysical churches, trying to find my Higher Power, or God. Nothing ever felt good, so I went back to Nature as God. Then at one church we met a man who introduced us to Sai Baba. I went to his house on a Thursday evening, and when I walked into the room and saw Swami's picture, I started to cry. Immediately I knew I had found what I was looking for.

In 1990, Christl and I made our first trip to see Baba. Our travel agent was a Baba devotee, but she still had a lot of old Catholic thinking in her head. She said, "When you get over there, don't expect any attention from Swami, and don't even *think* about staying in the ashram, because you are living in sin." So we stayed outside. I thought I *must* have been living in sin, because Baba ignored me completely. He'd walk down lines of people, and when he came to me he would look the other way, and then come back to the guy next to me. So I thought I must be pretty bad.

From there we followed Swami to his Whitefield ashram, where we met another couple. We thought, 'Well if we're living in sin, they must be!' They were gay, one white and Jewish, and the other black. We called ourselves the odd couples. Three days later, Swami called all four of us in for an interview. He took Christl and me into the inner room, looked at us with a smile and said, *"I put you two together. People out there look down on you, but we in the Universe recognize the two of you as a couple."* While saying this he had a hand on each of our heads. He said, *"I have much more to give you. Come back tomorrow and sit by the gate."* We did go back, and Baba proceeded to give us a lot of attention. At the time I was wearing a pendant of the Sarva Dharma symbol, showing the main world religions. He took it off my neck, took it apart and put it back. All I could do was cry. He pushed my head into his stomach and kept his arms around me. Then he made an announcement to everyone in the room. He said, *"This is a very, very good man."* The most cherished possession I have is that Swami, who I believe is Divine, said I was a good man.

He also blessed the gay couple, and gave them much love. One time he gave them five interviews in five days. We kept in touch over the years, and one has now died of AIDS. I believe that Swami doesn't see us as 'This one's married, this one's living in sin,' but as different light bulbs. Each bulb has the same current running through, and some are brighter than others. He removes the dirt and dust, so that we can shine more brightly. Christl and I now come to see Baba every year at Christmas time.

My father still had his hooks into me even after his death in a car accident. I still felt I had to do more, and be more. So I went to a lady in Phoenix who does Phyllis Krystal's method of cutting ties. It frees us from the negative ties that build up in any intimate relationship, which control our behaviour. It was the only way I could be free of my father. As an adult I was *still* trying to do things so that he would say, "Good boy!" and be proud of me. When I looked objectively at his life, I saw that my Uncle was the brains of the business and my father didn't really accomplish much, except as an entertainer and golfer.

My other addiction was cigarettes, and it took longer to kick that habit. My favourite thing was to taper off, so that the pain of withdrawal was not so bad. In the early nineties, whenever I came to the ashram, the desire to smoke went automatically. But it came back when I went home, and I was smoking a pack and a half a day. When I came to India I was using chewing tobacco, so as not to suffer from withdrawals. Baba put a stop to that. Two years ago I came with a big pouch of chewing tobacco. He made it taste so awful I couldn't put it in my mouth, and I threw it in the garbage. There were no withdrawals, and I haven't touched tobacco since.

After fifteen years regular attendance I dropped AA in the late 80s, as the group wasn't spiritual enough for me. I believe that God gave this programme to Bill Wilson, the founder, to help sick alcoholics. I wanted to have more spiritual meetings, but there were always so many new people coming in the door, we never got past the third or fourth step. So several of us would meet separately and do the later steps, the more spiritual part of the programme. We would look at our shortcomings, make amends to people we had harmed, and practice prayer and meditation. I had taken rehab meetings for alcoholic priests, and the toughest thing was to be able to talk about God with them. They seemed to think they had a lock on it, and God had nothing to do with their drinking.

I don't often go to AA meetings now, but I try to be God's instrument as much as I can. There has got to be a reason why I'm still here after all the scrapes I got into, and when I meet someone having a problem with alcohol I open up right away about my past. I'm not ashamed to say I'm an alcoholic. I tell them I've been in the programme thirty-five years, and maybe get them going and take them to some meetings. But they have to *want* it for themselves. One of my prayers is that I'll be used as an instrument, and people do come into my life. When I'm in the ashram I collect my little lambs, to use my wife's term.

Often I meet people who are confused by Baba and don't know why they are there. Many times I happen to be holding just the book they need, and I give it to them. I once met with a Catholic priest from Australia. He loved Jesus, but here he was feeling love for Swami and felt he was betraying Jesus. We talked for quite a while, and then I realized I had the perfect book in my hand. It was **A Catholic Priest Meets Sai Baba** by Mario Mazzoleni. I always seem to have something to give somebody.

Another time I was sitting by a young Indian man in *darshan*. I got playing with his two small kids, and he started talking to me. He was from Los Angeles, and said he was not into gurus, and was only there because his father believed that Baba had saved him from an operation. He'd had a heart attack, and woke up to find a packet of *vibhuti* (holy ash with healing properties, symbolising death of the 'ego') on the table, which healed him. He was so grateful he decided to take the whole family to see Baba. But his son did not care for this. In my hand I had Professor Kasturi's book, **Loving God** which I gave him. Three days later I was walking back from the canteen, and saw this man with his wife and children. He came running to me like I was a long-lost relative. The book helped him relate to it, and now he knew why he was there. This is how I get used.

There are so many positive experiences in life now. My wife Christl is Austrian, and one Christmas we went to

Vienna. It was like a picture postcard, with the lights, snowflakes, and glitter . . . very beautiful. But I was talking to Swami and saying, "Well, I see all the beauty, and hear Christmas carols being sung, but I'd rather be in a Baba meeting." We went into a big department store to get warm. There was a young lady behind a counter giving nail file demonstrations. I thought she looked familiar, but I hadn't been to Austria before. We went closer and saw an Om sign round her neck. Within an hour we were at a Baba meeting! These are ways Swami shows his presence.

Wherever I am I'm always talking to Swami; I figure Swami is with me all the time, and we talk. I often ask for things in *darshan*, and love to look into his eyes. On 26th December 2002, I asked him to give me eye contact and as much bliss as I could handle. I was holding a letter, and Swami took it, put both his hands over mine and stared into my eyes. I knew I'd been given a lot of bliss, and felt almost out of it, as if I'd had a very strong drink. I sat there for at least fifteen minutes and cried. I cry easily around Swami. It feels like a squeezing in the middle of my chest, and it goes up my neck and into my head and the tears come. When I left the *mandir*, I waved off a few friends that I usually talk to and went back to my flat. I sat on the bed, looked at his picture and couldn't stop crying. It was pure bliss. This went on for about an hour and a half. Then I decided to go in the kitchen and find something to eat. There is another Baba picture there, and as soon as I saw it the tears started again. So I felt I should get out of the flat. I knew they were taking down the Christmas decorations that morning, and I finally managed to go out and help. I felt fantastic and was filled with an incredible amount of energy. It was better than any booze.

We now make a living in Florida making sun visors. I got the idea in meditation, and saw it clearly. The next day I made one, and my wife laughed and said that nobody would ever wear that. We now make ten thousand of these a week. Without regret I look back at my drinking, business career and everything I've gone through as karmic. Hopefully I don't make any more bad karma, and can take some links off the karmic chain I'm wearing. Daily when I do my morning *puja*, (worship) I surrender everything that will be done that day to Swami, offering to him all my senses. Everything is dedicated to him. This is the way I try to live my life. It's been a great ride with Swami. I love him so much

My imperfections and failures are as much a blessing from God as my successes and my talents, and I lay them both at His feet.

- Mahatma Ghandi

Sad News of Dave from his Wife Christl, January 2013

David passed away on 2nd July 2012. I am still heartbroken over this. He had open heart surgery that turned into an infection with high fever, and he never left the hospital alive. He was 75 years old.

4

'What's it like in Heaven?'

You can hear my footsteps, for I walk with you, behind you, beside you. When you cry out in agony, 'Don't you hear my heart's complaint? Have you become so stony hearted?' my ear will be there to listen. Ask that I should protect you like the apple of my eye, and my eye will be there to watch over you and guard you. I answer to whatever Name you use; I respond to whatever request you make with a pure heart and a sanctified motive.

- Sathya Sai Baba

I met Grace at Sai Baba's ashram in January 2002. She agreed to tell her story, though she had to dredge it up from her memory as it seemed like a different life. Grace was born in 1948 in New England, U.S.A. She is beautiful, with long blonde hair, shining blue eyes and a lovely smile. She is gentle, with much sweetness and humility. With her husband John she lives in Puttaparthi, the small town which contains the ashram. They have lived there for the past eight years. What struck me was that she appears to be totally content with life. And this is remarkable after what she has been through. It is a story of transformation, told without a trace of self-pity.

Grace's story: In order to explain the addictions, let me clarify why it all started. I felt like I'd had a hard life. I don't want to do the poor me thing, but in my mind life was rough. My Mom left me, my brother and my Dad when I was a year old, then soon after my Dad re-married to have a mother for the children. Our stepmother wasn't a happy lady, and my grandfather said she used to maltreat us. He had to secretly take us out of the house in the middle of the day, and we went to live with the grandparents. I was happy there.

Then my father married a new lady when I was seven. Gramps thought we should go and stay with them, but I didn't want to. Anyhow, my brother and I had to move in with Dad and his new wife, and she didn't like me. I think she was sad because she knew that Dad was still in love with Mom and I was a constant reminder, looking just like my mother. She hated me. She kept a big stick in the drawer, and used to pound me on the head with it. Dad didn't believe it till he saw I was black and blue one day. It was a very unhappy household.

As an adolescent, I was thinking that I didn't know what love is and it might help if I could find someone to fall madly in love with. So I found this guy, soon got pregnant, and we decided to get married. I thought I really loved this man. I was only sixteen. On the honeymoon I was pregnant, not feeling well and he would be out all night. I found out that he was sleeping with other girls. Now I was really screwed up in my head and rejected again. Then I gave birth to a beautiful son and went into post-partum blues. I was deeply depressed.

I noticed that all the women he was running around with were really thin ladies, so I thought, 'If I get really skinny, perhaps he'll love me.' I figured that if I could get rid of my food, I'd get skinny. So at the age of eighteen, I was bulimic before it became popular. I thought it was my very own invention, and didn't even know other people did that. I got very thin, down to 87lb. When I felt like making myself feel good I'd eat a whole lot of comfort food. That's what it's all about. I'd think, 'If I could have *anything* I'd like and as much as I want, what would it be?' Then I'd get all this nice food that I'd been dreaming of, gorge myself on tons of it, go drink a lot of water, stick my fingers down my throat and throw up. This happened three or four times a day for years. Nobody knew. This way I felt like I was in control of at least *something* in my life. There had to be a part of my life that nobody else could touch. It was definitely an addiction.

During this time my marriage ended, and at the age of twenty I married my second husband. He drank too much, and was possessive and controlling. He was basically a nice guy, but drove me nuts telling me that I couldn't wear this, or I couldn't do that. My life was under his control, not my own. We had a lovely daughter, and after her birth I went into post-partum blues again. So many things were going on; it was hard to figure out what the problem actually was. Confused, I couldn't understand why I was always upset, why nobody would talk about things, and I was expected to forget about the problems and pretend everything was okay. I got more and more stressed out.

One day somebody said, "It's all in your mind." So I decided to go to a psychiatrist and figure out what the problem was. Back then they didn't know much about addiction and that drugs were habit forming. The psychiatrist started giving me anti-depressants, and was constantly changing them to find one that would work. Then all of a sudden, they told me to stop taking them. Well, if you stop taking a handful of drugs, you're going to have withdrawals. Nobody told me, and maybe they didn't even know. I started not sleeping at night. Then I really went off, and thought I was going nuts, because I was going through the horror of withdrawals and didn't realise what it was. So I had to get more drugs to keep me going.

As well as my mental problems, I thought I had a heart condition with pains in my chest. I was becoming a hypochondriac. It turned out to be pains caused by the bulimia, from making myself vomit several times a day for years. The doctor said there was nothing physically wrong with me, that it was all in my mind, not acknowledging that I was going through symptoms from trying to come off these addictive drugs. So I said, "Well, if I'm crazy then put me in an institution and straighten this out. Let's solve this once and for all." So at the age of twenty-two, I committed myself into the State Institution.

Soon I started to become institutionalized. Now that I was in hospital I had easy access to more pills and it snowballed, with a little more of this, and a little more of that. I was taking a handful of drugs before the year was over . . . Valium, sleeping pills, anti-depressants and Seconal. It was such a fog I can't even remember all the drugs I took. They would line all of us up three times a day to take them. Ritalin was one of my favourites. It's a strong stimulant and then I couldn't sleep, so they gave me sleeping pills. Soon I was loaded with anti-depressants, speed, sleeping pills . . . you name it. It got to be fun after a while, because I became an expert in changing my mood with a little pill.

For seven months I stayed there, and then I went home. My husband's family had been looking after the children. I only saw them occasionally for years and that was painful.

But I couldn't cope with my life, and over the next two years I was in and out of the Institution four times. I got addicted to that place. In there I didn't have to cope, and anytime I had a bad feeling they gave me some medicine to take it away. People there liked me and talked to me, and didn't treat me badly. I got hooked on the niceness with people finally being good to me. But I was too messed up to handle the possessiveness and trouble from my husband. The psychiatrist thought the marriage wasn't working and advised me to leave him. When I came out of the hospital, I found a place to live on my own and left the children with him till I was settled. My husband proceeded to prevent me from having our children. He said I was running around with men, having found a young man in my apartment visiting, who was only a friend. It was all his paranoid imagination. He said I was a drug addict, and told the children I didn't want them. Of course, I *did* want my children and was a loving mother, and this was incredibly painful. So I took more pills.

Within months I had married again. I was now twenty-five years old. This time I chose a psychotic. He was a schoolteacher. Everyone in town loved him and thought he was a really nice guy, an amazing and wonderful person. I thought so too. But he wasn't. Talk about going from one problem to the next. He was *really* crazy; I'm not kidding. In the night he started trying to choke me. One time, in the middle of town, he dumped me off a Harley Davidson motorbike. When he'd bought the Harley he'd made a sissy bar and put it on very loose. Needless to say it fell off and I went with it. Only an act of God saved my life. People were asking me if he did it purposely so that I would fall off. I got the nerve one day and asked him. He got this evil look on his face, smiled and said, "Would I do something like that?"

Then he was laughing. I guess that answered my question.

During this time I got so desperate that I overdosed and was taken to hospital. It was a cry for help. I told everyone I'd done it, and didn't seriously intend to kill myself, though life didn't seem worth living. I had been trying to get my children back with me, so we could have a good family life. Well, it wasn't looking that way. My husband wanted a child, and I naively hoped that if we had a baby everything would be great and the whole family could be together again. So at twenty-seven I got pregnant again, and gave birth to a beautiful son. The post-partum blues returned, and the child was born addicted to the drugs too. He cried all the time. I had tried not to take too many drugs while pregnant, but nobody had told me they would affect the baby. Anyway, he was okay after a few weeks. So here I was post-partum blues again, husband choking me, with a little baby. And I was still addicted to all these prescription drugs.

My favourites were Codeine, Nembutal and Seconal. I had been given Codeine for back pain caused by the fall off the motorbike. I continued to ask for it long after the back pain was gone because I liked it. I'd feel high and suddenly everything was okay, I'd relax and sit around smiling. It made me feel creative too. I took it a couple of times a week. Seconal was my other favourite. It made me feel good for a long time before going to sleep, and then I'd have a really great sleep. I was addicted to these for years. I still didn't *know* I was addicted. I was confused as such a lot of crazy stuff had happened.

At this time I was alone a lot, didn't have any friends and didn't want to be with people. I often used to pray for help. Finally one day I thought, 'I don't think there can be a God. There can't be. In twenty-seven years I've had nothing but misery. So if there *is* a God, he doesn't care about me.' I had taken a few overdoses before, half meaning it, half crying out for help. But now I decided that I really wanted out. So I started saving pills . . . a big bottle of sleeping pills, a whole bottle of Valium and another bottle of something I had put together. I swear to God, that's a lot of pills. I told nobody about it and I thought, 'This is it. I just *cannot* take life anymore.' I remember that day. I felt really great. For the first time in ages I was feeling good. I went to McDonald's and had a meal. I wasn't fretting; I knew what I was going to do, and that at last the misery would be over.

That night, at 10 o'clock I took out the pills from where they were stashed away. I went to my bed and lined them all up with a big glass of water. I smoked a cigarette and I remember thinking that I would miss smoking. I loved my cigarettes! Then I thought, 'Okay, it's time to take them.' I swallowed three full bottles of pills. Then I thought, 'If you are there God, please forgive me. I don't think you *are* there, but if you are please forgive what I've done. I just can't be here any longer.' Then I lay down and went to sleep.

Next thing I remember, I was being woken up. My husband had the sense to realise I wasn't breathing and threw me in the bathtub and ran cold water on me. They rushed me to hospital thinking I was dead. At the hospital they rang my mother and told her to hurry up, as they didn't think I'd be around for much longer. I was in a coma for days. I had truly not expected I would be alive after this. To wake up and find myself still there was amazing. By the grace of God I survived. When I came to, the first thing I did was to ask for a minister. When he came I asked him what it was like in heaven. He said, "You tell me!" He came back two days later and we talked a lot and became friends.

Then another psychiatrist came and said they were sending me to a psychiatric unit in a regular hospital, as they felt I might injure myself. It didn't bother me; I was used to it anyway. There was a nice lady in the ambulance and she said, "When you get out of this hospital I want you to start taking Yoga classes with me." I said, "Okay" and soon forgot about it.

Finally I returned home. Things just got crazier. After the suicide attempt I had been given a counsellor. My husband was still being violent and was hurting the baby too. He admitted to the counsellor that he was doing it. Years later he went on to sexually abuse our son. One day I called the counsellor very upset as he had hit me again, and they took me to a place of protection. Then he called the hospital and reported me missing. He put on a good act of being the good husband and me the crazy wife, and the police convinced me to go back. I knew it was the wrong thing, but I went. After the police had left he laughed and said, "I just said that to get you back." He said he'd kill me if I did that again. However I plucked up courage to phone the counsellor for help. She told me that if I didn't get myself and the baby out of the house, she believed he *would* kill me. This time I got away for good. I was now twenty-eight years old and separated from my third husband.

However some positive things had been happening. When I woke up in the hospital after trying to kill myself, something had changed. There was something inside me that was never there before. It was a new kind of strength and I felt that as I was still here, it had to be for a good reason, because I *shouldn't* be here. I now believed that there *must* be a God and it gave me the strength to go on. The bulimia fell away without any effort. When I was happy, which was only when I was in hospital, I didn't do it, but apart from those times it had been with me every day. Now I decided to stop all the crazy stuff I was doing and thinking, and try to find the person I really was. She had gotten lost. I was always exhausted, and was so messed up I never thought about my health or nutrition. If I was tired I went to the doctor and he gave me something to wake me up. I knew it was time to change all that.

Soon after I came home the woman in the ambulance phoned me. She said, "Do you remember me, I was in the ambulance with you? I want you to take my Yoga class." For some reason my husband allowed me to go, and a few months after my suicide attempt I started the class. The man was a great Yoga teacher and I loved it. He talked to us about things that were outside of my experience, and I was interested. He talked about gurus and Eastern spirituality and someone in the class lent me a book on reincarnation.

My Yoga teacher told me that when it's time for you to find a guru, one would come. A year later in 1978, a guru came from India to Boston and I went to see him. He took me in as a disciple and initiated me into *Kriya Yoga* and meditation. From the beginning my meditations were good, and my mind began to get calmer. I started to change and took less and less drugs. Guruji was a wonderful person and I loved him a lot. He taught me so much and I became interested in the way of life in India, in gurus and even in God.

At last I understood and accepted the fact that I was addicted to all these drugs . . . Codeine, Valium, antidepressants, and Seconal. I knew I had to come off them but the time had to be right. I had been through withdrawals before so I knew the symptoms, and now I felt that I had the strength to go through it. I'd been on pills for so long that I'd forgotten how it was to live without them, and wondered if I'd ever be able to survive without some crutch. For the first time since I was sixteen I was single, and learning that I didn't *need* a man. I didn't marry again for six years.

Around Christmas time I went to a retreat in California with *Guruji*, with all my medicines. When I came home after the retreat I phoned him, needing support. Over the phone he gave me a mantra and got me to repeat it several times. When I hung up, something inside me said, "I don't need any more medicines." At that moment I got blissfully high. I felt so good that I abruptly stopped taking my pills, trying to go cold turkey, but that didn't work for long. So I told the psychiatrist that I wanted to stop, but couldn't sleep, and they said they would help me through it. By now I had pretty much educated myself on how to get off these things. After two months I was clean, sleeping at night and feeling good. Within two years my life had totally turned around. I haven't taken any drugs since, and later the cigarettes went. My life was back.

In 1979 a friend gave me a book and said I must read it. It was **Man of Miracles** by Howard Murphet, about an Indian Holy man known as Sathya Sai Baba. This book changed my life. I knew he was for me and straight away wrote him a letter. I told him about my life and said that I would love to come and see him. Grateful to *Guruji* for all his help, I knew it was now time to leave him as I had found my true teacher. After coming to Swami, miracle after miracle began to happen in my life. In 1979 I also met John, who was to become my husband. At last I was to experience a loving, happy relationship.

But there is always a test. After getting clean, I went to a dentist who extracted two teeth and dislocated my jaw. It took three years to find out what the problem was. It was causing severe pain in my jaw and head twenty-four hours a day. This has never completely gone away. The doctors kept telling me to take painkillers but I refused to take more pills except for the occasional aspirin. Though I've lived with a headache for over twenty years, I have the strength to cope with it.

John and I married in 1981, and I started a Sai Baba group. My husband wasn't interested. All the time I was reading about Baba and wanting to go to India. In 1987 I told John that I wanted to go, and him to come with me. He said, "Well, that will take a miracle. We have no money, there's no way *you* can go, let alone the two of us." I said, "If Swami's everything he's supposed to be, we'll get there. Get your passport anyway." I couldn't find mine anywhere, and hadn't seen it for years. I thought if it turned up that would be a sign that I'd go to India. My daughter knew nothing about this, and a few days later she came from her room saying, "What's this I found at the back of my drawer Mom?" It was my passport. Ding! In my mind *that was it,* we were going. So I wrote Swami a letter saying that I wanted to come with my husband, but we had no money.

Soon after that I had a dream that my real mother was writing me out a cheque. My intuition told me that this meant something. So I wrote my mother a letter saying that I wanted to go to India, and asking if she could lend me some money. She had plenty of cash, but I had never asked her for anything. I knew that she hated gurus and India, but I put it in the mail and left it. Soon I had a phone call from Mom. "*Why* do you want to go to that God forsaken place? *Are you out of your mind?*" I'd expected that. Then she softened and said, "Well, if you've really got you heart set on it I'll buy you a ticket. But I don't want you to go alone, so I'm going to send John to watch over you." She sent us three times after that. I don't know why. She bitched every time.

So in 1987 John and I made our first trip to see Baba. We received so much from him and were happy. We were lucky enough to have an interview. My husband is a sweet, loving man and I was his primary concern. He asked Swami, "Has my wife paid off her karma now? Can you help her with her headache?" Swami replied, *"Next time."* I thought that was great; I would be healed. We came back the next year hoping, but not realising that Swami's timing is different to ours. It was *nine years later* that we had our next interview. That's a long wait. Basically, I was no longer thinking about next time.

Back in the interview room Swami asked me, *"How are you sir?"* I replied that I was not so great. He said, *"Why? What's the matter?"* I said, "A head problem." He didn't seem interested and started to talk to other people. Then he turned to me and said, *"You are always taking medicine."* I thought he was off, as I didn't take anything now. He said, *"Don't do that anymore."* Then I realised I was on antibiotics all the time because of a sinus infection from my jaw problem. He looked at me with compassion and said, *"How is it? How is the pain?"* I replied that it was bad. *"I know it is,"* he said. Then he appeared to go into a trance. Next he showed me on *his* head where the problem was, and suddenly reached over and put his hand on *my* head. He kept rubbing where the pain was, saying, *"I will help you. No more medicine."* My husband started weeping, because he knew how bad it was, although I hardly ever talked about it. After that the pain got worse for a while, but now it's much better. In due time, I know it will go completely.

Baba says, "People now have more faith in medicine than in God. Life is built on capsules and tablets. Though you may dine on the best of foods, pills are certain to ruin health. You should not make these temporary makeshifts a permanent habit."

Through all my pain and problems, addictions and marriages cigarettes were my best friend. I thought I would *never* give them up. I was probably twelve when I started playing with tobacco. I only quit when we moved to live in Puttaparthi in 1994. There came a day when I gave Swami the only letter I ever wrote about giving up cigarettes. I told him that it was my best friend I was talking about, and I had searched my heart and didn't think I could give them up; but I wanted to. After he took the letter I cut down to about three a day. And I swear to God, I could *not* get the smell off my hands. I went to *darshan* every day to see Baba, and sitting so close to people I started to get paranoid that people would smell the tobacco on me. The smell was getting stronger and stronger and driving me nuts. I would keep washing my hands and even put alcohol on them, but it made no difference. I didn't want to smell like a cigarette in *darshan*.

So I had someone bring me Nicorette patches from the States. Then I picked a day, not telling my husband, and decided to give it my best shot. I had made up my mind I didn't want this addiction, and took it one day at a time. After ten days I got really edgy wanting a cigarette, so I tried a patch. It took the edge off. Over the next few months I only used about ten patches and I got cranky and ugly. My poor husband! I'm usually a quiet person, but now at night I would talk, talk, and talk. John had to tell me to shut up. For four months all I did was talk, but I conquered it. It took determination, the patches and mainly being around Swami every day. I have an addictive nature, but one by one I've overcome all of my addictions.

My relationship to God had always been ambivalent. I wanted to believe but I never really did. I went to Second Baptist Church as a child, but never believed what they told me. They said that if you were baptised you were not allowed to sin anymore. I was just a little girl, and I wondered how you could go your whole life and not swear or do anything bad. I thought, 'If that's what God says and I get baptised, then I'm ruined, because I know I'm going to do *something* naughty.' So I wouldn't get baptised. However I always thought that if Jesus were here on this Earth I would have to go and see him, if it was a real story. I didn't think it was, but I always wanted it to be. When I met Sai Baba He made me believe in God, because he made the darndest things happen, and I had no choice but to believe. So many miracles have happened to change my life.

Of course if I had my life over I'd like my children to be happy. I would have liked to be with them. But I can't feel guilty anymore. Finally I said, "No, that's over, I've paid my dues." I believe that I came here with a purpose and my kids too, and it is our karma. They chose their life, with me as a mother, for their own lessons. I was always kind to them and did the best I could. But I'm sorry they had such a hard time, and I love them more than I could say. I hope that one day they can forgive me, and heal and be happy, and love themselves as well as me.

John and I decided to stay in India in 1994. We bought a small flat in Puttaparthi near the ashram and love our life here. I go to *darshan* every day and that is my spiritual practice. I have a strong connection with Baba, and my inner guidance has never let me down once. I try to do the right thing every second of the day. I've had many experiences that show me that there is a God and I'm on the right path. There are still tough times but I can rise above them now. The experiences I went through have made me strong. For the last twenty-seven years life has been good.

I saw that if I could make it through everything that had happened to me, I could do *anything*. I'm pretty stubborn when I want to do something and don't get swayed by anyone now. My husband loves me to pieces and knows I'm a good person. He still has me on a pedestal after all these years, and tells everyone how wonderful his wife is. But I don't let *anyone* walk all over me now, and my husband can't get away with anything. But I try not to be hurtful. I have a straight line to my conscience and follow that. I couldn't be happier. People say that I seem so balanced and normal, and come across as having reached peace of mind.

My only desire now is for God-consciousness . . . enlightenment. That's the reason I'm living here now. I want to realise my own Divinity. I am grateful for everything that has happened in my life. Swami knows me better than anyone, and always gives me what I need. It was all worth it to get me to where I am now. I'm waiting for the day that he'll come up to me and say, *"Do you remember when you said, 'If you are there God, please forgive me?' It was me that heard you."*

It *had* to have been him that saved me.

All Truths in the universe will manifest in your heart, if you are sufficiently pure. The harder the circumstances, the more trying the environment, the stronger are the men who come out of these circumstances.

- Sathya Sai Baba

Update from Grace, February 2013

I'm happy to say, and I attribute this to living in Baba's presence for so many years, that I remain free from all past addictions. During those years with Swami, I had trials and tribulations that many times tempted me to revert back to old habits. And I am proud to say that with God's grace I was able to find my inner strength, and quickly realise I didn't need crutches anymore. I learned that it takes knowledge of the God within or without to know you are bigger than the addiction, and you control it. I *am* addicted to my husband and new little kitty, but we won't tell anyone that.

5

The Perils of Night Duty

The body is the temple of the Lord; keep it in good and strong condition.

- Sathya Sai Baba

Hilary was born in London, England in 1940. She is youthful looking, healthy and has enormous stamina, allowing her to work long hours as a massage therapist and counsellor, and to do voluntary work in hospices with cancer patients. Who knows if she would be able to do all this, had she continued to smoke heavily? She is a dynamic, lovely woman and a great example for us all.

Hilary's story: After my very first night duty as a student nurse, my fellow students invited me to come and have a cup of tea and a cigarette. I said that I didn't smoke, but they said I would *need* a cigarette after doing a night duty. So as I wanted to be like everyone else, I had my first cigarette. I was eighteen.

This incident started thirty-seven years of smoking. I didn't think I was addicted; I enjoyed my cigarettes! They were part of my life, whether socially, or on my own. Over the years, the number I smoked increased and reached twenty a day. I wouldn't let myself smoke any more than that otherwise, I told myself, I would have a problem! I didn't ever think about stopping until the 80's, more than twenty years later. By then a lot of information about the ill-effects of nicotine on health was emerging. I didn't think it applied to me, as I didn't think I had a habit. How addictions can delude.

I decided to try to stop smoking at various times over the following years, whenever there was a blitz in the press about the dangers. I tried hypnosis, which had no effect at all. Then I had acupuncture, and small studs were left in my ears, which I could twiddle whenever the desire to smoke occurred. That didn't work either, but I didn't have the heart to tell the Acupuncturist that I would be her first failure, as she told me that everyone she had treated hadn't smoked again. So I had failed once more, and to me this was a clear sign that I needn't give up, and I didn't really have a problem. How arrogant and how ignorant I was.

I first came to visit Swami in 1993, followed swiftly by another visit in 1994, and again in 1995. When I made the third visit, prior to arriving in India I talked to Swami about the possible problem I would have while I was in Puttaparthi regarding my frequent need to '*nip out for a smoke*'. I prayed that for the duration of my stay he would help me not to want any cigarettes, as I was coming to try and improve the spiritual side of my life, and didn't want physical demands to interfere with this. As a precaution, I decided to get a month's supply of nicotine patches to see me through my three-week stay in India. I smoked all the way over during the flight, and in the hotel room. Thirty-seven years is some habit.

On the morning we left Bangalore, I stuck the first nicotine patch on my left upper arm. Immediately I had a 'fizzing' sensation in my body. (I've asked other people who have used patches and nobody has had this sensation, in fact they've had no physical sensations at all.) I thought 'Oh good its working,' and then forgot about it. We had morning *darshan* of Swami, and my day was fine with no desire to smoke at all. I kept checking that the patch was still there by patting my left upper arm. Later that day I met some friends in the village for supper. When the meal was delivered to the table, the fizzing in my body increased so much that it was becoming unpleasant, and I said I would have to take the patch off. I felt on my arm, and the patch wasn't there. It could not have fallen off as it was like a plaster. So I checked my other arm, knowing full well that I hadn't put it there. I checked my clothes and inside my top. There was no sign of the patch anywhere.

The next day, while resting before afternoon *darshan*, I was enveloped in a burning fever that made even my hair hot to touch. A room-mate tried to cool me, but I was so hot it was impossible. This passed after a couple of hours. And I have never had a cigarette since then; I have had no *desire* to have a cigarette; I have had no withdrawal symptoms at all. Now I cannot bear to be near, or in the presence of anyone who smokes. I cannot claim to have given up smoking at all. Swami took away my desire to smoke, and I think that the fever was to burn the addiction and possible side effects out of me. When I came home and told my children that I no longer smoked, they said that it was indeed a miracle.

Prayers for worldly ends do not reach God. They will reach only those deities who deal with such restricted spheres. But all prayers arising from pure love, unselfish eagerness to render service, and from hearts that are all-inclusive, will reach God. For God is the very Embodiment of Love.

- Sathya Sai Baba

Update from Hilary, March 2013

I am still very definitely a non-smoker. I find I am also very intolerant of having to walk behind anyone who is smoking in the street, and inevitably need to cross to the other side of the road to avoid having to inhale their stale smoke.

I work in a hospital environment, and find it sad to see people having to walk with oxygen tubes up their nose, or needing an oxygen cylinder everywhere they go because of the toll that smoking has had on their body over the years, and of course on their way of life. I thank God every day I see this that I am no longer a victim of this invasive habit.

6

Culture Shock

'Where there is a will there is a way' is absolutely true. At first the will is your own. It has to be strengthened by the will of God until you convert it into the Almighty Will of God. You seem to be playing a particular game, which you do not really desire to give up. You can change the game if you will. You are not weak and helpless. Every strength and power is within you.

- Sathya Sai Baba

Rajesh has lived most of his thirty-four years in America. Since October 2000 he has lived in India. Meeting Rajesh it was hard to believe he was addicted to crack/cocaine. He looks so pure, youthful and angelic. Bubbling with energy, he's a picture of health and vitality, a handsome man with big liquid eyes, which would light up when talking about God. We nicknamed him "the chipmunk" because of his cheeky, toothy smile. He talks little about his past, but was willing to share the following story, in the hope it might help others struggling with addictions.

Rajesh's story: I was born of Indian parents in the South East of America in 1968. That part of the world is pretty conservative and prejudiced towards coloured people, so it was tough on me from the beginning. My parents had moved from a traditional Indian culture to 1960s America, and looking back I can see that there was nowhere I could fit in. That took various manifestations, including being an angry and frustrated child with a profound feeling of alienation.

At the age of twelve I was offered alcohol and marijuana. The first time I drank I had two beers, and next time it was five triple hard drinks and I got sick. But I was happy to fit in somewhere at last, and it made me feel like somebody totally different. I had found a new way of life and a culture I could relate to. Gradually, over the next four years I changed my identity from someone trying to do well at school, to identifying with the drug using, partying crowd. My grades progressively dropped, and I was caught drinking at school. I got involved with the neighbourhood gangs who were into mischievous things like stealing, skipping school and getting high. My parents tried to deny what was happening, and I tried to hide it, but by the time I graduated high school at sixteen they had figured it out.

I made the full break into being an addict in my first year of college. It was not a conscious choice. At the age of seventeen taking various substances became an everyday thing, and I started to use cocaine and LSD. I'd always drunk a lot and smoked pot, and at nineteen I was introduced to crack/cocaine. Then I stuck to crack as it was relatively inexpensive, and I liked it. That was the big downfall, as it is extremely addictive and completely took over my life for the next six years.

Even so I did manage to work, but lost jobs frequently and got into stealing. First I stole from my parents, and that's when they knew for sure that something was wrong. And I would borrow money from them with the tacit understanding that they would never get it back. I think that the most important thing to an Indian family is to deny the situation and pretend it's not happening. I felt they were more worried about what other people thought than what was really going on. They did get angry, but their denial of my behaviour allowed it to continue. On the other hand they stuck through the ordeal with me more than most parents would have, and I'm certainly grateful for that. If they hadn't kept supporting me time and time again, I may not have come out alive.

Finally, when I was twenty-one they couldn't take it anymore, and said I had to go. They could no longer leave me at home by myself. I was a full-blown crack addict, which means that I could not be trusted. The desperation for the drug was high, and my mind was being clouded and destroyed day by day. There was no rationale in my mind and I had lost all moral feeling. Deep down I knew what I was doing was wrong, but I wouldn't allow myself to see it. I just had to have what I had to have. So I did crazy things. I stole money and expensive things from the house, and my parents didn't know what would be missing next. They kicked me out as they didn't know what else to do. My mother worried herself sick about what might happen to me, and they still rooted for me and were willing to be there for me . . . at a distance.

A friend of mine in Memphis Tennessee had a business cleaning carpets, and I joined him. It meant moving further away from my parents. It lasted four months. I spent the money as soon as I got it, and my health deteriorated more and more. I got down to around 110 lb. and looked emaciated and drawn. I got into a bunch of trouble because I couldn't pay the bills, and everything was crumbling around me. Then one day I had a serious car accident in a brand new Mazda truck that I had talked my father into getting for me. My parents were still trying to support me. But after that it all caved in, they told me I had to get away, and I knew I had to run. My parents were moral people and I had stretched them too far.

In 1991 at the age of twenty-three I moved across the country to Portland, Oregon. I was on my own for the first time and had nothing material left. I spent one year homeless, and slept in shelters or on the streets. Because of being in poor neighbourhoods it was dangerous, and my life was threatened several times. One time I had a gun put to my head by a gang, got beaten up and all my money taken. Another time I had a knife at my neck over some drugs. I never begged, but I stole and also worked. I was a waiter, and often had people coming by the restaurant to give me my drugs. I would stay up all night doing drugs and drinking, and get up just in time for work the next afternoon. I'd have my only meal at work, and most days I'd get high in the bathroom. My health was deteriorating badly. You can't eat well when you are doing crack, so eating was haphazard.

Rarely did I allow the supply of drugs to run out, because when I had no drugs the emotional pain was too intense. I couldn't bear it, and had found an effective way to avoid it by smoking crack. It was an everyday, all day process for me. If I wasn't using I was going to get some, or I was thinking about *how* to get some. It preoccupied my mind twenty-four hours a day except when I was sleeping, and I imagine I dreamt about it too. The only reason I worked was to get money to get high.

But every night before I went to sleep, deep in my subconscious, I knew something was wrong and that it had to change. But the disease of addiction is insidious and you can't see what is happening. It was as if I was only doing a normal thing, though on some level I knew I wasn't. I used to feel the problem was always something other than the drugs, like if some person in my life would change, or if I got a better job, things would be fine. I didn't pin it on the fact that I had a serious drug problem. But when I went to bed at night I would know it, and I'd say, 'I'll never do this again.' It happened every day, hundreds of times, before the Grace came to me and I took the leap. The more I did drugs and the more things I did that I'd said I would never do, the worse I felt about myself as a human being. So I continued to anaesthetise myself so the pain would not surface. I had the sense to know that my life was in the pits, and that I was dragging others down with me. My parents were getting drained trying to help me. I called them from time to time. Every time the phone rang they were afraid they would be told I was dead.

I spent a year like this on the streets of Portland. I was losing jobs left and right and any semblance of a life. I was getting kicked out of places, and started to develop a reputation among restaurants. Something big was going to happen and I can only speculate, but I probably would have died soon had I continued. Then in February 1993 something changed, though I can't tell you what it was that opened inside of me. Looking back, I think that a deep but denied belief in God was driving me. But I was so far from a sound mind that I couldn't connect with anyone, let alone God. I can only say that someone was looking after me when I didn't know it.

The way it took shape was through a Twelve-Step programme. I had been along to Narcotics Anonymous (NA) while still using, but was only half-serious. Anyone in Twelve-Steps will tell you that you have to be *much more* than half-serious. For years I had gone to meetings occasionally, so I went seeking help there. I had been going to the meetings a lot saying I was clean. Of course other addicts know when you are lying, but they kept encouraging me saying, 'Oh good, glad you're clean, come back again.' I felt that either these people were accepting of me, or else they were stupid. Either way it was okay, because it was a place I could get away with stuff, and those places were running out.

At the same time I heard about a drug programme that was free, so I went to the Welfare Office to find out about it. They said that you had to be unemployed to go on it. The one thing I was holding onto was the fact that I could work. The insanity of my addiction made me think it was more important to keep my job than do a programme, so I said no thank you. Then two months later something clicked inside and I thought, 'I just *have* to do this. I've already lost everything anyway. I have to get into this programme, and I have to change.' Every day I phoned to see if there was a spot in the treatment centre. And I started to pray that if there was a God I needed help, and wanted to get into this programme. Within a week they'd found a spot for me. Usually it takes two months.

That night I went to a Twelve-Step meeting and told everyone I was going to do a drugs programme. This time I was serious. I stayed in it for three weeks, and came out clean. Now the challenge was to *stay* that way, so I started to go regularly to Twelve-Steps where I had good connections. At the meetings people talked about God a lot and in the beginning I had problems with that word. Having grown up in the Bible belt where people throw the hell word around, I had a resistance to it. Being brought up a fundamental Hindu, in a right-wing Christian, area added to the confusion. But it started to dawn on me that there was a Higher Power, and for a year it was the only term I felt comfortable with. Now that I was serious, this Power came into my life. Now I was ready to do whatever was going to work. My parents and other people had tried to help me and nothing had worked. But in NA there were people like myself, and I could see *them* changing, which was inspiring. If they could do it, I knew I could too.

A year later I met a wonderful spiritual man who became my sponsor in NA, and he really worked with me on God. That's when my relationship with God started to happen. He told me that if I wanted a good life I would have to do some work, and do things I hadn't been comfortable with, like praying. I was willing to try it. The Twelve-Steps are about developing a relationship with a Higher Power, clearing out past patterns and developing new ones by surrendering to a Power greater than ourselves. I did the work pretty intensely for two and half years, and stayed clean. I thought about God, I wrote to God, I prayed to God, and began to see immediate results. I was changing internally and got better and better.

After a year-and-a-half a guy in the programme said to me, "You're a pretty smart fellow. You have a life now; you're not living on the streets, putting stuff into your body and poisoning yourself. Why don't you go to college?" This had always been a dream for me. I'd flunked out before due to drugs, and felt incapable of studying. I wanted to prove to myself that I could do this, so I agreed and had an amazing four-year experience. It was fun, and my fears of flunking out were soon put to rest as I started getting A's. As I had just woken up to life I wanted to explore myself, and find out what I really loved. Here I was able to design my own programme and took an interest in the culture I had previously rejected, including the Indian scriptures. After the first year I got a scholarship for academic excellence.

All the time I was doing the Steps and turning everything over to God and I could steadily see how my prayers were answered. I often said the Serenity Prayer, which is always a part of Twelve-Step meetings:

> *God grant me the Serenity*
> *To accept the things I cannot change,*
> *The courage to change the things I can,*
> *And the wisdom to know the difference.*

When the pain came up I would pray, and rely on the support of the people in the group. I still had deep feelings of rejection and unworthiness, but now I had God and my studies to replace the drugs and restore my self-esteem. Now I had a reason for living. Sometimes I felt serene and good, and it was clear that when I did the work on the Steps and prayed, there would be positive results. I concluded there must be a God. Also there were people in my life in the same process, and their lives were drastically changing too, so I couldn't buy into my own doubt.

After two years of college I moved out of Portland, to finish my last two years of school in a small town. This was a big shift because it meant leaving that NA programme. This had become my family and an identity for me, so I had a hard time going. I felt that after all these people had given me I had to give back. I couldn't have given up crack alone, and I'm really grateful to them. But in the new town I was beginning to butt heads with some people in NA, and had the feeling that I didn't fit any more. What had to change was my reliance on others, because eventually I had to find God within myself. One of the Steps talks about improving a conscious contact with God through meditation. I was realising that I didn't have that.

Even during my drug use I had always been drawn to meditation. It's hard for a crack addict to concentrate, but sometimes I would take my recorder to the beach and meditate to sitar music. There was something in me, maybe from a past life, which knew meditation could bring me peace. When I moved out of Portland I found the Buddhist Vipassana meditation practice, and loved it. I had grown up mistrusting gurus, so was happy to find a practice with no guru involved. Unlike the Twelve-Steps, which are about surrender to God, here there was no mention of God.

The result was that I got too much into my head. This was not good for me, as that's where I was defunct, always going off into mental spirals. For a year I was dried up, and lost touch with my feelings and connection to God. I didn't realise it at first, then started to see that I was having serious problems with the practice. But it seemed to be the only thing holding my life together, and I went through a lot of internal struggle. I feel that it is important for addicts to be in the heart. Our minds are addictive, so we need grounding. I know now that my path is that of the heart, but Vipassana was an important stage in my spiritual life.

On the tenth day of my first Vipassana course I spoke to another participant. The first nine days were in silence, but on the last day we could talk. He said, "I know we're not supposed to watch each other, but you can't help it, all eating and living together. You seem serious about what you are doing, and I want to tell you that there are a couple of teachers on the planet right now that I suggest you go to. They are the highest teachers around. One is Sai Baba and the other is Ammaji. They are both in India." I politely replied, "Oh, that's lovely." I had no interest and was thinking, 'Don't tell me who's *high*.' Dave was a writer and had been a devotee of Sai Baba for twenty years. He was nice enough to send me emails about Baba, and as he lived in Canada I didn't see him again. I left it in my email for a year before looking at it. When I did, the first thing I read was that Baba said Buddha and Jesus were not avatars. I knew the concept of avatar, descent of Divinity into human form, but didn't know if it was literally real or spiritual symbolism. I was offended, and thought, "Who is *he* to say that Buddha wasn't an avatar!" At that time Buddha was the closest I had to a guru. Nothing about Sai Baba attracted me. First of all his appearance put me off. He was so different to anyone I'd ever seen and I thought he looked strange. I thought he was trying to prove something with this unusual garb, bushy hair and materializations. To my mind it all seemed egotistical. So I threw all this stuff away.

One day my sponsor from Twelve-Steps called me and said he had late stage pancreatic carcinoma, a cancer that would kill him within six months. Here was this vibrant, incredible man, with so much energy, dying at fifty-four. I couldn't believe it. He was my spiritual mentor. At the same time I was leaving college and getting disillusioned with Vipassana. Everything meaningful in my life was being taken away, and I was only four years into my life of being clean and sober.

The one thing I had to hold onto was a six month trip to India that had been planned with my mother. My family is from Andhra Pradesh, and it was my first journey to see them. We arrived in India in October 1998. The idea was to spend the first two months with my mother, visiting family. It was exciting as at last I was going back to my roots. On December 15th we got to my Uncle's place, and he immediately suggested that we should go and see Sai Baba for Christmas. I told them that I did *not* want to go. But my mother was getting older, and we didn't know if she'd ever be able to come back to India. So I couldn't say no. It was a horrid experience getting there. The train was dusty, dirty and hot and I was still not adjusted to travelling in India. We arrived in Puttaparthi on Christmas Eve, and it was hot and crowded. We finally found a hotel room that was horrible, totally dirty, and four of us had to share a small room. I was feeling terrible.

That afternoon my Uncle dragged me along to *darshan*. As it was Christmas there were probably 50,000 people there. We found a place and sat squashed, cross-legged on the ground amongst this mass of humanity. My first impression of Sai Baba was of a huge figure in orange sitting on a chair, when everyone else was sitting on the floor. It confirmed every fear I had about him. We had to sit there for hours. I felt nothing but discomfort and resistance, and decided that I had no use for this ashram. But I had to bide my time and stay till the twenty-sixth when we were leaving.

After *darshan* I went out into the village and saw a sign saying Pizza and Veg-burgers. I wanted some Western food, so I went into the hotel. Sitting there was a woman I recognised from the Vipassana course. She was Dave's wife, the guy who had sent me the emails a year earlier. She remembered me, and said that her husband was in the bathroom. I was shocked to see Dave, and couldn't deny that it was a strong coincidence. We talked for two hours about avatars and Rama, Krishna and Baba and he persuaded me to go to *darshan* again in the morning. That night I went to bed early, looking at Baba's picture and saying, "If you're God, why did you give us such a dumpy place to stay?"

I was woken up at 3am and went back to the temple, thinking that it was a really far-fetched idea for God to take a human form and come to Earth. I didn't trust him. As I sat waiting for Baba to come I remember saying in my mind, "If you are God, I think you've forgotten about me. I need your help because it feels like you've disconnected from me for the last two years. Why haven't you been there for me anymore?" Dave was sitting next to me. He said, "I know you have doubts and questions. If you ever want to communicate with Baba you can write him a letter." Strangely by the time Baba came out, somehow I'd started to think he was okay and looked nice.

Next day we went to the canteen to get tea before leaving on the train. Above where they serve the food is a huge picture of Baba. As I looked at him, his eyes clearly moved back and forth and stared at me. It took me aback. Things like this didn't happen to me. My spiritual experiences were more of a feeling nature and I didn't have visions or flashes . . . except once. My girlfriend at the time was a Yogananda devotee and I had gone with her to a service one day. There was a picture of Krishna there. When I glanced at His face His eyes had done the same thing, and I did a double take. Now eighteen months later it had repeated itself with this being who people said is the reincarnation of Krishna. Something happened to me that day, and my scepticism was badly dented. Coincidences were happening, and I had a glimmer of hope.

So I asked my uncle to wait, and quickly wrote Baba a letter asking him to guide me to Liberation. I don't know where *that* idea sprang from. How to get it to him? I only had thirty minutes left before catching the train. I knew Baba lived in a building near the *darshan* hall and there were some trees nearby. So I decided to put the letter in the tree, thinking that if he's God, he'll know where it is. As I walked away, the security people came and took the letter, but I didn't care. It was happening on some deep level beyond my conscious awareness, and I had no idea what was going on. We left the ashram and went back to the family home.

My mother returned to America and I went to Bombay to meet my girlfriend, to find she had sent me an email saying that she wasn't coming, and we were finished. The relationship was all I had left to hang on to, and now that was gone too. I didn't want to go back to the States with my tail between my legs and nothing accomplished, and something inside told me to stay in India. So I went to an Ayurvedic clinic for a detox, and all the time a voice in my head kept telling me to go back and see Baba. When I finished my treatment I returned to the ashram, arriving on the sixth anniversary of when I got clean.

On my first day I got a good place right in the front for *darshan*. I wondered about the letter I'd put in the tree. Had I sold my soul to Baba? I didn't understand what I had done asking for Liberation. Again something seemed to take me over, and I borrowed a pen and paper and wrote another note. I wrote, "Okay, if you are my guru please take this letter to give me confirmation. If you aren't then don't take it." I wanted to know his response, but at the same time I wasn't too keen on giving him the letter, and I had a prime position . . . a place where he would have to pass. After a long wait Baba came along, and I held the letter close to my body, unsure if I wanted him to take it. As he came closer he was on the other side of the aisle, not near enough for me to reach out with the note. Then he suddenly turned, looked right at me and gave me a great big smile. He crossed the carpet, came over to me and took it from my hand. I immediately thought, 'Okay it's done, he's my guru.'

I thought that my life would change the next day. I expected him to give me a spiritual practice and tell me what to do with my life. It didn't happen that way. I spent five weeks at the ashram in Bangalore, had an interesting and enjoyable time, but still didn't feel connected to Baba. I was struggling, as he didn't give me a clear path. I thought that was what a guru was supposed to do. I tried to do *namasmarana*, repetition of a Divine name, but it meant nothing to me. So I did another Vipassana course and tried to figure it out there, but that wasn't working for me either. So after six months in India, feeling lost, I decided to go back to America.

The experience in India receded and felt as if it was all a dream. I had a photo of Baba on my mirror and occasionally referred to it, but he wasn't in my life in any way. I felt more and more closed internally, and even less like I fit in anywhere. And I was getting angry. So I called out in anguish, "**God, Baba, whoever you are, is this what you want for me?**" And that's when things started to change. I had this Indian tee shirt with OM SAI RAM on it, (a greeting used by Sai devotees) which I only wore indoors as I didn't want any awkward questions. One day I had no clean clothes and wore it to the grocery store. A man my age saw me, and his jaw dropped to the floor, and he was mumbling, "Puttaparthi? Puttaparthi?" He had just come back from a visit to Sai Baba. So we got talking, and he told me about the local Sai Baba Centre. I was desperate for companionship. At the time I worked in a restaurant where people drank and got high. That wasn't in my life anymore and I didn't fit in, so I was happy to go to the Centre.

When I arrived it was strange to see this group of Americans singing devotional songs about Krishna and Shiva. It was familiar, but had no meaning for me. After a few meetings they asked me to come and lead a song the following week. I took a cassette home and learned some *bhajans*. For the first time I felt what it means to sing from your heart, and praise the name of God. Then I started to go religiously twice a week. It felt great to be connected again. Soon I went to the annual Baba retreat in the mountains near where I lived, and a transformation occurred.

Everyone was singing and telling their stories for the whole weekend. As I was gazing at a huge picture of Baba, I felt my heart warming and totally opening to him for the first time. The feeling of elation I experienced lasted for two days. I was naturally high, and everything was surreal. That's what I had been looking for when I used drugs. The difference was that this feeling lasted, and it was a totally loving experience. I called everyone in my family and was able to fully express my love for them. And it didn't hurt afterwards. I didn't lose all my money, or have the police running after me. Now I was feeling my heart again, and longing to be with Baba. His 75th birthday was coming up in November 2000, and I wanted to be there, but at the same time I felt undeserving. I thought, 'Who am I to come to his 75th birthday?' which I had heard was a very auspicious occasion.

In April 2000 I signed a lease for an apartment and bought a car. Things were settling down, so I thought I would go to India after a year. All the time I was praying that I could go see Baba. One day my roommate said, "What you need to do is sell everything and go see that Baba, because you keep talking about the 75th birthday all the time." I replied that I couldn't see it happening as I had no money, owed taxes, had just taken on a year's lease on an apartment and bought a car. But things started to happen right away. A fantastic job presented itself, and a free apartment in a luxurious setting, the lease sold straight away and I was free to go to India within two months.

In October 2000 I arrived in Puttaparthi. This time I stayed, and in 2001 I had two interviews with Baba. He didn't mention anything about the drugs or my past. We were a small group of men and he said, "*You are all very good boys.*" That said something to me, because I believe he knows everything I've ever done. For him to say that confirms that I'm not my past, and I can get on with my life. I haven't thought about using drugs now for years. There is *no* inclination, and that's his Grace if I think about how much I needed them nine years ago.

Now I look on it as an experience that I set up for myself on a soul level, so that I could learn to be more loving and compassionate. Before I saw myself as a victim, always thinking, 'Poor me, why did this happen to me?' Most addicts never get out of this. I used to be unhappy that I didn't fit into the world. Now I'm really happy about it. In situations which would have made me feel terrible, I now feel so much love from within, as I know the Divine is in me. I used to be addicted to people, attention, food, TV . . . anything to numb my mind. There is no longer such a need for external things.

Now I've been here in the ashram for two years, and he's

answering every prayer, clearing darkness out of me and filling my life with joy. I'm not the same person. As I talk about the past it's like I'm talking about somebody else. The biggest change I can see is in my level of confidence. Whereas I felt *such* an undeserving person when I thought about all the stuff I was doing, now I see that *I* wasn't doing it, it was God doing everything through my life; and these experiences were valuable. Addicts are low in self-confidence because we abuse ourselves and do all the things we said we'd *never* do, and hurt ourselves and everybody around us. So we think we are worthless. I don't often beat myself up any more. I can let go of the past and see it as an experience that had to happen, and I don't need to live with those patterns anymore. Now when the fear and undeserved-ness come up I surrender it, and it soon goes. There are long periods of contentment.

My belief is that most addicts are looking for God, but they don't realise they are doing it in a destructive way. Drugs are an unconscious attempt to reach God, but they don't work. They always bring us back down again, lower and lower. With drugs I was looking for a fulfilling life, but all I ever got was trouble, confusion and chaos. When I turned to God my life rapidly began to change and I found direction, purpose and fulfilment. Looking back on the ten years since I got clean, I can clearly see the results of God coming into my life. First, He showed me how to be responsible by giving me a job, and then took me off to the perfect college for me. He showed me that I could fulfil my highest dreams if I consistently ask for help and guidance, and have the courage to follow His directions, which are always those of my own heart.

While I was still confused He brought me to His lotus feet in the form of Sathya Sai Baba. Life is very full now. I have a beautiful relationship with true intimacy, which I could never have dreamed possible. My wife loves God as I do, and together we are steadily progressing in the path of love. Since coming to live near Baba I have found a sense of inner contentment and joy, and he has opened within me my deepest desire to know my true Self, my inner Divinity. I know I have a long way to go, but I also know that I have come a long way, and he is truly taking me home. Drugs eventually led me into a self-made prison. God unlocked it, and as my friend is walking me every step of the way to what I've always been looking for — freedom.

Freedom is independence from externals. One who is in need of the help of another person, thing or condition, is a slave thereof. Perfect freedom is not given to any man on earth, because the very meaning of mortal life is relationship with and dependence on one another. The lesser the number of wants, the greater is the freedom.

- Sathya Sai Baba

7

In the Pink

By drinking intoxicating stuff, one loses control over the emotions and passions, the impulses and instincts, the speech and movements.

- Sathya Sai Baba

Kay is a picture of purity with her shining porcelain skin and clear blue eyes, serene as an unruffled lake. She appears peaceful and happy, and I had noticed her walking silently around the ashram long before we met. Later on a visit to Glastonbury I ran into Kay. I was talking about this book, and she volunteered to tell her story of addiction to cannabis, alcohol and men. Another surprise for me ... you really can't tell a book from its cover. The covers change as we do. We all have the possibility of transformation.

Kay's story: I was born in Dumfries in the South-West of Scotland in 1968, and grew up in a small mining community of three thousand people. My mother was seventeen, and my father was eighteen when they married.

As I grew up I witnessed a lot of violence between them. My father often hit my mother or us kids when he'd been drinking heavily. He got into rages and would lash out, especially me as I challenged his opinions and spoke back. If I didn't do as he said, he'd threaten me with beatings, and I'd be sent to bed. Then if I made a noise he would come in and pull off the bedclothes, bare my buttocks, and hit me repeatedly with a slipper or his hand. He told me not to cry because I deserved it. It was painful for me, but I learned to switch off the physical pain by bringing my consciousness away from the body. I grew numb to the beatings, and afterwards would cry myself to sleep, or lay listless wishing I could escape or die.

This behaviour was commonplace in our community, so I didn't know it was anything out of the ordinary, just the way we were taught right from wrong. It was part of the culture. If anything happy happened it was celebrated with alcohol. If anything sad happened, people would commiserate through alcohol as well. So I grew up in a dysfunctional family and community, seeing the grown-ups around me coping with life by resorting to a bottle.

I was introduced to alcohol at an early age. I started drinking wine at the meal table at nine, and by the age of twelve I was drinking to get through stressful situations. I started smoking, and drank anything I could get my hands on. My friend's parents owned a pub, and we'd steal from there and go somewhere quiet to enjoy getting drunk. I needed to escape the reality I was living in at home. Sometimes my parents would notice, but mostly they were too caught up with their own dramas. At family gatherings we would all be drunk. But I mostly got drunk with my friend, and it became a crutch all through high school.

When I was thirteen, my parents separated. This was a crucial juncture in my life. Father left and mother went to college. I was happy to see her gaining confidence by getting education after years of being beaten up, but sorry that my home life was falling apart. As a clever child there were expectations of me to perform well at school. I was expected to go to University, but knew I couldn't cope with that. Out of nine exams I only passed four, despite the pressure. I just wasn't interested. I had no idea how to deal with life, especially how to relate to people in social situations. A large chunk of myself was missing. At the age of sixteen I left home and went to college, and made friends with a girl who was mainly interested in drinking. We shared a room, and instead of going to college we preferred to get drunk and smoke cannabis. We thought our behaviour was normal and couldn't see how messed up we were. We just wanted to party.

Then I got a job at Marks & Spencer which was good, as there was a discipline and I had to apply myself. But I was leading a double life, working in the week and getting plastered at weekends. I was also having sex with various men to fill the huge gap in my emotional life. When I was drunk I'd meet a guy and spend the night with him, getting a quick fix for intimacy. Occasionally a relationship might last a few weeks, but they were mostly one-night stands. I was giving myself away, desperately reaching out for someone to love. After these liaisons I usually felt ashamed, resentful and disempowered. I'd always wanted the first time I made love to be special. However I lost my virginity at fifteen, when I was drunk. It was a complete violation of my dreams, and as I could never go back to being a virgin, I felt it didn't matter what I did now. I knew very little about my body, and was expecting a man to teach me how to be a woman. They couldn't show me that. By sixteen I was covering my emotional pain by escaping into sex and booze.

But I managed to keep my career together, and worked for two years at Marks & Spencer. I was good at my job and enjoyed it. But I wanted to be more creative, and moved to a ladies fashion store, and started work there as a trainee manager. By now I was making a good salary and spending it on drink, clothes and partying. I was outgoing, and enjoyed flirting with men and having a laugh. On the outside my life looked good, but my personal life was a mess. I couldn't maintain a home and kept moving from one place to another. When I got into the pits of depression, I'd nervously laugh at myself and the situations I was in and think, 'My God, what am I doing?' I would have loved to be clean, but was in denial about being addicted to anything.

At the age of twenty I decided to move from Dumfries, and applied for a transfer to Aberdeen. I landed a position as manager and moved into shared rooms with people at work. That was when the drinking escalated. We were all young and far from our hometowns. At weekends all we wanted was to go and get totally smashed. Soon I realised my drinking was a problem, and I was dependent on it to get me through. As a manager I had greater responsibilities, but the hangovers were getting worse. I often didn't want to get up to go to work, and it was becoming difficult to function. After a binge I'd spend time alone reflecting on getting my life sorted out. I wondered how. There was nobody to turn to for help, as my family was so messed up themselves. Financially I was in chaos, and finding it increasingly difficult to feed my lifestyle.

On Friday nights I used to go to a cocktail bar and drink Southern Comfort, and get completely out of my face. Then I'd have to go to work on Saturday morning. I was suppressing so much depression through alcohol, but I rarely allowed anyone to see it. Externally I appeared as a bubbly girl with a good job, beautiful clothes, hair done up, with expensive make up to make me look attractive and sophisticated. I found it hard to connect with others in a sober state, and always felt the pressure to perform socially. I wanted to come over as a vibrant and fun person. I looked good, but emotionally I was a mess. I only felt the pain when I was alone, and when it came to the surface I smoked cigarettes and drank lots of coffee. I hardly ever cried; I knew how to stop that, and I realise now that caffeine, as well as cigarettes and alcohol deadens the emotions. All my friends were like me, and used booze as a survival mechanism to get through a life which had been tough. The only time we could let an emotion show was when we were out of our heads. All this was slowly dawning on me.

After six months in Aberdeen I had itchy feet again. I found a job in Glasgow and moved there. It was an hour away from my hometown, and I started to go back and get involved with people there. I began taking amphetamines and cannabis and liked the effect of dope (cannabis), as there were no hangovers and it was a different state of consciousness. This job enabled me to go to London on buying trips, all expenses paid. There I used to meet a friend and go to acid (LSD) and ecstasy parties, and have a wild time. Playing this game of working hard and partying and mixing all these different substances, I was burning myself out.

It started to kick in and affect my work, and I couldn't hide it any longer. My bosses knew I was having problems, and I had to approach them and say that there was a lot going on in my personal life. It was the first time I had talked to anyone about the dysfunction in my family. Physically I was drained and exhausted, and emotionally I was breaking. I remember sitting in the office one day and repeating to myself, "This is all meaningless." After that day I never went back to work.

Deep down I knew I had to sort myself out. I was only twenty-one and burnt out. As my mother was away working, I went to live in her house and signed on the dole. Now I didn't have the money to maintain that lifestyle of living in the fast lane. My doctor prescribed anti-depressants. This gave me a break, and I slowed down and started to look at life with a bigger perspective. I was still drinking, but not to the same extent. I was relying more on cannabis at this time. It was more expansive than alcohol and opened up my consciousness. Drinking for me was social, about dressing up and pretending to be someone else. With cannabis I sat by myself, smoked and reflected and would sometimes draw.

I came off the anti-depressants, thinking they weren't doing me any good. After six months break I found a job at a Centre for Robert Burns, the Scottish poet. It was a nice job with a slow pace and few responsibilities. I spent a peaceful summer, and then I met a man. I had always been seeing someone, but each relationship soon ended in major conflict, a mirror of my parent's relationship. But this was different and we stayed together for two years. Steven was an alcoholic and smoked a lot of dope. He had a good job, and when we moved in together I stopped work. It was the first time I'd had a home of my own and I devoted a lot of energy to looking after the flat, in fact it became an obsession. We didn't have much money, and spent it on cannabis and alcohol. I smoked and drank every day and got irritable and agitated if I didn't. I wouldn't have said I was addicted. To us it was normal living, a way to get through the day and deal with reality by escaping from it. But I *was* addicted.

Steven and I were completely dependent on each other. We were never honest about our feelings and dealt with them by getting drunk and stoned together, and we laughed a lot. We did love each other but also shared a deep sadness. He had a violent streak, with outbursts that reminded me of my father, and I took the role my mother had played. After an intense two years it ended when he beat me up.

My mother was there at the time. It was my twenty-fourth birthday and we all went out to a bar. Mum went home drunk before us, and Steven and I started an argument at the Chinese take-away on the way home. By the time we got back to the flat in the taxi we were shouting at each other. Inside we were both fighting and hitting out, and then he smacked me in the face and pushed me into a cupboard. I remember spinning out and coming back and I was screaming in pain. My mother woke up and just said, "Kay, get into bed!" So after some verbal abuse from Steven, I went into the living room to sleep with my mother. I was sobbing and apologising to her. She just said, "Go to sleep Kay."

When I woke up one side of my face was completely swollen, and I couldn't see out of one eye. I looked in the mirror and that's when I realised how far we had sunk with our behaviour. It wasn't the first time, and it was the one thing I'd said would never happen to me. Now a man I supposedly loved and who loved me was beating me up. I decided I couldn't take any more. My mother invited me to stay with her, and I walked out of that flat with hardly any possessions. It was a turning point in my life.

I moved to Plymouth in the South-West of England. As I was shaken up by the incident with Steven I had a rest for a while. For my birthday my brother had given me a book by David Icke, **Love Changes Everything**. It was the first spiritual book I had read. He didn't give a concept of God but talked about energy, and I was able to understand about energy being all-pervasive as I'd had psychic experiences as a child. I'd also had some expansion in consciousness through taking drugs, but it was temporary, and left me feeling bad afterwards. I found the book inspiring and bought two more, one on meditation and one on chakra therapy.

I wasn't smoking dope or drinking much at this time, and I started to do the chakra exercises. It was lovely sunny weather, and it was time to be on my own, relax and immerse myself in a different level of being. I found it easy to visualise the different energy centres of the body, and I could feel energy flowing through my body. One day I had an amazing experience. Suddenly I was in unison with all there is. Everything dissolved and a tingling went through every cell in my body. Each cell was vibrating, and I was merged with everything around me in total union. Time no longer existed, and even days later I was seeing everything with intense clarity and awareness. It was completely beyond words or any drug experience I'd ever had. I realised that this was what I'd been seeking through sex and drugs. There was a feeling of love and bliss, and now I *knew* there was a God. I could never have believed it with blind faith. I had to have an awakening experience.

This had an incredible impact. I was able to look at people and see and feel the inner light of their souls. I could see the fragmentation which made people seem separate. After being in this state of ecstasy and inner awareness, I came back out of it into a state of dealing with what we call reality, which I knew now was non-reality. The separation returned. My life changed immensely, but the addictions didn't go straight away.

For two years after that my creativity exploded. I started to draw a lot and express my spiritual awakening. I needed to explore my artistic abilities and decided to go to Art College. I found a flat in Plymouth and started a course. I wasn't drinking much but smoking a lot of cannabis, reading spiritual books and painting some amazing pictures. A friend who was also a cannabis smoker introduced me to a book called **Vision of the Divine**. It was about Sathya Sai Baba. When I saw Baba's picture . . . ooh! It was a similar feeling as when I had the awakening. So I started to avidly read his teachings and they completely resonated with me. I knew it was truth, and wanted to live my life according to these teachings, but it seemed out of reach as it was so *clean.* Here I was still addicted but desperately wanting to live a life of happiness, love, truth and joy. I read more Baba books and talked with my friend about his experiences with Baba. 'There is no way could I ever live up to that,' I thought.

Slowly I had been getting more excessive with drinking and smoking, and eventually was in such a mess I could hardly function. I couldn't get out of bed in the morning without smoking a joint, wasn't eating properly, and was finding it hard to have any social contact as I was in such a depressed state. One day I woke up thinking that I couldn't stand this any longer. I cried for a long time, and prayed for something to happen. I was on my knees and completely surrendered to Baba. I didn't know what else to do.

That set off a new chain of events, and I decided to talk to my Tutor at college. She was sympathetic and suggested I take some time out. At the same time I made contact with Steven and found out that he'd got clean with Alcoholics Anonymous. We talked on the phone and he understood exactly where I was at, and how it feels to have had enough.

He offered for me to stay with him for a while. Although it was scary, as it had ended so violently, I felt we had something to clear with each other, so I went. For the first three days in Scotland I stayed in Edinburgh at my brother's flat and came to a decision. I decided there would be no more cigarettes, cannabis, drinking, coffee or tea, and I would become vegetarian. I gave up all these things in one fell swoop. My brother was supportive and helped me detoxify. I stubbed out my last cigarette there, and quite suddenly I was clean.

Then I moved into Steven's place. He was in an Alcoholics Anonymous programme, and was supportive as he was also in the process of recovery. He'd had an awakening too. I never felt drawn to AA, but did the Twelve Steps on my own, and they helped. One day I bought the Findhorn magazine. It was about avatars and had articles on Sai Baba, one by Jenny, the author of this book, talking about her healing of addictions. For the nine months I was there, I kept it under my pillow, and read everything I could find about Baba. Steven and I had a beautiful time together. We spent time in nature and enjoyed cycling and going for walks. We took lots of saunas. These were things I'd always wanted to do but never got around to because it was such a pretentious life I'd been living. This was a real everyday life. Physically, giving up all these things was easy. I felt fantastic, and it was so good to taste food, eat well and look after my body and health for a change. Emotionally it was hard. I had to get to grips with the depths of sadness and anger I felt, and Steven and I were honest and talked about our feelings. He wanted us to heal the past and the way we had broken up, and that's what we did. The nine months were spent in a completely different space, with him sober and me clean and enjoying life.

However, it became evident to both of us that the relationship was not to last. I had a strong passion to go back to Art College and he was happy for me to return and finish my course. We left each other in love this time. I returned to Plymouth and devoted all my time and energy to the course. I was also having counselling. It was an intense time, and I expressed strong emotions in my paintings. I was no longer drinking or smoking, and was celibate and this enabled me to see things with a deeper clarity. I was supporting myself, living in a bed-sit with a lovely family. Life was good.

I wrote a letter to Baba asking for the healing of my family, as I loved them very much. My friend Simon gave it to Swami in Bangalore in April 1996. I was at a point when I was confronting my parents about the abuse I'd suffered as a child, and they were finding it hard to deal with. There were long periods when they didn't contact me and my father was hostile, but I knew that I was being true to myself and that these repressed emotions had to be dealt with.

At the same time I was learning more about Baba, and decided that I had to go to India; but I had no idea how I was going to get there. Out of the blue, in September 1996, my Aunt presented me with a cheque for £1000. She had been saving it up for me. I knew that was my ticket to India. Before I made the trip I contacted my parents and a great deal of forgiveness started. I realised I was holding on to a lot of hatred and resentment, and that I couldn't change what had happened. When I told myself things should have been different it only hurt me, and I started to view the situation from a new perspective, seeing what they had been through. I had to stop being so selfish. There was no point in blaming them for what had gone wrong in my life, and I saw it was time to take some responsibility. Gradually compassion for them grew and things got better, especially with my father.

In 1997 I went alone to India for two weeks. It was an incredible experience. I went to *darshan* every day and afterwards would sit under the meditation tree on the hill overlooking the ashram. Since my experience of spiritual awakening I had been wary of meditation, as it had been so overwhelming. Now I started to meditate deeply again. Sitting under the tree, I wrote letters of apology to people I had treated badly when I was using alcohol. I was ashamed at how irresponsible I'd been, and knew I could have behaved better towards people who were kind to me. I posted them from Puttaparthi, and all of them were met with love. When I returned, my father came to stay with me for a week for the first time ever. We had lovely quality time together. It was uncomfortable at times, as I wasn't drinking and smoking, and he was. That was difficult for him, and made him more aware of his habits. But much healing occurred.

I was asking for guidance from Baba for my next steps, when I came across the teachings of Dr Goel, who has written on meditation and his *kundalini* experience. It was a revelation, and I realised what had happened to me when I was in bliss after the chakra exercise. I had thought everyone experienced that when they meditated, but now I realised it had been a *kundalini* awakening. Suddenly it all made sense, and I could understand that *kundalini* energy was moving through the chakras and dissolving the old mental formations. The periods of emotional outburst were natural, as were the periods of deep realisation, as the spiritual energy cleared the channels. Until now I had felt like a victim of life, and was always getting angry. But now I saw that it was a natural process.

In 1998 I was at Dartington College doing a degree in

Visual Performance and Arts Management. I started to meditate three times a day. This helped me be calmer and more often in the Witness State of consciousness, seeing everything that happened in a way that was accepting and embracing of it all. By the end of my second year I felt the need to go and see Dr Goel, who was also a disciple of Baba's. I approached my tutors and was told it was the wrong time and I might blow my degree if I went. But I was determined to go, and said I was booking my ticket. Then one of my tutors came to me with a suggestion. She offered me the possibility of going to India for three months and doing a project on my journey. I agreed to this opportunity, and my father gave me part of the money to go.

I arrived in Guruji's ashram, and two days later he left his body. I never met him. So I stayed and documented his Mahasamadhi, the ultimate union with the Divine, the final stage of Yoga. I had a month of profound experiences. All the spiritual questions I'd wanted Guruji to answer were actually answered by his death. I had felt the need for confirmation that I had experienced a true *kundalini* awakening. But with his death I knew I didn't need anyone else to tell me it was real. I spent a further month in Baba's ashram, and finished my project, which I dedicated to him.

For four years I had been celibate, and now I met a man. For the first time I had a relationship that wasn't based on drink or smoke. It was based this time on truth and honesty, but there was still some dependency there. I was still looking outside myself for approval, and I could see that I needed to love myself and this body, rather than looking outside myself for love. It made me recognise that I felt much shame about my past promiscuity. I became aware that no man could teach me how to become a woman. Somehow that's what I had been looking for. How could a man know what it's like to be in a woman's body and teach me? It was crazy. Something clicked within me that helped me to see that we are all souls living in these bodies, and we've been given different genders to learn something. So I started to explore natural fertility awareness and the menstrual cycle. I got into harmony with my own bodily rhythm, and it was liberating and empowering.

Life was rich and stimulating. I was going to regular *satsangs* at the Ramala Centre in Glastonbury. This is a beautiful Sai Baba Centre and exudes peace and light. There I took an Education in Human Values course, which is a system of teaching children human values and how to live a good and happy life. It was developed by Baba and is having profound effects in many schools all over the world. My creative life was active and I was busy making artwork for a Goddess conference in Glastonbury. I had an exhibition in 2001 and it inspired and helped a lot of women. I moved into the Ramala Centre. It was good to be living there, practising meditation in that beautiful space every day and living Baba's teachings as I'd always wanted.

My great dream was that there would be a healing in my family, and that one day we would all get together. There was no way I could see that happening when I had written the letter to Baba with these prayers. It was a time of turmoil and confrontation with my parents. But after doing a course in healing, I had the opportunity to give healing to my mother, father and brother. They all had spiritual experiences, and I connected deeply with my father at a soul level and it was mind-blowing. At one point in my life I could have killed him for the violence and brutality he inflicted on us, and now there he was laid out in front of me, vulnerable. He told me that when I was a child he was emotionally disturbed, and that the alcohol motivated the attacks. I was able to give him healing and feel love and compassion flow through me into his soul body. The hatred dissolved and there was only love.

My mother and I had an up and down relationship, though we loved each other greatly. She had found it hard to connect with me as a child, and I felt emotionally distant from her. When I gave her healing I felt myself melting back into my mother, and she felt a profound sense of warmth. My brother also had a lovely experience. He was the only one still resistant to us all getting together. Then on November 23rd 2000, Baba's 75th birthday, my brother graduated from Edinburgh University. The whole family was there, and we were able to hold hands around the lunch table. It was amazing and a complete blessing from Baba.

Again I went to India in 2001 and stayed for three months, visiting Amma and other ashrams as well as Sai Baba's. It was great for my confidence travelling alone by train. I had so many beautiful experiences and synchronicities, meeting people and sharing our journeys. I spent five weeks with Amma and she blessed my work. At Baba's I started to develop work for the next Goddess conference called *"In the Pink,"* a celebration of the heart of the Mother. My creativity was flowing, unhindered by the suppressing effects of my previous addictions.

In July 2002 I went to a workshop with Byron Katie in London, and this provided me with important tools to deal with the remaining negative feelings towards my father. I stood in front of hundreds of people and had a session with Katie about the beatings I had received from him. I cried a lot, and doing her method, "The Work" I started to see things differently. She suggested that I make a list of hurtful things I had done to my father. This was a different approach, as in my eyes *I* had been the victim, not him.

Soon after this, I made the journey to Scotland to visit my family. On the train I made the list and wrote a letter. My father met me at the station, and when we were home I read to him what I'd written:

"Dear Dad, for years I have re-lived you hitting me in my mind and this has been mental torture, as I could only see you as someone who hurt me. I need to take responsibility for this abusive thinking, and apologise to you for what I have done. I have hated you and at times wanted to kill you. As a child I could only ever see the bad things you did, and never honoured the good. I desperately wanted you to love and nurture me, and it was a living nightmare to experience my inner conflict when I rejected your expressions of love. When I returned from India, you attempted to express your sadness that I didn't phone you. I didn't listen to you and was only interested in defending myself. I have suffered enough of this inner torture and am open to being in an honest relationship with you, where I can express myself freely, without fear of punishment. I look forward to this new relationship based on honesty and love."

I kept eye contact with him while reading this, and at the end we smiled at each other. A few moments later, tears poured down my face. Dad asked me why I was crying and I said that I felt a huge relief, and I loved him. He replied that he loved me too. I asked him for a hug. It felt so good to be held lovingly by my father. After this I felt incredibly calm and light and we walked peacefully to the lake where he fished as a child.

I feel so much more at peace now than I have ever done. Resolution has taken place, thank God. The biggest growth in my life has been learning to love myself and embrace my femininity. Swami has taught me to live a life that has value, and to respect and love myself as a woman. When in India, I like the separation between the men and women in the ashram and love watching how close and easy the Indian women are with each other. Sitting with thousands of women and being in that amount of feminine energy is beautiful, and I found it to be greatly healing.

I can see now how my addictions were a way of getting out of the body to escape emotional pain, as I'd done to escape physical pain as a child. My healing process was about consciously getting *into* the body and practising spiritual teachings in everyday life. To me being spiritual is about being conscious *in* the body. Being addicted was about getting *out* of the body, numbing it from any feeling, thought process or problem. Sai Baba has helped me to transform the anger, fear, and grief within me. I know how it feels to get into the pits of despair and depression. The addictions were a way of embracing the darkness.

Now it's a completely different life. Baba was there for me when it felt like everyone else drew away. He accepted me as I was. He didn't point the finger at me and say I was an alcoholic, or addicted to drugs or sex. It was only me that was judging myself. He opened his arms and greeted me with love. Through my weird and wonderful journeying with him and his teachings, he has healed the traumas of my childhood, re-united the family and empowered me to live a life of truth. Instead of using various substances to get me through the challenges of life, I now rely on God as my true support.

When women are true and brave, kind and compassionate, virtuous and pious, the world can have an era of peace and joy.

- Sathya Sai Baba

Update from Kay, April 2013

After a lot of detective work I finally got hold of Kay's phone number, and she picked up first time. I was happy, and not surprised to hear that she is doing well. She hasn't touched cigarettes or cannabis since we spoke ten years ago, and says she can't go near it. Alcohol was never her drug of choice, and she was not addicted to it, although she did drink a lot at times. She has the occasional glass of wine now, maybe for a celebration, but not to get drunk. There is no craving to go on drinking for the effect.

Kay's relationship with men is an on-going process of healing. She recently split amicably with her partner of several years, and they are still friends. She has lovely male friends now, who are nice to her. The wounds are healing, it all takes time. Her spiritual practice is self-enquiry, and living open to the moment and what life has to bring. Later this year she has plans to live at Findhorn, the famous community in Scotland. Her creativity is simmering away and she feels inspired now to write as well as paint. She sounds happy.

8

'Rollercoaster'

"When people pull back from worldly pleasures their knowledge of the Divine grows, and this knowing causes the yearning for pleasure to gradually fade away. But inside, they may still hanker for pleasures. Even those minds that know the path can be dragged away from it by unruly senses."

- Bhagavad Gita Ch. 2 v 59

Carl was born in Hanover, Germany in 1968. I met him in Puttaparthi in January 2004. He had picked up The Ultimate High, opening it where Rajesh, another cocaine addict, talks about Vipassana meditation. Carl was about to do the same course, but now decided to stay at the ashram. He was hyper and intense, having stopped injecting cocaine only days before. His story illustrates the determination not to give up trying, despite many relapses. Carl went to the AA meetings in Puttaparthi and over two months he visibly relaxed and lightened up. As of March 2005, he is still clean and doing well.

Carl's story: I started using drugs when I was sixteen. First it was alcohol, but I never liked it much. Then I was introduced to marijuana, and loved it straight away. My mother got together with a guy who smoked a lot. I noticed the smell of hash in our apartment, and told her. After a while we smoked together, and it was never a problem to smoke at home. She just warned me not to get caught by the police, or smoke outside the house. She had started smoking again with the new boyfriend, who smoked every day. By the age of seventeen, I smoked every day too.

I was a punk, and hated everything. I was in trouble at school, and hung around with friends who had the same rebellious thoughts as me. We protested about everything, and smoking was a way to escape the pressure. We met every day, and our hobby was smoking and doing nothing. School was no fun anymore; I hated it. When I was eighteen we moved from Hanover. I stopped school and learned carpentry for the next three years. I smoked all day and wasted most of my time. I went to punk concerts with my friends, and stayed up all night.

But we wanted to feel something stronger, and at the age of nineteen I started using other drugs too. First there was speed, then cocaine for partying. In the beginning I was euphoric. I took mushrooms and LSD big time, and started to think there must be something other than the real world, as my first LSD trips were so mystical. But when I came down it was depressing, because I had to come back into this reality. I started to have difficulty with this, and my depressions were growing. I lived in a dream world. I was close to giving up carpentry, as I had trouble with the guys at work who were older than me and 'normal'. I was a learner, always having to do the worst work. So I went to a doctor, and he signed a paper to say I didn't have to work. It was a big relief. I just went to school once a week to take the carpentry exam; I passed and got the certificate to be a carpenter.

At this time I started to snort cocaine. I was bored with life and wanted some kicks, and I was soon addicted. When I didn't have cocaine I got depressed, and had problems with my girlfriend. I couldn't save money, though I had a job on the side. My moods were changing and I became more aggressive. Then I went on vacation for two months with my girlfriend to Portugal, and there was no cocaine around. I felt good about this, but we met a dealer and lived at his place, smoking marijuana from morning to night. It felt unreal. I wanted to get back the feelings I had with LSD; sometimes I had felt completely one with everything on those trips. But it was not *possible* to get this all the time. I was searching for enlightenment.

Life was depressing. It was just about going to work to earn enough money to party at the weekend. At the age of twenty-two I started to do heroin. I felt helpless. There was no teacher, or anyone to talk to. I was only interested in reading about drugs, and being a drop-out was my one goal in life. Things got worse with heroin, but it took a year before I was really addicted. In the beginning I was only smoking and snorting it. The kick was very high; I was far away at that moment and that's what I loved. I felt that nothing and nobody could touch me; there was no pain anymore. I felt I had a lot of power, and no problems. Of course that was an illusion. My girlfriend broke up with me. I tried to get her back, but with my drug use we'd had many bad times, and I was aggressive and depressed.

Then after a huge weekend of partying, mixing all kinds of drugs, I visited a friend and he said, "Hey, let's go get a syringe and do some with a needle." From that point, things got worse. It was the first time I felt a *physical* addiction. I woke up in the morning and felt terrible. The mind addiction was there before, but now my body started to need it. It was a big change. I didn't have to think about all the emotional garbage now. There was only one thing to think about . . . how to get the stuff. I was on heroin for a year, then did cold turkey for a few weeks, then would start using again. This roller coaster went on for a while.

There were other drugs too. I didn't go a day without smoking marijuana, and took strong painkillers and sleeping pills when I couldn't get heroin. I took a loan from my bank and all the money was going into my veins. Sometimes I worked, and sometimes I couldn't. The addiction had made me start stealing and dealing. I stole a lot from my mother. She went to Australia for four months and gave me her credit card. This surprised me, and wondered if she knew what I was doing. But I couldn't resist the temptation. I used the card a lot, and always told myself that this would be the last time. I hated myself for it.

Then I went to a doctor who gave private prescriptions for addicts to get the opiate codeine. They put in something so it wasn't possible to inject it. He gave me codeine as a heroin substitute. It took away the pressure to get money. It gave me energy and took away the pain, and as it was pure there were no side effects. I became highly addicted to this too, but I felt better mentally as I didn't have to run after the heroin.

Then ecstasy came along. The first time I took it was at a party, and it was the first time in my life that I had felt so much love and happiness. It was amazing. After my third ecstasy party I decided to stop heroin. I went to a friend's place, stayed in bed and did a cold turkey. There were terrible cramps and vomiting for a week, then depression. But I knew that after a week I could go to Amsterdam, take ecstasy and get rid of my depression. That kept me going. Ecstasy is so strong. I stood in the street in Amsterdam, and was nearly exploding with love. I felt totally connected with people and they felt the same. We shared everything. After a long period of depression, it was the first time I could see the sun on the horizon. It felt as though something really good had come into my life.

But after taking so much ecstasy, the depression was horrible, because it takes you so high. After a while I couldn't do any more parties. My money was gone, I had nothing to eat, and the depression was even stronger than with heroin. So I relapsed again. This was the worst time for me on heroin. I had been offered a place for therapy, but had to wait six months, so I thought, 'It doesn't matter now, so I can really go for it.' I took more and more. I couldn't work as my body was too weak. My mother gave me her card again, and I lived on it. She wanted to help and thought this was the best way. She closed her eyes to the addiction.

Then I went into hospital for two weeks. After the second day, I was so weak it wasn't possible for me to move out. I couldn't sleep, but I knew that if I didn't stay I would die. I wanted to really try this time, as my life was completely run by heroin. I had no friends; it's not possible to have friendships when you are on heroin, and you can't connect with people who are not using. All I had was my drugs and my TV. But this time it was the end of using heroin.

I came out of hospital too depressed to work. I began smoking hash to escape the suffering. For a year I couldn't look into anyone's eyes; the guilt was too much. Then I started partying taking ecstasy and coke, and I met some people selling morphine pills which they stole from the hospital. I didn't want to feel anything and got hooked on these too. At the same time I met a girl and fell in love for the first time in years. I couldn't tell her the truth about my addiction, but I stopped the morphine after three months. We both smoked marijuana every day. I thought that all there was to life was passing time, and trying to get some pleasure. I didn't know anything about spirituality or God.

Then I met my girlfriend's father. He had been visiting Sai Baba for twenty years. He gave me a book, **The Holy Man and the Psychiatrist,** by Samuel Sandweiss. That's how Baba came into my life. It was easy for me to accept. From the first moment I knew that he was a special being, and I was very happy. Now I knew there is a God, and this was new for me. We visited a Sai Centre, and I felt welcome and experienced good energy there. But I didn't go back. I read about Baba and liked the teachings, but it was difficult for me to live even a little piece of it. I didn't feel connected and felt so much guilt about my life.

There were many problems in the relationship, and it broke up. I was still suffering from my heroin days. I owed a lot of money to the bank, and was unemployed with barely enough money to survive. I was caught up with the everyday problems of life . . . working, money, and problems relating with people. In particular, I had problems with my mother. I loved her *and* I hated her. The ties were so strong. For years I had lived alone with her, and she used me like a partner. I always felt I had to carry her, because she was depressed all her life. She never had friends, and came to me with her problems. It was too much, and I didn't know how to deal with it, so drug taking was a good way to dump it. The first three years that Baba came into my life were difficult, and there were a lot of drugs . . . but no heroin.

On my thirtieth birthday, alone on holiday in Tunis, I

stopped smoking cigarettes. This was the first time I had prayed a lot. I prayed to Baba, and then read **The Easy way to Stop Smoking** by Allen Carr, and it worked. It was the first time in my life that a prayer helped. This was a big experience. But it was still not possible to live his teachings. I was always lying and manipulating, was really introverted, and found it hard to relate to women. I was searching but I wasn't finding. I lived alone in a big house in the country, went to work, went home, and was alone.

Then a year later, in January 1999, I got the money to go and see Baba. When I arrived in Puttaparthi I felt the love, but was feeling so bad about myself. After one difficult night in the shed, I met a guy and we shared a room. Slowly I started to relax. Small miracles happened. The guy had to leave, and I needed someone to share the room with, or I'd have to go back to the shed. I prayed to Baba to send someone, as I felt I couldn't cope with that. Next morning I was sitting in the room and a man knocked on the door, asking if there was a space. He was confused. He had been sent to the sheds, but on the way an Indian man came up to him and told him strongly, "North 5, D23." That was my room, and he turned up at the door. It was a miracle for us both. We were sure this was Baba setting it up. We got on well.

Every day I felt the bliss and energy in *darshan*. One day I was sitting there after Baba had left and my whole body was vibrating. It wouldn't stop, and I was scared. But people told me that Baba sends you energy, and sometimes the body has problems absorbing it, so I stopped worrying. I smelled him too. I was told he had a special smell like flowers. I could smell it when Baba was twenty metres away. My heart opened a little bit, and I felt now my life would change.

But I still had many fears. I went home, and back into depression. There was snow on the ground, and I couldn't talk to anybody. But I had money, and after four weeks I booked another flight. After never travelling, suddenly I was going back to India. When I got there, I met some Germans and talked about my life, and opened up about my addiction. Baba let me touch his feet this time, and looked into my eyes, and I felt the bliss. I had prayed for this. I could feel a big opening in my heart. I swore to God that I never wanted to take drugs anymore.

When I returned home, I stayed clean for nine months. But the pressure was high, being alone all the time. That was the big mistake. I didn't know enough about addiction, and didn't realise it was harmful to isolate myself. I had nobody to talk to about God, or my addiction. My friends smoked and drank, but I didn't. I just ate lots of sweets, chocolate and Coca-Cola, and gained a lot of weight. I learned a lot more about how addiction works later, when I went to Narcotics Anonymous.

Then one day at work I fell from a roof and broke my arm, half an hour before the lunar eclipse. I couldn't work, so I moved to Hanover and started therapy. Here I relapsed, losing control completely with cocaine. I was isolated, and when you take hard drugs there are no real friends. You don't want to share; life is only about getting the drug. Wanting desperately to do something about it, I took a loan from the bank and bought a ticket to Puttaparthi. For the third time that year I was there for a month. I had huge guilt about relapsing, and beat myself up about having no willpower to resist. Baba loaded my batteries and filled me up with love. Again he stood in front of me, and I touched his feet, which made me very, very happy.

Back in Germany I was clean for three months. I relaxed and did some healthy things. But I lived with a guy who smoked marijuana and drank, and all my friends smoked. After a while I started smoking again. When I smoked marijuana all the good feelings evaporated. I tried to meditate, but didn't feel anything. My perspective changed, and I told myself that life hadn't really improved. Work still stressed me, and I only did the job for money. I met a girl for a few weeks, but it soon ended. Feeling sorry for myself, I lost control *again* with cocaine. But Swami called me back to India, and didn't give up on me. Knowing I wouldn't use in India, I injected cocaine in the airport toilets on my way to see Swami.

But first I went to Jaipur where I stayed two weeks, and the worst cocaine withdrawal depressions went. But I smoked constantly as my friends were dealers. I met my future wife in Jaipur. Then I went to Puttaparthi and saw different healers, and found that my last eight incarnations were in India. This man said, "Don't worry, that's why you have problems in the Western world." It was a relief for me, as I had always felt an outsider in society. Running after a new car, TV, fancy clothes and endless consumption never touched or attracted me. I never wanted a career. It was a relief to feel that this was okay. Even though the depressions were still coming, I could feel that I was growing on each visit to Baba.

After a month I came home, earned a lot of money and soon had enough money to go to Chicago to see my American girlfriend. We had a good time, and then I went back to Germany. Later we met in India. The first few weeks were in Delhi, and I hated it. Then we went to Puttaparthi, and my girlfriend hated it there. There was nothing I could do, and she left after four days. Again I felt the love from

Swami, and had a good time and more healing sessions. Then I re-joined my girlfriend in Delhi, and we had some good, and some very bad times. We split. I felt bad that the relationship wasn't working.

One weekend I partied with cocaine, and it resulted in a cocaine psychosis. I flipped out at work and left. I couldn't talk about it to anyone. I stabilised a bit, and then started shooting cocaine again. This time I lost control like never before. My girlfriend called and asked if she could see me. I was in despair, and thought maybe this could bring something good into my life. So I went to Chicago for two months, and stopped the cocaine. I admitted to her that I had a coke problem, and went to my first Narcotics Anonymous meeting. I liked it but still thought I didn't need help. I didn't tell the whole truth to her or myself, telling myself I could stop whenever I wanted. Although we had signs the relationship wouldn't work out, we were both happy that we had found somebody, and decided to live together in the States. It was an attempt to escape from my unhappy life in Germany.

But first I had to return to my hometown. I had only been back one day and I relapsed. Every day on my way home from work I said, "No, I'm not buying anything today." But I always did. This was the first time I felt I couldn't do anything about it, and I confessed to my girlfriend. We decided to be together, even though I had no money and I was lost in addiction. My mother paid the flight back to Chicago. This time I started with NA seriously. But because of my visa, I had to leave the country or marry my girlfriend. I saw so many signs that I shouldn't do it, but we got married. From that moment on, we *only* had stress. It was the first time I had ever lived with a woman, and there was no place for me to hide.

I didn't tell *anyone* the truth. My sponsor in NA didn't know everything, and I could feel my addiction working again with a desire to go home. The connection with Baba was gone, and I wanted to get rid of the stress in my usual way. So I changed my ticket and went back to Germany. I relapsed on the first day home on my way to my mother. And I moved in with an old friend who was borderline alcoholic. The place was chaotic, but I had good work with this guy, and he closed his eyes to me fixing cocaine. A friend lent me money, and I fixed it away.

In desperation I prayed that Swami would take me out of this body. I didn't want it anymore. It was slow suicide always living on the borderline, because a kick is almost an overdose, and I always wanted to get a stronger one. But I was praying every day. Every time I injected I prayed to Baba, and put everything in his hands. Then I found the cheapest flight I've ever seen to India, and I bought the ticket before I could spend it on cocaine. Even though I was angry with Baba, I could tell he was saving my life. The last time I used cocaine was 5th Jan 2004, the day before going to India.

I was amazed how easy it was to come down from cocaine in Puttaparthi. I felt guilty, but Baba gave me so much love, and I had some wonderful healing sessions . . . release work, EFT, hands-on work, and cutting ties. I got a lot of energy from this, and for the first time had the feeling that everything was right, even leaving my wife. I saw that what happened was the best thing for me. The times before, coming down from cocaine was much harder. In the ashram I never think about drugs, because of Swami's love and the connection with God. It's only when I went back to Germany I would feel disconnected and get stressed.

In February, still in Puttaparthi, I started the preparation for cutting the ties with drugs, and a lot of memories of drug taking came back to me. It's a guided visualisation technique. I used a symbol of a black hypodermic needle, which was in one circle of a figure 8, with myself in the other. Then for a week, several times a day, I visualized an electric blue light running around the figure 8, separating me from the needle. The morning before the session with Jenny to cut the ties, I was sitting in *darshan* thinking about the highs I'd had. I asked myself if I wanted to do it again, and I realised that the highs were so brief, and the pain was so long. I felt certain that it was over.

Then I went to do the session. I had to visualise trying to destroy the needle. It was difficult. First a hammer leapt into my hand, and I hit the needle, trying to smash it to pieces. Some builders outside started hammering loudly at this point! Then I buried the pieces, but they kept re-emerging. I was getting stressed, so I called on Swami to help deal with it, and he immediately jumped into the circle with the needle. He swallowed it, and transformed it into gold. He sat in the other circle of the figure 8 and looked at me. Then I was sure that everything had been taken away.

Swami then came into my circle and stood behind me, putting his hands on my head. I was getting emotional, and felt a lot of energy moving in my body. I called out, "I can trust him. I know he will take care and guide me." I was close to tears. Then Psalm 23 . . . 'The Lord's my Shepherd . . .' came into my mind and prolonged the emotion, and I felt a strong vibration in my face. I fervently thanked Baba for taking the last roots of the addiction and called out, "I know he'll take care of me, and I'll never have to use drugs anymore." I was crying. Then Swami gave me a hug, and returned to his place. I sat in the energy for a while, as I was being filled with beautiful vibrations. I knew I was on the right path and had nothing to fear. I was smiling, knowing that Baba is behind me and I don't need to know the destination, but have complete trust. I was able to forgive myself for my life with drugs, and see that it was all part of my destiny.

When I came back to my room, my mind doubted if it was all my imagination, and whether I deserved it. But my heart knew that everything was true. The following day was the Hindu festival of Mahasivrathri, and Swami produced two large golden lingams from his stomach. These are egg-shaped objects, symbolizing the eternal universal consciousness. It was a great experience to witness this, just after I had cut the ties with drugs.

I received so much love and support from people on this trip. Some were recovering addicts too. I had many fears about going home to face the debts and problems that waited for me. I knew that living the old lifestyle would make it too hard to stay clean. This time going home was different because I felt Swami in my heart. Sometimes I thought about drugs; it was always when I felt bored and disconnected. My yearning was to get super-strong feelings, but I know it is always followed by the opposite, and I didn't go near the places it was sold. Something always happened that reminded me of the connection to Swami when I was thinking about drugs. I could see how he was taking care of me, and would remember the image of him with his hands on my head. I was never seriously tempted. I trusted totally that Swami was taking care; and it was very clear that he did.

All the problems I feared facing on coming back were smoothed out. Before I'd left, the bank was going to take me to court for debts, but now there was a letter saying I just had to pay a small amount each month. It was no problem. My roommate never bothered me with drugs, and I soon got a new place to live with a man who had no addictions. It was easy. I went to NA twice a week, and made the coffee and prepared the room. That commitment helped me to go regularly. I met a woman there and we started a relationship. I can take things much easier now, and for the first time I feel I can be a good partner. The end of the year was difficult with my girlfriend, but it didn't bother me. When we went to see Mother Meera my girlfriend was in a bad mood and wanted to end the relationship, but I stayed cool and relaxed. Her mood passed and all was well. Even if it goes wrong and she goes, I know that Swami will stay. I'm not afraid of losing her. Before, I thought that if a woman left me my whole life was finished.

This year was one of the best in my life. I rarely got depressed, and if I did something would happen to bring me out of it, like an email from Puttaparthi friends, or a phone call, and there was support in NA. This time it was crucial *not* to do it alone. I *have* to go out and be honest, and talk about my problem. It's extremely difficult for me to go to somebody when I feel bad. There is so much guilt, but it's helpful to go to a meeting, and hear that other people feel the same.

At first when I came to see Baba I was flying high. I thought that everything would be beautiful, and all stress would be over. Life is not like that. Now I'm more grounded, more at peace. My mind is calming down, and at times I can just observe and say, "Hey, it's only the mind." Intellectually, I know we are not the mind, and I see that more and more. The connection to God is much greater. A lot of guilt was taken away, and now I think I'm not a bad guy. I'm reading the Serenity Prayer every day, and praying for Baba's guidance. I feel so blessed and grateful. So much love has come into my life. These days, I'm mostly happy. It's a *big* change.

Spiritual hunger is the ultimate meaning of every activity in life. The dissatisfaction and restlessness that remain even after obtaining all the necessities of life show that everyone, consciously or unconsciously, does suffer from spiritual hunger and it is not appeased until the spirit within is released.

- Sathya Sai Baba

Update from Carl, February 2013

I relapsed in 2006 and suffered three weeks of pain. But since then I'm really in the Programme, working the steps and staying clean. In 2010 I had to do interferon therapy for eleven months because of my Hepatitis C, which I have had since 1993. I could only do it because of my friends and fellows in Narcotics Anonymous. It really was a hard time, but two weeks ago the doctor told me that the Hep C will never come back. I'm grateful.

At the end of 2011 they found cancer of the intestine. This was a big shock. Many friends told me to do the surgery right away, but I had a ticket to India, and came to Puttaparthi in January and was so happy there. End of February 2012 I had the first surgery, and in June a second one. Yesterday I made a computer tomography and everything is fine. I'm happy. The surgeries were really strange experiences. I had to take a lot of painkillers, even Morphine, and got addicted again. This was hard-core. I didn't want it, but had to take it because of the pain. It was so strange to get wasted again. My thoughts and feelings changed, and there was nothing I could do about it. I was lucky because I got a lot of help from my fellowship and my girlfriend. After I stopped I did a little cold turkey again. One side of it was good, because I really know that I don't want to be on drugs again.

I have just done Step Five in the NA programme, which is a great relief. The programme really works. I have had a girlfriend for a year and half and it feels good. I still have problems with women, but we are good together and she is not an addict.

And all the time Baba is with me.

9

'Go to AA or Die'

Drink is so pernicious a habit, that when man puts the bottle in his mouth, he himself gets into the bottle and cannot escape. First man drinks wine; then the wine drinks more wine, and finally the wine drinks man himself. He is sunk and drowned in drink. Liquor destroys the humanity in man.

- Sathya Sai Baba

Ruth was born in 1943 in the US. As well as being an alcoholic in her past, she has worked professionally with drug and alcohol problems, and has extensive knowledge of Alcoholics Anonymous. She worked as Director of the Women and Alcohol Project in Cleveland Ohio, and has done trainings on women's issues and addiction, Prevention Projects in schools and the community, and has talked on TV and in the media on addiction. She is a bright, highly intelligent woman, with a quick wit and ready smile. She has changed from a totally self-preoccupied person to one who likes to serve others. She has been sober for nineteen years.

Ruth's story: Alcohol wasn't part of my family life at all. Ironically, my mother made me a plaque of the AA Serenity Prayer when I was young and explained it to me. She thought it was wonderful. It must have been a premonition.

> *God grant me the serenity*
> *To accept the things I cannot change,*
> *Courage to change the things I can,*
> *And the wisdom to know the difference.*

My drinking started at college, but I didn't drink like most people. The first time I had hard liquor I got so drunk they had to carry me down the mountain. I don't remember any of it. No one else got drunk at that party. When I started drinking I didn't want to quit. My tolerance was higher than others and I was macho about it, boasting that I could have twenty-seven beers and not be drunk. I was amazed when people only had a few beers when they were partying. When *I* got drunk, I didn't stop. If I was with friends, and there was no alcohol around, it wasn't any fun. As I look back it wasn't *about* fun, it was about drinking. So I changed my friends as I wanted to be around people who drank, and that gave *me* the right to drink. We were cool. I could spot other people into alcohol from across the room. We were all preoccupied with talking about partying, drinking, and being hung over.

In the mid-sixties, I got a job selling. Women didn't do that in those days. I was a trailblazer, and it was a great job for a drunk because you could cover. I was leading two lives. The people at work didn't know about my drinking life, and it didn't slip into my career too much at that stage. But on St Patrick's Day I went for lunch with my boss and got totally blitzed, getting him into trouble with the owner of the

Company. Driving back to work I was stopped for a DWI (driving while intoxicated), a major offence in the US. In those days they let women go. Women could slide through and cover their drinking easier than men, but the stigma was greater. If I went to a bar I would be considered a lush, and get picked up easily. I could feel that in bars. So I started drinking by myself, because I didn't want to be attacked and used and slandered.

I liked to drink at lunch if I could, and being on the road I could get away with it. I changed jobs a lot. First it was the only way to advance my career, as they didn't promote women; and second it was a way of covering my drinking. I started to lead a life of covering everything, and denying it to myself. Life is like a mobile, in or out of balance. One minute it's in balance, then you put a paper clip on one end (addiction) and the *whole thing* tips — relationships go out of balance, work life goes out of balance and spiritual life is non-existent. I'd actually given up all hope of a spiritual life even before drinking. I didn't like the Christian Church; I thought it hypocritical, and saw that people were not practicing the teachings. They could not answer the fundamental questions I had about life, and being arrogant I thought they were stupid.

However I progressed in business, and loved adventure and travelling. But drinking affected that, and soon I couldn't handle those explorations. Fifteen years later the addiction was so overpowering in my life that *all* I wanted to do was drink. I chain smoked too, getting through three packs a day. If a friend wanted to go out I'd find an excuse not to go, as then I'd have to drink slowly. If someone cancelled coming over I'd feel good, because I liked to drink till I passed out. I didn't have the mechanisms to be able to stop. I remember once having a few wines when I was out and thinking, 'What a nice glow. I wish I could be moderate all the time.' But it was torture, and I knew I could never do that.

I first noticed there was a problem when I used to visit a couple I liked. They didn't drink but automatically got out the Scotch for me, and I had to be careful, not wanting them to see how much I drank. Also I would buy booze in different places, because God forbid if one store saw me buy too much. I had a routine of shopping so it never showed up. I lived alone, and would even hide the booze in my own home. If I hid the booze in a blackout I'd be tearing the place apart trying to find it, with no recollection of where I'd stashed it. This happened constantly. Why? We only hide what we are ashamed of, and shame ran my life. Everyone usually knows everything anyway, and you can't really hide anything.

Once I was invited to a coke party. I thought they meant Coca-Cola, so I got good and drunk ahead of time as I thought there would be no booze. It was a cocaine party, but by then I was so anaesthetized by liquor the cocaine had no effect. You could never find a time when I had no alcohol in me, so I didn't get into the drug scene because it never had any effect. Life got greyer and duller, till it was simply a matter of existing. The goals and excitement waned, my personality changed, and I looked awful, but I didn't know these things. Just once in a while it sneaked through that there might be a problem.

Lots of crazy things happened. One time I sold a Volkswagen car. I was drunk when the people came over, they paid cash, and being in a blackout I forgot where I'd put it. So I called them up and accused them of stealing it back again. This wonderful couple was devastated. They came over and were almost crying, telling me they were good, honest people. Wherever I went it was turmoil. Once I went to the doctor because my knees were swollen and hurting. They couldn't find what was wrong, and gave medication for arthritis. When I came out of a blackout one night, I suddenly got it. 'Oh, I see!' I remembered that I got up from the couch *every night* and fell over the coffee table, which was knee high. When I got sober, my 'arthritis' totally cleared up.

Another time I went with my ex-husband to a friend's place to go canoeing. For some unknown reason I got mad at my ex and ran out of the room. I was angry, and wanted to get home a hundred miles away. I ran through the forest screaming late at night, very drunk. They were out searching for me and praying, very concerned. Next day I was devastated and embarrassed and, of course, dropped them as friends. Different friends told me they didn't like me calling them drunk in the middle of the night. I was horrified as I wasn't aware I'd done it. One time I had a job selling coffee machines, and was so hung over one morning I didn't know how to work it. The customers were giving me pitying looks, and asked me what the problem was. They must have been thinking, drugs or alcohol? Of course I didn't sell the machine.

These things were not funny at the time; they were terribly humiliating. They were periodic reminders that my life was out of control. Trying to control my use was like carrying five suitcases of cement, and without some kind of programme, not using was impossible for me. Drinking was a nightmare, and trying not to drink was a nightmare. If I tried to stop I got bad withdrawals, I was dizzy and couldn't think. Anything you have to control means it's out of control, and I had rules around my drinking to *try* and control it. It didn't work. I didn't have many friends left by now. They either hated me or thought I was crazy; and my drinking cronies didn't care about me.

Eventually life got so miserable that I wanted to kill myself. One night, coming out of a blackout, I found myself planning suicide and I knew that I might go through with it. But I had two cats, and couldn't think what to do with them, even in my drunken stupor. Love for *anything* can stop you. In desperation I called a counsellor I'd known way back. She talked to me most of the night to keep me on the phone, and gave me the name of a psychiatrist. The next day I went to see him. He basically said, "*Go to AA or die!*"

I pulled a face, and said I wouldn't go on any Recovery Programme. He said he couldn't treat alcoholism; that psychiatry didn't work for this disease. He said it takes a group. But he saw I needed something and I believed in medicine, so he put me on Antabuse, medication that makes you sick if you drink. For a while I stayed sober, till I realised that if I stopped taking the Antabuse I could have a binge. So I went off and on it, getting more and more confused till finally I had a huge reaction. At the time I was starting a new job, and my brain just wouldn't work. I was talking like a broken record. The pressure was way too much, and I probably injured my brain. Finally I told the psychiatrist the truth. He was perceptive, and saw that nobody could tell me what to do. I was stubborn, independent and rebellious, like many alcoholics. He thought that if I could discover on my own about the disease, I might have the motivation to give up. So he sent me to seminars on Alcohol and Mental Health, pretending to be his secretary.

After fighting everyone who tried to help me, I finally decided to go to an AA meeting. Fighting had made me miserable and I had to surrender, get into the river and learn to flow with it, rather than swimming upstream. It was too exhausting. To get sober and have a life worth living eventually I had to tell myself, 'I give up. I can't handle this problem. I believe it's physical, and I can't do it alone. I need help, be it God, (I didn't believe in God) or a group of people.'

When I walked into AA I saw people laughing, with bright eyes, having a good time. They told stories about being as drunk or more drunk than I was. *Then* I began to believe. Seeing that people can recover gave me hope. I didn't particularly *like* these people at first, but I knew that I didn't get along with anybody. My thinking was so distorted that I decided to *use* them to learn the skill of getting along with people. They became my best friends, and I went to meetings every day. By going to a lot of meetings, hearing stories, being around people who are sober, and hearing how they want to live, my mind structure changed. That's how I started recovery. I was forty years old.

I started to work the Steps and discovered that they have a power within them. I research *everything*; it's one of my faults, and AA was no exception. The founder Bill Wilson wrote **The AA Big Book** when he was three months into recovery. How can you write a book that is so successful and used all over the world only three months after giving up drinking? You can barely remember your name. It had to have been divinely inspired. It is the only truly successful long-term programme that exists today, and has been going since the 1930's, based on The Oxford Group, in Miami Ohio. They were a Christian group but had a lot of Eastern influence. The founder was studying Hinduism and worked with Carl Jung. Later I came to believe it is based on Vedic philosophy and is identical with Sai Baba's teachings. Unlike the Western view, which is success-oriented and builds up the ego, AA says to get rid of the ego, that our thinking is distorted, and it's all an illusion. You have to surrender to a Higher Power. You can't control your addiction. Everything you tried yourself failed. Once you give up and say there is something greater than you, it helps.

Working these principles was the beginning of my spirituality, even though I was an Atheist. It doesn't matter if you call the Higher Power God, Jesus, Sai Baba or whatever. In the Steps it is called, 'The God of your understanding.' If you still have a problem with the word, say that God means Good Orderly Direction. In AA others are always there to help you. When I'd get cranky or emotional they would say, "Give it up. Are you going to hold on to that? It was an emotion. Be over it." They taught detachment from painful thoughts and feelings. When I first went into the programme I relapsed every few weeks. I had a horrible time getting sober. I went in and out, struggling, lying and sneaking a drink. But I kept on till it worked. Unlike most alcoholics I can't remember my last drink. The craving was taken from me at a certain point. Then I had to work hard to learn how to live properly. I had to learn to improve *myself,* not focus on judging and blaming others.

By the time I accepted spirituality I was living in North Carolina in the middle of the Bible belt, and there wasn't much AA there. So searching for something, I did a metaphysical course, and I had two hundred and eighty metaphysical books in my library and read them all. I learned to do readings, and developed psychic skills. I did this for five years and started to believe in a soul, but not God. I had an automatic rejection of anything that came near to the religious structure I'd dismissed. I used to get mad when people talked about God, till I realized it was my stuff and I had to get over it. I pieced together a philosophy I thought was my own, a pot-pourri of eclectic ideas. What it turned out to be was identical with Swami's teachings.

The first time I heard of Baba was when a good friend in Atlanta sent me an email saying he'd found an amazing guru in India. He told me of the phenomenon of Sai Baba's footprints appearing before him on the rug. I knew he wouldn't make this up. He said that unbelievable things were happening around Swami. He also sent a quote from Baba. When I read it I was jumping up and down in excitement. This was what I believed! After reading all those metaphysical books, just a few words from Swami came flying through in that email *and I got it!* I knew it was the end of my search.

So I drove down to Atlanta one weekend for a Sai Regional Conference. It was a whole weekend of *bhajans*. I don't like singing, I hate hymns and I don't like ritual, but the minute I walked in there I was overwhelmed by an incredible energy. People were friendly, showing me rings that Swami had manifested, and grey ash (*vibhuti*) that had appeared out of nowhere. These were things that in my imagination I thought *might* exist. Now here they were in front of my eyes. People's eyes shone with divine love. Now I know them as regular people, but Swami's love was filtering through them. I just couldn't believe the *bhajans*. I felt as though I would disintegrate, because the energy was too high for me and I had to leave before the end. They gave me a tape of the songs, and I listened in the car and cried all the way home.

I knew I had to be around devotees to learn, and I went to Atlanta every week. I got involved in service projects and studied the teachings like crazy. Only three weeks after the

Conference in 1999, a bunch of coincidences landed me in India. I'd had no intention of going. Some devotees tried to book me a seat with them, but they said the flight was full, and I'd have to get on the waiting list. I rang the agent to tell them not to bother, but a seat had immediately come open and they had booked me. So I took that as a sign. From that point on there has been one miracle after another.

Our group was called for an interview. The first thing Baba said to me was, "*Husband?*"

"Gone, divorced." I said. He looked at me seriously, cut the air with his hand and said, "*Gone, past. The past is a seed, the future is a seed, and the present is a tree. The past is gone.*"

He detached the past from me. All the baggage I was carrying about my ex-husband was gone, like the faraway memory of a movie that didn't really happen. He *did* that. The minute I got back from India people told me I'd changed. I didn't look angry anymore, and my eyes were sparkling.

Then he said, *"How are you?"*

Every emotion I've ever had whizzed through me. I didn't know how to answer . . . depressed, miserable, happy, sad, agitated? For a second, they all flew through me. So I said, "Okay."

He started to laugh and said, "*Okay? Just okay?*" and I felt like crawling under the chair.

He asked me what I did. I said that I was a photographer, and used to do social service. My primary career had been in medical clinics and the drug and alcohol field.

He shook a finger and said, "*That's not social service. It's okay, but it's not social service. You helped the rich. Social service is helping the poor, the sick, the elderly and the children. You did not do that.*"

I took that as a mandate to help indigent people when I returned.

He asked me who the richest person in the world was. Bill Gates came to mind, but I knew that wasn't the answer he wanted. I said, "You Swami." He laughed, "*No, no, no, The richest is the man without desire.*"

Then he went to others, manifesting rings and giving away orange robes. We were in there for half an hour. When he was leaving, he walked by me and a feeling came over me that I must not miss the chance of a lifetime, or more than a lifetime. I felt that God was walking out, and I must not miss this opportunity. I didn't plan it, or even know I thought it, but putting my hands up in prayer I said, "Swami, I want to serve you." He pointed his hand at me and did some writing in the sky. I'm very glad I said that. If I had walked out without speaking up, I would have had an interview instead of a life with Swami. It was the surrender I had learned to do in AA, and will practice for the rest of my life. That was the main significance of the interview for me. I had to turn my life into the care of God as I understood Him.

When I got home, my head was spinning. It had all happened so fast. As soon as I got back from India I went into hospital for surgery. In the recovery room I woke up wanting coffee. When I'd quit drinking I had immediately substituted it with caffeine, and drank it from the moment I got up till I went to bed. I *loved* coffee, and it had no effect on me except when I went for more than an hour without it. Then I had a major withdrawal headache. I knew I was addicted, but didn't care as compared to alcohol it seemed a minor problem. After the surgery I craved a cup of coffee, and they had to bring it to me as I was so uncomfortable. The doctor told me I shouldn't be drinking so much coffee, as it was bad for my heart. A week later I had a dream.

Swami was sitting on the porch of my house in North Carolina, for sixteen hours. I remembered the time period distinctly. He was drinking my coffee, asking for more and more. He kept saying, "Oh, it's so good! Please give me more of your coffee."

Swami does not drink coffee. A few days later I started shaking, and was nervous, jittery and couldn't sleep. I went back to the doctor thinking something was wrong from the surgery. I told him my stomach was upset, and I was jumping out of my skin and couldn't sleep. I wondered if it was the drugs he'd prescribed. He questioned me in depth and said, "It sounds like you're drinking too much coffee. I warned you." I said, "I don't get symptoms drinking coffee, only when I *don't* drink it." He told me to stop, so I tried. To my amazement, I didn't have a headache and I calmed down. My addiction was totally gone and there were no withdrawals. To this day I love coffee, and can drink it in moderation, but I don't *need* it. I'm not addicted anymore.

Then with my mandate from Swami, I joined the Sai Centre Seva (Social Service) committee, and found an indigent nursing home in a poor, multi-racial neighbourhood. There are few of these for poor people, and this one was well run. Many of the inmates had no family, and the devotees began to visit. We went in and sang the old songs that generation knew. They were heavily drugged, and seemed somewhere else, but you could see them come out of that world and smile, clap or just blink. There is a soul in there, and they responded. The songs triggered memories. We painted nails, did simple crafts and took little gifts. To give joy, even for a second, gave us so much back. We also went downtown and gave sandwiches to the homeless. I try to do as much as possible through the Sai Centre, but also do personal *seva*. I keep nutritional bars in the car for people who stand by the freeways downtown asking for food. I never give money but hand out a few bars. I say nothing but look them in the eye, smile and acknowledge they exist. Nobody likes to look at the homeless, and they feel invisible. Doing that makes my day, but I still don't feel I do enough. I pray every day to do something good with my life, and to do it quietly.

The basis of AA is service. The premise is to work the Steps to get a spiritual awakening. They say that the *only* way to recover and *stay sober* is to help others. It is the basis of the programme. You help other alcoholics or drug addicts. You can't carry the person, but you can carry the message. We had a prayer at the end of every meeting, *"Pray for the alcoholic, whether they are in the room sober or drunk."* I never saw a group of people more willing to help each other. If someone's moving house, they will get a truck and all pitch in. If there is a funeral in the family, two hundred AAs may turn up. They will help wherever there is a problem. You have to get out of yourself to stay sober. It's a way to give love, and we know that to give love is to get it. Relationships don't work if we are only looking out for ourselves. It backfires. But if you are doing something outside of yourself, there is a union that is beautiful, spiritual and loving. It's not just the right thing to do. It's our only survival. Without doing that Programme and helping others, I'd be dead.

It's the basis of Swami's teachings too. I can't find any difference between his teachings and those of AA. He says, *"Hands that help are holier than lips that pray."* I *must* serve others. Before, my whole life revolved around getting the booze, because I thought I couldn't live without it. I was only thinking of that. If you don't get out of your own way, you'll kill yourself spiritually, emotionally or physically. AA knows that there is no real recovery without spiritual intervention. It's a conversion . . . the whole structure of your brain changes. In the group we could never predict who was going to 'get it' and who wasn't. Most people don't recover, but a good number do. We used to call it, 'The light' and that this ball of light would bounce round the room and fall on at least one person there. You might think, 'That guy will never get it, he's so angry and obstinate' and suddenly, boom! He got it! It was nothing *we* did; we were just there to allow it to happen. To watch that is a miracle.

Miracles have come into my life. For fifteen weeks running *vibhuti* manifested in my songbook at the Sai Centre. It came on my altar too. And I have been cured of at least two major diseases. Six months ago I was diagnosed with Alzheimer's. So I did voluntary work for the Alzheimer's Association, using my public speaking experience to give talks on TV and in the media. I wanted to tell people what you *can* do, to see that there is a real person in there, and take away the stigma of the disease. Then I had a dream:

Swami's head came off and rolled past me. He grew another one and was laughing at me saying, "See, new head!"

I had no idea what that meant, and I asked my friend who said, "He just cured you." All my symptoms went away. I kept getting better, and went to the neurologist for another test. He couldn't find any Alzheimer's.

Through stress tests the hospital found a major blockage in my heart. They arranged for a cardiac catheter and scheduled me for surgery. When they went in they couldn't find a thing, and had to send me home. I asked them how rare that is. They said it was pretty rare, and got edgy with me. I have no problems with my heart now.

Giving up smoking was painful. It took me six months, using patches, nicotine gum, and willpower to cut down. I would not quit trying, no matter how many times I relapsed. I prayed a lot, and went to Smokers Anonymous. Then I had another dream:

I was in hospital in a wheelchair, with emphysema. I was bent over from smoking, and being wheeled out to the back section where I could smoke outside.

It had such an impact that I simply *could not put another puff of smoke in my lungs.* I'd had pneumonia several times, and been to top pulmonary specialists about chronic bronchitis. Of course *I* knew what the cause was. For the next three months I didn't inhale. I couldn't. That finally broke it. When I gave up they discovered I had Coeliac disease, which is masked by smoking. Without quitting nicotine, I could have died of that too. How many fatal illnesses can one person have and be cured? It's getting to be comical.

It's important to remember that it's always possible, even when sober for a long time, that we can be 'side-whacked'. People can relapse after many years, and AA emphasizes that you have to keep on using a spiritual programme. I pray every day that I'll never use again. I'm not complacent. If you don't keep practicing daily, your brain can take over with the things you learned as a child. The pathways in the brain are still there. I need that daily looking inward, and with prayer and meditation I rise above those patterns. If I get back into illusion I'm so miserable. I want to live on that other plane, beyond illusion, as much as I can. For my spiritual support I go to both the Sai Centre and AA. To me their principles are identical, because they are based on Truth.

"Why does the Divine attract? Is it to deceive or mislead? No, it is to transform, transmute, reconstruct, reform.... a process called samskara. What is the purpose of the reconstruction? It is to make that person useful and serviceable to society, to efface his ego, and to affirm in him the unity of all beings in God. The person who has undergone samskara becomes a humble servant of those who need help."

- Sathya Sai Baba

Update from Ruth, January 2013

I'm still sober, and now semi-retired living in the Mountains of North Carolina, teaching photography at a local community college. I do online webinars on spirituality, and private sessions internationally on healing and spiritual topics. I have been twenty-nine years sober.

www.dragonflyhealing.com

10

Switching Off

Television sets are installed in every room in the houses of the rich. From the moment television made its appearance, the mind of man has been polluted. Before the advent of TV, men's minds were not so much polluted. Acts of violence were not so rampant previously. Concentration on TV affects one's view of the world. The scenes, thoughts and actions displayed on TV fill the minds of the viewers. Unknowingly, agitation and ill feelings enter their minds. In due course they take root and grow in the mind.

- Sathya Sai Baba

Eddie was born in Malaysia in 1953 of Indian parents and was brought up Roman Catholic. He came to England in 1971. My impression of him is that his mission on Earth is to make people laugh and be happy. He is bubbly, joyful and fast-talking, and a pleasure to be with. He and his wife spend much of their time offering love and healing. This story illustrates the obstacles created by television for those who are seriously on the spiritual path. Clearly for Eddie it is important to be away from all impure and negative input.

Eddie's story: On the seventh of July 1994, during

meditation, I saw a television and a large "X" appeared over it. My impression was that I was being told not to watch television. During this period I'd say I was an average viewer, and liked documentaries and films. I would put the TV on in the evening, after work. I was also meditating up to five hours a day and reading. However, I didn't stop the TV habit, but mentally bargained with Swami that I would only watch educational programmes or documentaries. Seven months later, on the 23rd of February 1995, I had a dream.

I was waiting for Swami to come. Meanwhile, I was watching television, which fascinated me. I heard a knock on the door, which I knew was Swami. Before I could think of opening the door, the television came on and I forgot that Swami was waiting outside to be let in. This was repeated twice, and every time the television came on, and I forget to let him in. After the third knock, when I did not respond, he burst open the door and walked in. I saw that it was Sai Ma (Mother Sai). She said that she had come for the slippers (representing the feet of the guru, to which we surrender). I wept as I ran to her, falling at her feet asking her to forgive me, as I understood my grave error. She said that she came to forgive me.

I understood that the slippers symbolised the grace of God I had received, and that they could be taken away for disobedience. It was a lesson that the word of the guru should be obeyed implicitly, as he had already warned me that television was a distraction for me on the spiritual path. Initially I tried bargaining with him, as I missed watching TV. But whatever the teacher says is for our own good, and after this dream I realised the great importance of this instruction. I hadn't considered it an addiction, but it *was* a habit coming between God and me. So the television set had to go. After the dream it wasn't difficult to give up, as I knew

I had to obey Swami.

At the time I was meditating when I came home from work, then I'd eat and watch telly or read. I'd meditate again before sleeping, and at 5 am when I got up. When one meditates, the energy starts to clear the excretions from the mind, and clears whatever negativity one has absorbed that day. When I stopped watching TV meditation was more effective, as there was less cleaning up to do, and more of the energy could go into strengthening me. Also meditation helps to increase focus and concentration, whereas TV and films disturb the mind and over-stimulate it. It's often left on all the time, and even if one's not actively watching, one can take in the impressions passively, as in passive smoking. Negative images and words are stored in the subconscious. I didn't think of it as an addiction, as it's considered normal to sit in front of the box for hours every day, and everybody does it. What did they do before TV was invented? Has it become the opium of the people?

Swami calls television *'tele-visham'*. *Visham* means poison in Sanskrit. Much that we see and hear on TV is negative and it all goes in like food, and is stored at a sub-conscious level. This affects our mind. The input through our five senses can be pure or impure, so we have to be careful and filter out the negative. Television was taking a lot of the energy I could have used. It wasted time, and when we watch day in day out, many negative things become accepted as normal. We become inured to violence, bad language, corruption and all kinds of damaging behaviour.

For eighteen years I had been smoking cigarettes, and had struggled and tried everything to give them up. I would cut down from twenty, to ten, to five, then some stress would occur and I'd be back to twenty. After an experience in meditation, one of the mental conditions that broke was smoking. It was so easy; I just stopped with no suffering. I was non-plussed, and didn't understand it until I had a dream a few years later, where Swami showed himself smoking. Then I realised that he had taken on my smoking addiction, as he sometimes takes on the illnesses of devotees. It was his Grace.

Giving up my 'normal' life of watching TV, smoking and going to the pub has not been a sacrifice. The rewards have been unbelievable, now that Sai Baba is navigating this ship through the rough waters of this world. Gradually, all the desires and attachments coming between God and us have to go. Then we can connect with the inner contentment and joy, which is *always* there.

Spiritual food should not be interpreted as something you take by way of your mouth alone. We have five different sense organs . . . ears, eyes mouth, skin and nose. What you smell, see, hear, touch and eat will all constitute what you take in as food.

- Sathya Sai Baba

Update from Eddy, March 2013

I spoke to Eddy by phone and asked if he had a TV now. He laughed, and said, "Not for about twenty years!" So he is still television-free, and busy with his wife teaching workshops on several healing modalities, as well as doing healing work.

11

A Moment of Conscience

The greater your troubles, the greater the chance you have to show the Lord that you are a spiritual Napoleon, a conqueror of yourself. There are so many imperfections within us to be surmounted! He who becomes master of himself is a real conqueror . . . to gain this wisdom of God is the only purpose for which you were sent here; and if you seek anything else instead, you are going to punish yourself. Find your Self and find God . . . By discrimination, by right action, learn to conquer every obstacle and attain self-mastery.

- Paramahansa Yogananda

Mui was born in 1955 in Sydney, Australia. After a miserable childhood, where she was lonely despite having five brothers, she got heavily into drugs. Her story is disturbing, and shows the depths of degradation a person can reach when profoundly unhappy. It also shows tremendous courage in the way she overcame her addiction to heroin, which is so tenacious and destructive. The woman I spoke to bears no resemblance to the one described in the first part of the story. I found her to be happy, totally at ease with herself and others, emanating a natural confidence and emitting a radiant spiritual glow.

Who but the Divine could engineer such a transformation?

Mui's story: I have almost no memory of childhood before the age of thirteen. I only remember my mother being sick and delirious in the bedroom, and asking her if she was going to die. I was shooed out of the room. My mother was a hypochondriac, so absorbed in her various illnesses that she had no time for us, especially me the only daughter. I never had any fun or closeness with her, and there were no guidelines to help me grow into a young woman. She was too busy being sick. I felt as though I lived in an alien family, and had nothing in common with any of them except my father. He was a musician and we shared a love of music. But he was rarely at home, always out trying to support us and pay the doctor's bills.

I was lonely at school too. I had no friends and no self-confidence. People would draw ugly, nasty pictures of me, and stick them on the back of my uniform, and I'd walk around school all day unaware of it, and no one would tell me. I could barely hold a conversation with anyone, always scared about what people would think of me. I left school at fifteen.

Just before my fifteenth birthday, still a virgin, I was raped by a neighbour and fell pregnant. My mother was in hospital, and my father noticed my clothes were too tight and I was always feeling sick, so he guessed my condition. They said that I *must* have an abortion, and I was rushed around to secret meetings, and made to feel like a wicked person. My father and aunt went to confront the man who raped me. He told them that I would sleep with anyone, and he hadn't touched me. They believed him, and thought I had been promiscuous. So I had the abortion, for which they let Mum out of hospital for the day. It was all very hush-hush and I was now the black sheep of the family.

Soon after this trauma I left home. When I told my parents I was leaving, my father threw me to the ground, kicking me with his pointed toed shoes, telling me that I was really upsetting my mother. I thought he had a strange way of trying to get me to stay. I moved into a flat with other young people and started smoking pot. I enjoyed it at first, but after a while I got even more nervous, and my self-confidence got worse. But I kept smoking because everyone else seemed to be having such a good time, and I figured something good would have to come of it at some point. The good part was that it made me laugh, and for the first time I felt included. This was new to me, and was what I longed for.

Then I started taking LSD. I didn't like it at all, but having no sense of myself, I went along with the others to try and feel that I belonged, and had some sense of purpose. For years I ate LSD like lollies every day. I hated what it did to me physically, but was yearning so much to feel alive that I kept persisting. It didn't work, as I was trying to get that sense of myself externally. It made me paranoid, thinking I was going to die, or someone was going to kill me, that nobody liked me, that I was ugly, and so on. During this time I travelled around fruit and tobacco picking in Queensland, doing any odd jobs to get money to party, and I became friends with Tim, a gay man.

One night I went out with him to visit his friends. Until now I had smoked anything I could get my hands on, but had never seen heroin before. A hit of heroin is called a taste, as if you are having a taste of something wonderful. He was about to have a taste, and was drawing the mixture into a syringe. I said, "Oh, can I have some?" He said, "No, I don't want that responsibility." But I persisted, "It's okay, I'll give it to myself, needles don't bother me." We argued for a bit, and I said I would take full responsibility, and would really like to try it. He shrugged and left me to it. I'd done a bit of nursing, so knew how to give myself an intravenous injection, and I took a small amount. It was the most amazing thing I'd ever experienced. For the first time in my life I felt that no one could hurt me, and I learnt the meaning of confidence. It was glorious, the most extraordinary thing I'd ever had. I thought, 'I don't know what all the fuss is about. I can handle this.'

A week later I asked Tim if we could get some more. Again the experience was incredibly euphoric. I didn't have the physical discomfort I'd had with LSD, or the paranoia of pot. I felt confident and it was wonderful. It was an inner circle of people that used heroin, so I instantly felt I belonged to some kind of family. Each week I went back, and started going without Tim. I have little memory of details, but I think I was sixteen. I had a part-time job in a supermarket, and after paying the rent I spent all my money on smack (heroin).

This continued for a while until I met some people who were moving to Darwin, in the Northern Territory. I thought that was great, as it was closer to Bangkok and Timor where smack came in more easily. I hitchhiked there, and slept on the beach till I met people who offered me a share in their house. They were using heroin, and I was excited as it was a couple of weeks since I'd had any. I wasn't addicted enough yet to be sick, but was a bit shaky, and really wanting it. Now I was living where people were dealing in it. There was such abundance of heroin I never had to pay, and it was of the highest quality, very pure. We lived at the other end of the street to the Darwin Hospital. Unknown to me, one of the guys in the house broke into the hospital pharmacy one night, and came back at some ungodly hour in the morning waking us all up. He opened his bag, and inside was every type of drug imaginable. It was like being in a candy store, and we were in oblivion for days.

Every time we had a taste of heroin, we had to go straight to the toilet and be sick. After that we could relax, sit around and be stoned all night and smoke lots of hash. My health was getting bad, but because I had this euphoric self-confidence I didn't notice I was getting sick, and didn't think I looked bad. I hadn't eaten properly for weeks, and went down to six stone. I'm normally heavily built. My face was caved in, and I was covered in tropical ulcers. If I got bitten by a mosquito and scratched, it got infected straight away. During this time I became promiscuous within the circle of friends I was mixing with. Everyone was the same. With that sense of euphoria you felt you could do whatever you wanted. We felt invulnerable.

But death was not far away. One day I met a guy who offered to take me to the old army barracks to get some smack. I hadn't had any for a couple of weeks and was feeling traumatised, sick and shaky. We drove there on his motorbike, and he mixed up a strong, pure hit. I started to pass out before we got on the bike to go home. He got scared, not so much that I would die, but that he would have a woman hanging off his bike dead, and the police would find out he had heroin. He put me on the bike and I have a vague memory of hanging on. He drove fast, dumped me outside the house and rode off. I was so close to being unconscious I could barely walk, went in, took all my clothes off, and my last memory is of sliding down the wall. I was told that my friends walked me round the garden for hours to keep me alive.

Unknown to me, a friend rang my mother and said that she should buy me a plane ticket out of Darwin, because if I didn't leave I would probably die. Mum called me, and I tried to persuade her to send the money instead, but she knew I'd spend it on drugs. I had run out of money and a place to live, so I had little choice. I have no recollection of the trip, or of her picking me up. When I got off the plane and walked past her, she didn't recognize me. She was looking for someone who looked like her daughter. When everyone had gone, we were still waiting for each other and I was the only one left. She realized with a shock that it was me. I was stoned and couldn't understand why she didn't recognize me. I thought I looked fine.

Back at home things were difficult. My mother was always sick, moaning and self-absorbed. She had some breast abscesses removed, and while the nurses were out of the ward she had taken a syringe and injected the infected material from one breast into the other, so that she could stay sick longer and get more attention from my father. She ended up having both breasts removed. Her stratagem failed and the marriage ended, and then I had to cope with her suicide attempts. I was there when she slashed her wrists, and another time she tried to jump off the cliff near our house, with me running after her, trying to stop her. And she overdosed on drugs, always when I was at home alone with her. I was usually stoned at the time, and had to call the police for an ambulance. I think I was eighteen.

Desperate to get away, I managed to get the money to go to New Zealand. I met some Maori guys in Christchurch who were into shooting heroin, and we took whatever drugs we could find, including Pethidine and LSD. One night one of them broke into a doctor's surgery. There was a knock at the door at 2am and the police came tearing in looking for Dan, who had a reputation in the area. We told the police we didn't have any drugs. I was stoned, and didn't know I had a needle still sticking in my foot. I must have stepped on it, and being so anaesthetized, didn't feel it. The policewoman wanted to look at our feet, so I showed her, and saw this needle hanging out. I freaked out and said, "Oh, I don't know how that got there, *I don't use*!" I had been good at hiding it, using veins in my wrists and under my toes and tongue, but there was no hiding this.

I had been terrified my father would find out, but they informed him and he brought me home to live with him. As I couldn't get heroin, I smoked hash and used LSD. My father found out and put me into a psychiatric hospital, where I refused to talk to the psychiatrist. Amazingly they let me go.

Before leaving Darwin, I had fallen in love. Simon contacted me now and we decided to move to Adelaide together. He got a job as a truck driver, and I worked in a hospital called "The Home for Incurables". I've no idea how I managed to keep the job as I did very little nursing. I was always stoned, and would spend most of the morning vomiting in the bathroom. The other girls covered for me. My partner started dealing, and we always had huge amounts of heroin in the house. A friend of ours was bringing it in from Thailand. On arriving in Australia he always came straight to our place to unload, by taking an enema and evacuating the condoms filled with heroin that he had swallowed before the flight.

One day our friends from Darwin came, and we were excited because they had some very pure heroin. When we got to their place, we found a woman had overdosed and was lying on the bed going blue. Everyone was shaking and slapping her, and throwing cold water over her. Eventually they brought her round and walked her around the garden. I took her little daughter upstairs to keep her away, as her mother looked dead.

Although I didn't have as much, I overdosed as well. I remember going from the bedroom to the toilet and being on the floor, throwing up. Next, I was going down a long tunnel in immensely bright light. Unlike the light from a bulb, it was integrated into the walls, which glowed. I knew I was travelling down a tunnel at *enormous* speed, and my whole body was turning over and over in slow motion. I was in absolute bliss. It was nothing like being stoned, far beyond that. I don't know whether the voice I heard came from within me or somewhere else. It said I had a choice; to keep going, or go back. The dilemma was that I felt so blissful that I didn't want to go back. But there was a part of me that knew I still had something to do, and I made the choice to go back. The moment I thought that, I wondered how I would let them know I needed help. Next thing I knew I was back in my body and whispering (I thought I was screaming) my partner's name. At that moment he walked past the door and heard his name, and saw me slumped over the toilet, very blue. I don't remember coming round or how they kept me alive, only that I didn't die.

One day the guy came in from Bangkok and I walked into the bedroom as they were doing the money business. There was a pistol on the ground. I'd never had anything to do with pistols and didn't like them; but I said, "Oh, cool! A gun! Can I hold it?" He had his shirt off, and I noticed he had bullet wounds on his back. I said, "Have you been shot before?" He casually said, "Oh yeah" and I assumed it was for drugs. I picked up the gun, and the energy coming from it was so horrible it completely upset me. I put it straight down and said to Simon, "That's it! I don't want guns in the house. *No guns in the house!*" He said okay. I knew he had a rifle and asked him to get rid of it. I thought he had, but it turned out he hid it on top of the wardrobe.

We used to make up pure heroin into large gelatine capsules, keep it in plastic bags and bury it under the tree in the garden. Late one night a friend came to visit, and we were asleep. Simon woke hearing someone creeping round under the tree. Before I knew what was happening he had the gun down off the wardrobe, and was yelling out of the window, "If you take one more step, I'll blow your brains out!" I couldn't believe what I was hearing. It's one thing to try and kill your*self* with this stuff, but this was getting too heavy for me. I shouted at him to stop, and then we saw who it was. It was getting scary.

Alarm bells were vaguely going off in my head, but we continued to use. Then one day a young couple, clean, healthy and innocent-looking, came and bought a large capsule of heroin. They looked like a sweet boyfriend and girlfriend, about fifteen years old. It was the first time my conscience had ever pricked me. One of the group lying around stoned said, "There goes a habit in a cap" and I thought, "My God, there was enough there for them to get addicted." My conscience started to nag me. I didn't want to be responsible for others getting addicted and ruining their lives. By this time I knew I was really sick and couldn't do without it. My whole focus of thoughts was about when I would have my next hit. Hanging out with friends, the conversation would be about how good the dope was, where and when you'd get some more, and telling stories of the best times you'd been stoned. We were constantly scratching, sniffing and "nodding off", head hanging, eyes closed, half unconscious. But I hadn't thought about giving up.

By now we were more hygienic, and one day I was in the kitchen boiling the syringes and putting them away. I turned around and there was a policeman standing at the window, watching. I didn't know how long he'd been standing there, and though scared I said, "Hello Officer, what can I do for you?" He looked at me with contempt and asked if Simon was there. I lied and said he wasn't. He said, "Tell him that I know what he's doing and where he's getting it from, and if it's the last thing I do, I'm going to get him!" I said I'd give him the message. They had been following the guy smuggling from Bangkok. I got such a scare that I realised if I kept doing this I would either die or go to jail. To me, going to a woman's prison was far worse than death.

At that moment there was a shift, and *I absolutely decided that I wasn't doing this anymore.* I was sick, skinny, covered in sores, couldn't eat or sleep, was continually sweating a foul chemical smell, and feeling guilty about selling stuff which might kill people. It was no existence. I told Simon I was leaving and stopping this life. I couldn't do it anymore, and thought about the best way to stop. Methadone, the heroin substitute, seemed a bad option, as I didn't want to get addicted to another substance. So I decided to stop cold turkey. Next morning a girlfriend offered me a flat, and within two days we had moved in. Simon decided to join me. I told Cathy what we were going to do and asked her to lock us in, check to see that we had water, collect the washing and bring cups of tea. I took full responsibility. She had done it herself, and understood that we would be pleading to get out, and going through hell.

It was horrific. For two weeks I didn't close my eyes. It felt as if matchsticks were holding them open. I went through extraordinary paranoia, thinking that people were trying to break in and kill me. I heard voices, hallucinated, and was so tender I couldn't bear the sheets or even the breeze to touch my skin. It felt like all the nerves in my body were exposed. It was torture. Cathy kept reminding me to drink water, but I didn't wash or eat. I thought she was trying to poison me. I was so sick physically that I'm surprised I survived, but after two weeks it started to get easier. Cathy made soups and I gradually got healthier, though still smoking plenty of cigarettes and pot. Physically the worst was over, but psychologically the cravings went on for a long time. I didn't know *anyone* who didn't use drugs, and was surrounded by people using. The craving was still strong, and I finally realized I had to leave this place or I'd crumble. My father had disowned me, but I rang him and he sent me a bus ticket to Brisbane.

Then I began to rebuild my life. I was nearly twenty when I stopped. I have often questioned why I went through it, and how I managed to stop. I can only think that I was fulfilling some karmic debt. Having so little love and care in childhood, I was searching for something to make me feel real. Some spiritual seeds *had* been sown. As a child I went to a Catholic school and thought the nuns were cruel and heartless. I rebelled, and didn't want to know about God if that's what Christianity was like. I wrote off spirituality and religion until I was eighteen, when I read ***Autobiography of a Yogi*** by Paramahamsa Yogananda. I found it amazing. From then on, I read Carlos Castaneda and other mystical and spiritual books.

After quitting heroin, Simon and I married and moved to a town in New South Wales. I have little memory of dates or the sequence of things. I'm surprised I have any brain cells left after all the drugs I took. We still smoked pot, but also developed an interest in meditation and got to know people who were more spiritual. Or so I thought. For a while I got involved in white magic and rituals, till I realized that some were not in it for the right reasons, delving into the darker side. So I left that crowd. I also left my husband, and with two small children in nappies moved around living on beaches. Then I found a flat in Brisbane. I was about twenty-six at this point. I kept meeting people who talked about a spiritual brotherhood called Subud, and I was attracted to it. So I joined. There I met Peter, one of the people involved, and fell in love. After an intensive three-month preparation in Subud, I went through a process of *opening* to God. Then I was given my spiritual name. I was happy to have a new identity.

I married Peter, and moved back to New South Wales. By this time I had given up smoking, drinking and eating meat, and we started a meditation group. By my early thirties I had two more children. One birthday Peter offered me a great gift for a mother with four small children, a weekend away on my own. It was a spiritual retreat at a friend's property. I didn't know what it was about, but was happy to get away for a break. On the first morning, I found myself walking round a huge sheep property at 5 o'clock in the morning with a group of people I didn't know, singing *bhajans*. We were led to the hall, and entered to find a huge picture of Sai Baba. I looked at this guy with fuzzy hair and an orange robe, and thought he looked strange, but didn't think much more about it.

Within six weeks, my friend Sue had gone to India to see Baba. He took her under his wing, gave her interviews, and she came back with remarkable stories. I gradually saw amazing changes occurring in this lady. The others in our meditation group became interested in Swami, and I watched them all go to India, one by one. My yearning to go was building, and it came to the point where I was *so* thirsty for him that I couldn't stand it. An American lady had been staying with me, and I'd helped her out of a difficult situation. She had lived in Puttaparthi for eighteen months, and spending so much time with her increased my yearning to visit Baba. After returning to the States, she sent me enough money to go. He uses many of us as instruments and brings us to him at exactly the right time for our learning and healing. This lovely lady was such an instrument.

Meanwhile horrible things had been happening, and I was traumatized. My husband had met another woman and left me with four small children. It didn't make me want to take drugs again, but I wanted to die. I had a good teacher in my mother and one day, in front of my husband, I took the scissors and cut my wrists. He had me committed into a mental institution. For the whole night I did nothing but chant Swami's name, "*Om Sai Ram, Om Sai Ram.*" The next day they let me go. I remember sobbing and crying to Baba, "*You'll have to be my mother, my father, my husband, lover and friend.*" I felt that I'd lost everything, and that I'd had very little in the first place.

Looking back I believe that everything that happened in my life was taking me to Sai Baba, and that it was him that stepped in and gave the impetus to give up heroin and that lifestyle. Now, having the money, I tried to find a companion to go with me to India but no one could go. I realised that I had to go alone, and was extremely nervous. But I knew that Swami was helping me build self-confidence by travelling abroad alone, and in 1994 I went for two weeks. I felt greatly healed and strengthened, but nothing dramatic happened.

An elderly lady I'd been reading to payed for me to go again in 1995. This time Swami called me for an interview. When I entered the room I reverted to childhood. I felt like I was four years old, and behaved like that. I didn't stop talking. Nevertheless, he treated me with a firm and loving hand, much like any father would. I was surprised that I wasn't shy at all, and felt supremely confident in his presence; it was a confidence I had never known before. It felt as though Baba was my mother, father and everything, and that finally I had come home. A few days later, I was sitting in the front row weeping when Swami walked back after *bhajans*. In my mind I was repeating to him, "You have to tell me what to do." Swami looked at me the whole way down the aisle, with *such* love. It felt like the love of a thousand mothers. I dissolved and couldn't stop crying. For the first time in my life, I felt a true mother's love.

Since those trips to India I've done a Welfare Course, and worked with women escaping domestic violence, taking drugs and having a terrible time. Because I have Swami, I didn't jump into their emotions with them, and had a sense that I could help them start a new life. I understood them, but remained detached. When I walk down the street I can literally smell if someone is using drugs. If I see an addict on the street I immediately repeat Swami's name, '*Om Sai Ram, Om Sai Ram,*' and ask him to help them. Even the mention of his name is so powerful it might be enough to reach them.

My attitudes to my family have changed. My mother hated my first husband and blamed him for getting me into drugs, but it was *my* choice. I'm sorry that I caused my parents so much worry. I had no concept of what it must have been like for them until I became a parent. My mother has senile dementia, and I can love her now, and understand that she was filled with incredible pain to have wanted to escape so badly from her life. I now have great compassion for her. My twin brother became interested in Buddhism and did severe spiritual practices on his own, and has become very strange and aggressive. The monks said this has happened because he has not had the proper guidance of a teacher and has gone off the path without realizing it.

I am very grateful that none of my children are interested in drugs; they think it's stupid. When I told my two eldest children what I had done as a young woman, my daughter wouldn't talk to me for two weeks. She couldn't believe that her mother had been that crazy, and she was angry with me. My eldest son had no negative judgements about it at all. The two younger ones don't know about my past and I don't see any reason they *need* to know now, as the person I was no longer exists.

In the worst part of the addiction, my body was emaciated and I had no sense of being anyone or deserving anything. I was completely empty without the drug, and very sick. I didn't realize it was destroying the shell as well as what was inside. Some of the people I used to know when using have died. The thing about heroin is that you have so much self-confidence. You don't think *it* (addiction) will ever happen to you, and even if it does, it doesn't seem to matter. It was a totally different life. Now I have natural self-confidence, many friends, and can tell my parents what I think and even counsel *them*.

It all changed at that moment of conscience, when I suddenly realised my responsibility for those young people buying heroin from us, and that this was only *my* addiction. I realised in the end that it was necessary for me to experience all these things in my life, for what reason only God knows. Looking back I can see that every step brought me to the realisation that *God* is the only drug that is any good for us. There is detachment from my parents, brothers and now even my children. Swami is the only thing for me, and my yearning for God is now indescribable. That's all I want. I don't want anything material, or rings from Baba. I just want what he has come to give us . . . *mukti* . . . or liberation from bondage. Without Swami bringing me to him I know I would be dead. I would have killed myself, especially after my husband left. That was the last straw. What I found about Swami is that he's the drug of all drugs. He fills me with more than anything else I've experienced.

The first time I saw Swami was on my birthday in 2001, when he looked into my eyes and spoke to me. And I was at his feet again in 2002 for my birthday. It seems that day is especially significant. I *have* been reborn since coming to him. I realize that the only thing that can *truly* heal us is the love of God, and that the fulfilment I had always been looking for was within *me*, not externally in the drugs. Now my only goal in life is to *find* the reality that I truly am, with God's Love and Grace.

"I gave many of you an unhappy childhood, including conflict or separation from your mother or father. In doing this, I removed from you the temptation to become attached to human parents or a specific family situation. That left you with only one option, that is, to attach yourself to me. Why do you not avail yourself of this opportunity, instead of continually seeking those relationships that can never satisfy you? Even if your childhood had been as idyllic as you would have liked, it is not your mother's love that you need. Ultimately it is not even the love of this Name and Form that you long for. Your deepest innermost urge is to return to yourself... to love yourself... to become the Being, the Awareness, and the Bliss which is all you ever were and all you ever will be."

- Inner message from Baba, taken from **Life is a Dream, Realize It**, by Joy Thomas.

12

Nowhere to Hide

Today cigarette smoking is the cause of many diseases like asthma, lung cancer, eosinophilia and heart ailments. The effects of smoking can be easily demonstrated. If a whiff of cigarette smoke is blown at a handkerchief, the cloth turns brown at the spot. If smoke can cause such damage to a piece of cloth, how much damage will it do when it gets into the blood stream? It ruins one's health and shortens one's life-span. Those who aspire to be true devotees of God have to give up liquor and smoking.

- Sai Baba

Cherie was born in Tasmania, Australia in 1953. I was chatting with her in Bangalore, just when I needed another story on nicotine addiction. I was surprised to hear that Cherie had smoked for so long, with her smooth skin and youthful appearance. She is pretty and sparkling, and looks much younger than her years. I can usually tell a smoker by their wrinkles and skin colour. It is aging. Nicotine is one of the most addictive substances, more so even than heroin, and this story illustrates the difficulties and rewards of giving up.

Cherie's story: I remember my first puff of a cigarette at the orphanage when I was three years old. Some of the 'Aunties' in the Home smoked and I asked them if I could try one. I was choking and spluttering, but it seemed the grown up thing to do. Then my sister and I went to stay with my real aunt and uncle on their farm during the school holidays. Neither of them smoked, but they always kept a little packet of Viscounts in the cupboard in case visitors came. One day my cousin Gary pinched them, and with my sister and I sat under the blackcurrant bush and smoked the whole lot. I was six. We had a good puff and felt very cool. I actually liked them.

In those days, smoking wasn't frowned upon. At high school some of my girlfriends smoked, and I'd always wanted to as it looked so cool in the adverts. I thought it would make me look older. As a sixteen-year old I looked much younger than my age. So when I left school at sixteen and worked in a shop, at last I had enough money to buy cigarettes. At a New Year's Eve party, I remember sneaking off to smoke so my parents wouldn't see me. But they did, and said that I might as well do it in front of them. Thus started my smoking career; it was to last over thirty years. Stopping was much harder.

In 1969 I started nursing six weeks after leaving school, and most of the nurses smoked. It was a comfort substitute and we didn't consider it to be bad. But I had a non-smoking boyfriend who didn't like it, and I did try to give up for a couple of years, discovering early on how hard it is. With the help of some pills that came out, I managed for six months, but when I went back on night duty, it started again. Once you've smoked, you always want to do it again.

Then I regularly smoked twenty to thirty a day until I became pregnant at twenty-four. I'd been living with this man for two years, and we married in 1978. My husband was a smoker too. The doctor told me that nicotine would make the baby small, and I really tried to give up. I couldn't stop, but limited it to between five and ten a day. It was a difficult birth, and my son weighed six pounds nine ounces. In hindsight, it probably did him a lot of damage, and he has had asthma since childhood. He smokes too. I kept it down while breast-feeding, then it increased naturally. I was always aware that when I smoked more than twenty I would feel sick, overdosed on nicotine. At parties I smoked much more and felt horrible the next day.

There were various unsuccessful attempts at giving up, but I reacted badly to not having nicotine. I got tearful, cranky and irritable, and so constipated that I ended up at the doctor. I tried naturopathic pills but that didn't help. I always tried to make it to the magic two weeks, after which I knew it would get easier. But I never made it. There was such a strong desire to smoke. Then one night I had a strange dream. There was a woman dressed in white, with an Irish accent. She said, "Cherie, it's time for you to give up smoking." I said, "Yes, yes, I'll do that soon." Still I didn't, but I tried. I was thirty-three. I was starting to feel guilty, times had changed and people were now being ostracized for smoking. It was considered an uncouth thing to do.

Soon after the dream I heard about Swami. The people who introduced me to Baba were smokers too. They said it was just one of their faults, and for a long time we justified our habit. When I first went to India I was thirty-nine. Smoking is forbidden in the ashram, so I had to go outside to smoke, and managed to get through five to ten a day to satisfy the craving. Two years later in 1994 I went to India again, and by now I badly wanted to give up, feeling like a leper in company that didn't smoke. At this time my marriage was breaking down, so it wasn't the easiest time to choose to quit.

We travelled to Kodaikanal, following Baba to his home in the mountains. I'd made new friends, and shared a big house with them. We were having a good time, but I was the only one who smoked. All I could do was to keep the numbers down. After *darshan* I couldn't wait to be far enough away from the ashram to safely have a smoke. One day I'd just lit the cigarette, when someone called out, "Here comes Swami!" I panicked and threw it away thinking, 'Oh no, where did he come from?' He went by in the car with a big smile on his face and waved.

The next day I waited till I got far enough away from the ashram, and lit a cigarette. Along came Swami again. I quickly threw it away, pretending to be holier-than-thou, with hands instantly flying into prayer position, *pranaming* to Swami, *definitely* not smoking. He laughed and waved. The next day I was very nervous about lighting this post-*darshan* cigarette, and as I got away from the ashram, I really looked around to make sure he wouldn't be coming, and asked if anyone had seen his car leave the ashram. I got as much information as I could, and went further than before to make sure he wasn't anywhere around. I lit up, and he came out of nowhere in the car. This time I didn't even have time to throw it away. I stuck it behind my back thinking, 'Oh Swami, You've caught me three times.' As if that shouldn't make me give up. But it still didn't.

Then Swami left Kodaikanal, and we all went to his ashram near Bangalore. Ashram life continued, and as I was sitting one day waiting to go in for *darshan*, I thought about how much I would like to give up smoking. I'd heard people say that writing to Baba helps, so I decided to write a note. I had a piece of scrap paper and wrote, 'Dear Swami, please help me give up my addiction and my desire to smoke.' I knew it wasn't just the addiction I had to let go of, but the desire too. So I folded it up, got line number one right in the front, and sat waiting for Swami. He came out and as I saw him, I thought, 'I don't think I want to do this today,' and tucked the note in the fold of my sari. Swami walked by ignoring me. Next day I was sitting in exactly the same spot. Again, I didn't think I could do it, and hid the note in my sari, asking Baba to bless a photo, which he ignored and walked by. The third day I was in the same spot again. It was bizarre! When he came up the steps, he stopped and really eyeballed me. I thought, 'Oh no! He wants my letter. What to do? I have to give it to him.' He looked severe and had a '*You're giving it to me today*' sort of look on his face. But he went over to a friend, Vimansa, before coming over to me. This time I had the little dog-eared note in my hand, reluctantly holding it out just a little way. Swami stood in front of me and started to sway. As he swayed, it was as though there was a string attached to my arm, pulling it towards him. I had a silly look on my face and was thinking, 'Oh, I don't want to do this!' As soon as it got far enough, he gently put his arm out and snatched it out of my hand, with a big grin on his face that seemed to say, "*Gotcha!*" Everyone around laughed because it looked so funny.

I knew then that he would take the addiction. I had a couple more that day thinking, 'Well, tomorrow that'll be it! I won't be smoking.' I went to bed, and in the night felt as if I was in hospital. I was barely conscious, but it felt as though a lot of activity was going on in my body, and I was having injections and being medically treated. I could feel Swami's presence the whole night. It was like coming out of an anaesthetic, when everything has a surreal feel about it. I felt when I woke up that he had been cleaning the addiction out of the body. When I got up I had absolutely no desire to smoke. Usually the first thing that always came into my mind on waking was to light a cigarette. Today it didn't happen. I was aware that I didn't want a cigarette, and that I wouldn't want one later. The desire was gone, and I didn't miss it. It was like that for a year.

At Christmas I went back to India and had a dream that I didn't understand at the time.

A friend came to me for my birthday and gave me a packet of Marlborough cigarettes and a Redhead cigarette lighter, with the logo of a redheaded woman on it. I was surprised, as he was a vehement anti-smoker.

"Here's your birthday present" he said.

"But I don't smoke," I said.

"But you might need them," he said.

"Well I won't need these," said I crossly, and put them aside.

My marriage of almost twenty years had ended at the beginning of the year, and I went through a divorce . . . yet I didn't need to smoke. But when I started dating again, the desire to smoke came back. It must have been the stress. A lot of my friends still smoked, and I thought I could just have one and it would be alright. The craving got stronger and stronger, and I badly wanted a cigarette, so eventually I gave in and had one. Then it became two, then three, and I was hooked again. After a couple of months the relationship broke up, so I smoked more. It seemed to fulfil something nothing else could. It gave me the feeling that this is something I can have for myself, like a reward system, which is strange thinking considering how dangerous it is for the body. This happened six months after the 'Redhead' dream, and I was hard on myself for taking it back up. It gradually increased back to fifteen or twenty, and it was getting to the point where my health was suffering.

I tried many times to give up. The nicotine patches and chewing gum seemed to make it worse, because it only addressed the nicotine addiction, not the desire to smoke. I thought, 'If I'm going to have these toxins in my body, I'd rather do the smoking.' Swami came to me in a dream once, maybe trying to help me not feel so bad about myself, and to show that he knew:

As I was getting on a bus I saw Swami there, with a long cigarette in his hand. He put it out as I got on the bus.

A few months after I'd started to smoke again, my friend in the Redhead dream re-married. He had only been married for six weeks when he committed suicide. It was very much out of character, but there was no doubt that he had done it. I went to the funeral, and to the wake afterwards at a hotel. By now I had forgotten about the dream. As I was talking to his ex-wife, I turned around and saw a whole wall devoted to this icon of the redhead that you find on matchboxes. My mouth dropped open at the realization of what Swami was telling me about my smoking. It was a kind of suicide. It didn't look like suicide, but it *was* slow suicide. Through the unnatural nature of what my friend had done, I was being shown the unnatural nature of what smoking would do. It actually made me laugh, as I saw how Swami is everywhere, even in my dream, and how he intricately links things in the most bizarre way. I was really gobsmacked that day. He showed me what smoking did. It didn't make me give up immediately, but it made me aware of what I was doing, and that if I continued it would cause me to die.

But I'm stubborn, and a lot of dramas were happening. Only after five more years of smoking did I get to the point where I thought enough was enough, and I had to try again. I prayed that Swami would help me. Now I was ready and simply stopped, determined to keep going. Every time the desire came, I had a drink of water or a mint, and distracted myself with housework, or phone calls. I told myself that if I put on a little weight it was okay. The first time I put on too much and didn't like being fat, so I tried not to overeat too much this time. I knew that after two weeks it gets easier, so I stuck it out. I knew that if I took one cigarette, I'd always want another. You just have to be strong enough not to take that first one.

It's been three years now, and I haven't slipped back into the habit. Since I stopped, there has been no desire to smoke until the last few months, when I had a big heartbreak. When sadness comes, I have to be careful not to revert back to old behaviours. I think the desire has something to do with the way I feel about myself. It's an addiction to the way I deal with things in my life. Smoking seemed to give a sense of nurturing; but it doesn't nurture you, quite the opposite. I had one temptation test, when I was feeling devastated a few months back. A girlfriend left her cigarettes at my place and I couldn't resist. I had two puffs, and it tasted so bad I couldn't believe it. I could still taste it after two days. It was scary to see how easy it was to pick up the cigarette, put it in my mouth and light it. My tricky lower mind had justified it by telling me that I shouldn't waste them! But it was a good experience, as it was so vile that I never want to do it again. I realized how yucky it is and how bad it smells. I'm safe now.

If I take one cigarette it's a never ending story and I don't want to go that way again. I have to learn to deal with life's problems in a different way. I don't have a desire to die now. A few years back, unconsciously, I probably did. Under stress I wanted to revert and contract into myself. There was so much sadness in me. I used to sit for hours and smoke, contemplating and going over sad thoughts and memories. I got stuck there. My father had put me in an orphanage, and I didn't meet my mother till I was forty-two. She recently died at sixty-six of congestive heart failure, which is related to smoking. She smoked when she was pregnant with me. Maybe I got addicted in the womb. The desire was in me from a very young age. All the women around me smoked and looked as if they enjoyed it. I really enjoyed it too. Now when there are dramas I go with it and think, 'This will pass' and it does. I just have to face the feelings and go through them, not avoid them. They soon pass if they are fully felt. I'm very happy not smoking, and would hate to do it again, and have to put myself through giving up one more time.

In 1995, when I'd taken up smoking again, after the year of abstinence, I was feeling incredibly guilty. I had a potent dream at that time:

There were some beautiful vines growing with fresh new shoots. Then the young leaves were starting to die (because of my smoking.) I had to go and stand in a queue for darshan. I was told that when I got to Swami I had to offer him something. I had a bag of bread, and decided I would give him that. It reminded me of the Lord's Prayer, 'Give us this day Your daily bread.' When I got to Swami I saw a big trough in front of him, and he was dipping the offerings in bleach to cleanse them. His sleeve had turned white. He was thoroughly cleansing. When I gave my bread, he fell on the floor and seemed to be having a seizure or stroke. I said, 'Swami, are you alright?' I realized that he was taking on some of my karma. Then he stood up and was fine.

Even during the dream I knew that he was taking on the effects of something for me. Now I think it was the smoking. As far as I know, I'm healthy. Who knows what may have transpired if I hadn't stopped filling my mouth, throat, lungs and bloodstream with poison, and if Swami had not taken on the ill-effects of thirty years of inhaling smoke?

Reason is a bad guide in spiritual matters, unless it is rinsed of all traces of ego. Else, it discovers arguments to support the point of view that is pleasant to the person.

- Sai Baba

Update from Cherie, January 2013

I have been well, and am in Puttaparthi at the moment. My life has been about learning to love the personality, and to accept all as meaningful for the awakening to my true nature. While at times this is easy, at others times it can be elusive as my awareness shifts. I did relapse into smoking again, and feel that it is only a matter of time that its grace will also leave me again. I have often felt it to be grace that has allowed me to smoke again, to receive the present moment inspirations I had while sitting alone, good or bad. Because of being so outcast from society, now one has to sit alone. In 2009 I met a wonderful man, with whom I am engaged to be married. The relationship continues to be full of present moments, walking side by side, and enjoying the experience of being in awareness in a physical body.

13

Ceiling on Desires

It is grace; those who suffer have my grace. Only through suffering will they be persuaded to turn inward and make the inquiry. And without turning inward and making inquiry they can never escape misery.

- Sai Baba

Marcel was born in 1942 in Edmonton, Canada. He is French Canadian. Marcel is an artist, and when I located him in February 2003, he was painting a statue of Sarasvathi, Goddess of wisdom and learning, symbolic of the wisdom he has gained through his experiences. He appears to be a happy man and solid as a rock. His face and eyes are clear and gentle. He gives his time to artistic projects around Puttaparthi, always willing to help and beautify the environment. Here Marcel tells his story of overcoming addiction to alcohol, amongst other things.

Marcel's story: I was two years old when my mother died. My father was a broken man and hit the bottle. He couldn't cope, and his new wife mistreated me, so my aunt and uncle took me in and adopted me when I was six years old. My adoptive parents were heavy drinkers, and there were often parties at our house. It was frightening to me as a kid. I used to get up at four in the morning when they'd gone to bed, and go round the house to check that all the cigarettes were out. I was very much against alcohol . . . until I tried it when I was fifteen. Then I knew what they were talking about. It hit the spot, and made me feel euphoric and powerful. It came naturally for me to start drinking, as it was a way of life for all my family.

I got married in 1970, when I was twenty-eight. My wife already had a ten-year-old daughter from her previous marriage. This girl could never accept me as her father, so there was tension between us. My wife and I were always arguing, and didn't hit it off because I was drinking like a fish. When I got rip-snorting drunk I became aggressive, and sometimes beat up on my wife.

But I had another side. I started doing Transcendental Meditation™. I wanted to do it because I realized that all the people in the world who had done anything with their lives had meditated. I wanted a discipline like that to see if something good would happen in *my* life. My wife and I were initiated in 1975. I was against it at first, because it was $120 each and I didn't believe you could pay for spiritual enlightenment. But we got our mantra, and I stayed with it for ten years. The promise was that if you continued with it that long, you would come to Christ-Consciousness.

In the same year our son was born. I stayed at home as house-father for a few years as my wife was a teacher, and could earn better money than me. I did the childcare, cooking and cleaning, and seven hours painting a day. My wife used to get angry with me because I spent all my time painting and drinking. When I meditated, paintings came to me full-blown, and I copied them, drinking heavily. After a while things started going haywire, as alcohol has a way of twisting things around and spoiling everything. We were divorced in 1980, when my son was only four years old.

I did to my son what my father did to me. I didn't *mean* to abandon him. I bowed out of the picture because my ex-wife re-married, and I thought he would be better off with his new Dad. I was drinking too much, and didn't think I was any good as a father, so I didn't see him for long stretches. I wanted him to take up with his stepfather and have a happy family life. He told me later that it affected him a lot. I knew *some*thing was wrong, but didn't know it was the alcohol. I was stupid, and it didn't click.

Alcohol is cunning and powerful and baffling. You go through getting high, over-drinking, and then go through the hangover. It's a rollercoaster. In interactions with people I always thought it was someone else who had a problem, never me. It made me aggressive and violent at times. I didn't admit that I was; but I was. After the divorce I had five years of heavy drinking. I fooled around, and was as promiscuous as hell. I used to have short blackouts for about twenty minutes, and towards the end started to feel like I was being possessed. When I'd had a few drinks it felt as though something took over my body. I was getting the beginning of DTs, (Delirium Tremens) and used to have this black *thing* on my shoulder when I had a hangover. I could see it out of the corner of my eye, but I couldn't identify it. It was scary.

In 1985 I was in my tenth year of practicing TM. In a way the promise came true, as something cleared, and I saw what was happening to me. One day, I realised with a shock that keeping a wine bottle under my bed every night was *not* normal. I started to ask myself, 'What the hell's going on Marcel? What are you doing? Going to bed with a bottle of wine?' It hadn't occurred to me before, and now it hit me with both barrels. I was afraid, and got down on my knees. I asked, "*If* there's anybody out there, give me a hand with this thing. I'm scared and I don't know what to do" I wasn't even expecting to hear anything, just calling for somebody to help me. And somebody *did*.

I didn't have a drink that day. I didn't even think about it. When I went to bed that night after work, I thought in surprise, "Hey, I didn't have a drink! Thank you! Thank you, whoever it is I'm thanking." I said the same prayer next morning. That went on for a week, and I didn't have a drink. Then one day I was passing a house called the Alano Club, and I saw people lounging around on the veranda. I thought it was a drinking club, so I went in. This guy came up to me and said, "Hello, I'm Jim, and I'm an alcoholic. Can I buy you a coffee?" I was shocked. I had walked into a common house for alcoholics, where they held meetings of Alcoholics Anonymous. I had never called myself an alcoholic; *definitely not*. It never dawned on me.

My AA birthday was February 15th 1985. From then on, I went to a meeting every day of the week, sometimes twice. They suggest you do ninety meetings in ninety days, and I did. I loved the honesty and humour. They would talk about the most ghastly things they had done, and be able to laugh at themselves. I liked that. I had always been taught to take myself too seriously. Those meetings kept me off the booze, and as straight as you can be when the mind still isn't clear, and your thinking is muddy.

I'd been going to meetings for eight months, when one day I was talking to my friend Sylvia, a fellow alcoholic. I said, "Sylvia, I really *am* an alcoholic!" It had suddenly struck me. I had been just mouthing it before. At meetings, everyone introduces themselves with their name, and states that they are an alcoholic. Then if they want, they tell their story, or share about their life. Up till then I had been saying, "I'm Marcel, and I'm an alcoholic, and I'd rather be quiet." After about a year I started to share about myself, and tell my stories. Then I got involved, and chaired meetings and did secretarial duties.

After I'd admitted I was an alcoholic, I told my doctor I'd stopped drinking. He was glad, as he said that I had an enlarged liver, and if I had continued drinking I wouldn't have lived much longer. I said, "Why didn't you tell me?" "Would it have done any good?" he said. "I think you would have drunk more and killed yourself sooner."

Alcohol messed up my thyroid gland, and I have to take pills now. Fortunately my liver recovered. I was lucky. The craving for a drink went the day that I prayed and stopped. It was lifted and I never looked back. It was such a blessing because I know a lot of people slipped and slid all over the place, going back and forth. Sylvia was one of them. I really *believed* after I got sober that I would never have another drink. I didn't dare take a chance with that. I wasn't going to play around with that stuff. It's powerful. That feeling has kept me clean and sober. But my brain was foggy for a long time, and the first year was easy, as I wasn't yet cognizant of what was going on. It was the honeymoon. Then the hard realities settled in.

One memory of my drinking days used to haunt me all the time. One morning I had a bad hangover, and I was carrying my small son up a flight of concrete steps at the University. He was uncontrollable sometimes. This particular day he wouldn't stop screaming, and I had a strong urge to throw him down on the concrete and eliminate him. Thank

God, something stopped me from killing my own flesh and blood. Later in AA, I did the fifth step with my son, "We admitted to God, to ourselves and to another human being, the exact nature of our wrongs." I wrote him a long letter when he was twelve, apologising for all the wrong things I did. He saw I was being honest, and it helped. Apparently we alcoholics negatively affect at least twelve people in our lives. They call it the Merry-Go-Round in AA.

I can't say that the first seven years of sobriety were easy for me. I moved from Edmonton to Victoria after my stepmother died and left me some money. I was doing nurses aid home support work, and liked it. And I was going to AA meetings regularly. Nevertheless, it was a time of white-knuckle sobriety, when I was hanging on by my claws. You bury all your problems with booze. You never deal with them, but put it off till tomorrow. When I stopped drinking, all these things came back and had to be dealt with, torn apart and put back together. That was real painful for me, because I stuffed a lot of hurt, guilt, fear and anger for many years. That door opens up when you stop drinking, and it can get frightening. I grit my teeth and hung in there, but I was going through hell. I kept saying to the old-timers in AA, "This is hellish; I hate it, all the stuff I'm going through." They would say, "Just keep on keeping on. It gets better." I got so mad at all the promises. But I did keep on, and it actually did work. After I'd cleared out the garbage, the promises came true. It was vital to have that experienced support system to give me understanding and hope.

For ten years, till 1985, I had been strict and meditated every day. After this I slacked off with TM and started to go to a group doing 'Transmission Meditation.' We met every week and meditated for one hour. Unlike TM there was no mantra. We visualized light coming in through the third eye, spreading through the body and out to the whole world. I really enjoyed it. We had meetings at Andrew's house and I used to borrow his '**Share International**' magazines. There was usually an article on Sai Baba, which always interested me. One day I asked Andrew if he knew where I could get any *vibhuti*, the sacred ash which Baba materializes. He said, "Yes, I've got some upstairs if you want it." I was thrilled, and he brought it down. He told me to put a pinch in water and some on my forehead. A few weeks later I asked him if there was anyone in Edmonton interested in Sai Baba. He told me that he went to a meeting every Sunday where there were a hundred of them! I started to go regularly. At first it seemed odd, with everyone sitting on the floor, men and women separate, and singing in Sanskrit. Most of the devotees were Indian, but I felt at home there.

In AA they always talked about the importance of finding your Higher Power, as you wouldn't be able to make it alone. As a recovering Catholic, I didn't like the idea of God. My idea of God was of a big father in the sky holding a sledgehammer to punish me. Now I decided to try out Sai Baba as my Higher Power. It worked. I would talk to him, telling him how I was feeling, and all the rubbish I was going through, and of course he had to listen. There is a saying that when the *chela* (disciple) is ready the guru appears. When I was ready, Sai Baba appeared.

In 1988 I made my first trip to see Baba. My stay was cut short to six weeks, as I got pretty ill with amoebic dysentery. They wouldn't let me stay in the ashram, as they were afraid I might die there. After a stay in a Bangalore hospital I had to go home. On the long plane journey back to Canada, I saw clearly that Baba had been shaving my ego, and I thanked him for it. He had ignored me the whole time I was there, even when I was sick and calling out for help. I had expected an interview and lots of attention. After all, I had been a devotee for two years, and I thought that was the least he could do for me. Ego! I soon learned.

Somewhat humbled, life continued and I stayed sober. Then in 1991, life presented a big challenge. I got up one day and couldn't walk. All the way to the kitchen I was leaning against the wall. My flat mate noticed and asked what was wrong. I said I didn't know, but I could hardly move. He took me to hospital, and they found I'd had a stroke. It came out of the blue. Luckily I came out of it with little damage. It was probably due to my heavy smoking, which took another few years to give up.

Then I went through a long, dark night of the soul. After the stroke, feeling weak and vulnerable, I fell in love with a girl much younger than me. I got addicted to *her*. She dropped me after a few months, and I went crazy. All the way through I'd been praying to Baba, "Please don't let me make a mistake here." He let me make my mistake really well. I was hooked. That's the worst addiction to have, to another human being. Of course I didn't realize I was heavily addicted. I thought it was love.

I went through an intense period of loneliness and despair for six months. I thought I was going to die of a broken heart. At the time I was working with John Bradshaw's book **The Homecoming**, on healing the inner child. Now I always advise people never to do that work alone. Without support, I fell apart. Everything started coming back to me, painful feelings of being abandoned and unloved as a child. As I was always crying and whining, nobody wanted to be with me. It was horrible. I was totally alone. I felt abandoned by Swami too. But I know I had to go through that experience, without knowing where it was taking me.

"Some of you feel neglected by me when disappointment or trouble comes upon you. But such obstacles alone can toughen your character and make your faith firm." Baba

I was going to Co-Dependents Anonymous by now, and my sponsor had given me a teddy bear, and suggested I talk to it as my inner child. One day, I visualised myself going into a lovely park. It was snowing, and there was a circle of people in warm coats standing around a little boy who was stark naked. He was crying. Everyone was pointing at him saying, "What's wrong with that little brat?" I went into the circle, picked up the boy and put him inside my coat. I didn't talk to anyone, but quietly carried him home with me. He cried a lot, and I paced the floor holding my teddy bear, crying for days. I couldn't go to work. Then one day I promised little Marcel that I would never abandon him again. I realized that it wasn't my parents who abandoned me. *I* was the culprit. I always talked harshly to myself. Now I made a promise to always listen when he was upset, and do my best to be a good parent to him. I've kept my promise, and now that boy is transformed.

He's innocent and beautiful, and I now see that he is God inside of me. I was constantly abandoning God within myself. I had to experience how hideous it is to be alone, so that something would click, and I would realize that I was playing this trick on *myself*. My ego was doing this to me. As soon as I had this awareness Swami came back into my life, and I could feel him again. Before, I didn't believe in myself. I knew now that I was worthy of love, no matter what I had done. Baba says that self-confidence is the foundation. Only then self-love can follow. It took three years to heal completely from that painful addiction to a woman.

In 1993 some friends invited me to go to India with them. I said I needed two weeks to think it over, as I was wary after my first experience. In my mind I said, 'I'm not going to be treated like that again Baba. I have respect for myself now. If there is a glitch with my passport or visa, I'll take it that I am not to come.' Everything went smoothly, so I went. This time it was different, as I had changed. I got front lines all the time and had personal *darshan* one day outside the ashram, when Baba came past in his car and smiled at me. Another time he made me pure white *vibhuti*. The icing on the cake was being called for an interview. It was a beautiful experience. He showed that he knew all about my life, but didn't embarrass me in front of the group. I asked if he approved of me putting him in my paintings and he said, "*Yes, yes!*" and blessed my career. At the end, when I was going out of the door I asked, "Baba, can I hold your hand?" He put his hand out for me to hold. Words cannot describe the feeling. It was the highlight of my life.

I got sick with 'flu after that for a week. There is a lot of energy in the Avatar, and I knew I was being cleaned out some more. But I was treated beautifully this time, and I know why. He was reflecting back to me that I now felt worthy of love, and had self-respect. I believe that we never get anything done if we don't have faith in ourselves. We need boldness and self-confidence. I think he liked my brassiness in wanting the best for myself. It's not the same as ego. I was feeling that I was as good as he is. I'm not as smart, and I don't have his abilities yet, but I see myself as a good man.

Another of my addictions was smoking. I gave that up in

2000, when Baba said that the plane was soon taking off, and if you weren't ready you might miss it. He had asked his devotees to give up certain bad habits, including smoking, as an offering to him. I wanted to be on board, and I gave up for Swami on my birthday. I told him I might not manage it, but I would try. I took it day by day, and went to Smokers Anonymous. I would still love to have a cigarette though, as I really enjoyed smoking and the desire has never left me. But I haven't smoked since then. I transferred the craving to eating, and put on weight, and now I'm tapering off on that. I've lost two stone in the four months I've been in India, and plan to lose another twenty five pounds back in Canada.

I don't have an intimate relationship now. I love everybody. I don't want or need a one-on-one relationship, but to be friends with everybody, and help everyone that I can. I would die for anyone. That doesn't mean that my ego always likes another person's ego, but I can love them. I sometimes send unconditional love to everyone. I had a dream, which taught me a lot.

I was on a hillside at sunset. I was sitting in a rocking chair and Baba was on my knee. He was small, and giggling and laughing as I rocked him.

I woke up and thought, 'You're God, I shouldn't be rocking *You*, I should be on *Your* knee.' It took me weeks to figure it out. Then I understood that whenever I have an altercation with someone, I should visualize taking him or her on my knee, rock them, hold their hand and talk to them. I did that, and it works perfectly. There are people I've had difficulty getting along with, but Baba says that God is in everyone, and we must love all without distinctions. He says, "Love all, serve all." Now I have an abundance of friends all over the world.

However I rarely see my biological family as they are all heavy drinkers, and it is difficult for me to be with them. They try to coax me into drinking, and though I'm not tempted, it's not a good thing for an alcoholic. I grew up with twin cousins. One was killed in a drunken driving truck accident, and the other is an alcoholic. My family thinks that Marcel is a snob, but I know that I have to keep a distance for my own good. I'm not attached to them anymore. I have my spiritual family now.

I don't do formal, sitting meditation much anymore. I attempt to make my life a living meditation. I repeat my favourite name of God all day, whenever I can, walking down the street or painting. Baba stresses *namasmarana*, repeating your chosen name of God, to be the best and safest method in this age. I took him seriously on that. That's my main spiritual practice. Sometimes I do Baba's *Jyothi* (light) meditation. In *darshan* I always say certain prayers. I promised I would offer myself as a sacrifice for my city, my province, and my country because I'm worried where it's going. It's getting really dark. In North America, the food is being altered and the air and environment is polluted. So are the minds of many people, and they seem to be at each other's throats for a few dollars. Every day I lay these problems at Swami's feet. I have a long list of people I pray for including my ex-wife and my enemies. I give Swami all my negativity; I can't hide it from him. He knows the deepest, darkest things about me, so I offer it to him, and it works. He takes all my junk. Not only is the negative offered, but *everything* that I do, not worrying about the results.

I can see a gigantic transformation in Marcel. I'm grateful for everything, and have learned a lot. William Blake said, "Let the fool persist in his folly and he will become wise." I'm not saying I'm wise, but certainly more intelligent and clearer. The changes have been gradual but sure, and given me immense confidence as I've overcome so much. First I gave up booze, then gambling, then promiscuity, then cigarettes and now over-eating. I couldn't have done that using force or pressure. I blow a fuse under pressure. I followed Swami's teachings and put a ceiling on my desires, doing it slowly, bit by bit over fifteen years.

It is said that a religious person prays not to go to hell, and a spiritual person has already been there. Because of my addictive nature I have learned about the painful consequences, and prayed not to transfer it to an addiction to attaining spiritual powers. I don't want to get caught up by visions or voices, psychic or healing powers. I'm not ready for that, and my ego would take over. But I *know* things that I didn't know before. When I was drinking I used to say, with great self-pity, "The only thing I know for sure is that I don't know anything for sure." That was the truth, and I really felt sorry for myself. Now I *can* say some things. I know that I love myself. I know that Sai Baba is God. I just *know* it. That's my transformation.

Above all, try to win grace by reforming your habits, reducing your desires, and refining your higher nature. One step makes the next one easier; that is the excellence of the spiritual journey. At each step, your strength and confidence increase and you get bigger and bigger instalments of grace.

- Sai Baba

Update from Marcel, February 2013

Marcel is well, and has now been twenty-eight years sober without relapse.

14

Hungry for Love

The food that is required for sustaining the body is conducive to health only when it is consumed within limits. Overeating poisons the physical system. Food may give satisfaction, or cause illness. By his food habits, man is becoming prey to disease. Food is essential, but it must be taken within limits for it to be wholesome.

- Sai Baba

Carol was born of Jewish parentage in New York, in 1941. She looks younger than her years and is a vivacious, sparkling woman with a ready smile. She is also slim and elegant. Appropriately for this story we first met over a delicious meal in the North Indian canteen in the ashram, and formed an immediate bond. We became close friends. Later she told me of her struggle with compulsive eating, one shared by so many people, and hard to overcome as we all need to eat.

Carol's story: The first time I remember thinking that something was wrong was when I asked my mother why I was so fat as a baby. On pictures I always looked twice as big as most babies. She said, "Oh well, you were hungry so I fed you." I was very chubby as a child and the other kids were always making fun of me. Right through my childhood I felt excruciatingly uncomfortable being so big. I never felt good about myself. I didn't have a good relationship with my father, and always felt frustrated at home and in my life. The way I covered it up was with food. I remember when I was twelve, I came home from school and there was a big loaf of bread on the refrigerator. I put lots of butter on it and ate the whole thing.

At the age of thirteen I decided to go on a diet, as I didn't like the way I looked. First I stopped eating dinner with my parents, and then someone suggested that I go to a diet doctor. My mother gave me the money to go and he gave me pills. I didn't ask what they were, just took them, lost my appetite and lost weight. I was happy. Later I realised I was on amphetamines. I got hooked and took them till my early twenties, going from one doctor to another, gaining weight and losing weight. At one point I had a friend whose father was a doctor and she was taking pills for me out of his cabinet, so I could continue. I was always speeding, and often used to eat *and* take the pills, which didn't work after a while.

I always had this idea that I wanted to be a model and be thinner than I was. I wasn't really that heavy, but constantly saw myself as fat. My head told me I didn't look nice, and my body was never the way I wanted it to be. When I was eighteen I did some modelling for a couple of years, and managed to stay real thin. I was a size eight. I got married to a husband who was on diet pills too. Then I got into the fashion business and cosmetic industry and *had* to be beautiful. I thought everyone loved me for the way I looked and what I wore. My husband saw me as a beautiful doll, and loved me for my appearance. He didn't love me for who I was . . . and neither did I.

In my early twenties I stopped the pills and tried a million different diets. The first one was with Weightwatchers. I went up and down in weight by about 50lbs, abusing my body with all the different diets. In between there would be periods of pigging out disgustingly, eating everything I had denied myself . . . gigantic pizza, ice cream and huge amounts of bread and butter. Sometimes I'd go to places where I liked the food and go and binge in my car, crying because I couldn't stop, and then throw the food out of the window as I was so ashamed of myself. Food would do everything for me. It was my drug, and when I couldn't cope with life I would just go to the food and eat. It was like I got drunk on sugar.

When I was twenty-five I went to Overeaters Anonymous (OA) in Long Island, New York. The first time I went to a meeting I felt I was home, because there were other people talking about their binges and what they did with food. Some people there weighed 500lb. I thought, 'Oh my God, other people do the same thing I do!' It was really nice for me because I was a closet eater, and nobody knew I was doing it. I would bring humungous amounts of food into the house and try to hide it, so nobody would find out. After gorging in secret, I felt sick and disgusted with myself. Then I'd walk around the apartment for days in my bathrobe, too depressed to go to the OA programme. People would call, but I wouldn't answer the phone. I completely isolated myself.

I was involved with OA for nine years and started losing weight, but I was getting anorexic. The diet they prescribed at that time, the Grey Sheet, was very strict and allowed no carbohydrates. I was jogging five miles a day, riding bikes, doing heavy duty exercise and eating a tiny amount of food, obsessed with my weight. I did enemas and took laxatives . . . anything to get rid of the food. I got down to 115lb.wanting to look like the girls in Vogue magazine. I simply wasn't built like that.

Eventually my marriage was in trouble. Every time I was upset I'd go to the food. Then I learned I could make myself vomit after bingeing to keep the weight down. It was like a monkey on my back that wouldn't go away, this cycle of starving, bingeing and throwing up. It was a horrible life. I did the 12-steps, but my vanity was so great that I couldn't stick to them. I wasn't winning in OA, and it was there I had first heard about anorexia and bulimia and got the idea to try it. It was also there that I knew for the first time there was a Power greater than myself that could restore me to sanity, and I really turned to that Power.

My first real experience of spirituality was in a marriage encounter weekend, run by the Catholic Church. My husband and I had one daughter, and wanted to try and save our marriage. The couples would spend time writing to each other, and then sharing what they had said. It was a listening experience. When it was over I had an experience of spiritual opening. This seemed to dispose of another of my addictions . . . shopping. I was compulsive about buying, always wanting things and spending money. I liked jewellery and clothes, and we could afford it. After this weekend it just stopped. I walked into a store and I wasn't longing for anything, which was amazing. I didn't spend a cent.

In 1980 a friend of mine lost her daughter to leukaemia, and went to see Sai Baba in India, staying for three months. When she came back she told me about it, gave me sacred ash and a picture of Sai Baba. I thought that her experiences were incredible. Maggie was a regular woman, not a *sannyasi* or anyone weird. Everything she said I believed; and she said that Baba healed her of her pain. I asked how much it would cost to go, and how do you get there? She said, "If Baba wants you there, he'll call you." I hung up the picture of this Holy man with the fuzzy hair in the kitchen. My daughter was embarrassed and wanted to take it down, but I liked it.

The marriage was going downhill, and when I was forty we divorced. I left with only two suitcases, leaving everything behind. My daughter decided to stay with her father, which was painful for me. I was now alone with only my eating disorder for company. The compulsion to eat got worse, and when I started I couldn't stop. I went to England and stayed with a healer friend, and learned healing and aromatherapy. Soon I met somebody, and went to live on an ashram on Long Island where I thought I would stay for the rest of my life. We studied the teachings of the Ascended Masters and I started having spiritual experiences, seeing lights and colours and having visions. I even saw angels. But I still had the addiction to food. It wouldn't leave me alone.

Then I was kicked out of the ashram as I was having a relationship, which wasn't allowed. It was devastating, as I wanted to dedicate my life to this place. I had nowhere to go and very few possessions. My mother loaned me some money and I went to a health farm, fasted and wondered what to do with the rest of my life. Then the woman who ran the place asked me if I'd like to do my healing work there. That was great, and I made a lot of money and people were helped by my treatments. But I was getting burnt out giving seven treatments a day, and got hepatitis and mononucleosis.

After recovering I offered to take a friend of mine to California, to be near her children. I felt guilty going so far from my own daughter, who was unhappy with her father.

I'd never been away from family and friends, and starting a new life was hard. So I was bingeing a lot and gaining weight. Then I found work with a doctor who did unusual healing work. He was a devotee of Sai Baba. On the way to California I had seen many rainbows, and he told me that it was one of Swami's signs. One day my friend took me to Big Sur, and as I was sitting in the monastery I heard a booming voice in my head. It was saying, "*Go to India!*" and it didn't stop. When I saw the doctor I told him I thought it must be Sai Baba, but I didn't have the money to go to India. He said, "Well tell him that if he's really calling you, you need the money." So in my head I talked to Baba about it.

I wanted to stay in California as I had work and things were opening up. But my car was stolen, and I had to go back to New York to handle the insurance. While there I got a job for Saul Steinburg, the publisher for a **Course in Miracles**. So I went to Course meetings and connected with old friends. One day I came into work really down, and Saul asked me what was wrong. I told him that I kept hearing this voice saying, "*Come to India*" and I didn't know what to do. He said, "Why don't you go? You'll always have a job here." As it happened I had just got the insurance money for the theft. The car was worth $600, and I got a cheque for $10,000. I knew it was thanks to Sai Baba. I had always dreamed of travelling around the world and hadn't been anywhere except California. Now I had all this money but I was afraid of going; however it felt like I had been given permission.

So I booked a ticket to fly on January 3rd 1984. My friend Maggie came to a New Year's party bringing all her saris, and an immersion heater that she said I'd need in India. All I knew about the ashram was that there would be crowds of people. Maggie said, "Don't worry, someone will show you the ropes." I was fat at this time, and bingeing. Maggie suggested I try to talk to Baba about my problem with compulsive eating.

Just before leaving I stayed with my mother, and she said, "Okay, go to India and get it out of your system." She was supportive. But I don't know how I got on that plane alone. It must have been Swami pulling me towards him. I went totally naïve and innocent, trusting that he was calling me. I didn't know much about him, and had never read a single book. I'd been given two books but decided not to read them as I wanted to see for myself. It was very clear I needed to go. I'd been teaching the Course in Miracles for a few years and believed in following inner guidance. And this guidance was strong!

I arrived in Bombay in the middle of the night. It was hot and smelled strange, and there were only men around. And I was late for the next flight and got bumped off. I didn't know what to do. The bus driver took care of me and found me a hotel, even giving his phone number in case I was in trouble. So I arrived hours late in Bangalore, and the taxi I had ordered was still waiting for me! He took me to a hotel where I could sleep at last, totally exhausted. However, I felt very well looked after.

The next day I met an English woman Sarah, who offered to share her taxi with me. She was married to a billionaire and had five suitcases. All I had was a few saris and some sweatpants. From the minute we got in the taxi till we entered the ashram, she didn't stop telling me stories about Swami. By the time we arrived I was full with Baba to the top of my head, after hearing about all these miracles. We shared a room in the ashram and she was so lovely, showing me how to wear saris and helping me out in every way.

On my third day there I was sitting in *darshan* still wondering what this was all about, when Baba looked directly at me from quite a distance. But I felt it. My heart opened and the tears were rolling down my cheeks. It was a wonderful inner experience of peace and joy; but I was still not seeing him as my guru. People suggested that I write a letter telling him all my troubles from the heart. I did this, and he came close to me one day and took it.

Unfortunately my room-mate also liked cakes, and sweet, sugary things. So we were pigging out in the ashram. We even had the taxi driver bringing us cakes to the room. One day I was carrying all these goodies back to eat, and all the mangy stray dogs were chasing after me, smelling food. I felt so badly about this that I decided I was going on a fast. So I collected lots of coconut milk and fasted, only drinking the sweet milk. I started to lose weight and felt I now had a semblance of order with my eating. I went from one extreme to the other again.

On the tenth day I was sitting in *darshan* with Sarah and her cousin, who was crying bitterly. She was ill. Baba passed by and told us to go for an interview. So we got up and walked to the veranda outside the temple, and waited for him to come. As he walked towards the seven of us I had eye contact with him for a long time. He told me to, *"Go in"* and we entered the room where so many devotees long to be, in his close proximity. He was very lovely and manifested *vibhuti* for people. This didn't impress me. I was looking on him as a human being who was very loving to everybody, like a good friend. He said to me, *"Your ex-husband is very bad. But I'll take care of giving you someone in your life."* Then he touched my head for a long time. I felt so much love.

On the way back to my room, my legs started to buckle and I had to sit by the bookstore for a long time. I started having visions and seeing beautiful colours. I was in ecstasy. This went on for weeks. He had shown me that he was far more than a good friend. I was falling in love in a sense, but still didn't see him as my *Sadguru*. I was hooked but didn't quite realise it. In the interview it hadn't occurred to me to ask about my food problem, as I was so overwhelmed by his love.

After two weeks I got really ill. Green stuff was coming out everywhere and I thought I was going to die. But I felt that even if my time was up, I'd now experienced everything I'd wanted. While I was sick I had a dream: *Baba came and put his arms around me.* I had never felt love like that in my life. Then someone knocked at the door waking me up, and I was in tears. It was a feeling I can't explain, like pure love enveloping me, enfolding me. After this I always felt Baba in my heart.

I stayed in India for two months and spent part of the time travelling, knowing that Baba was taking care of me. He saved me from some dangerous experiences. I saw many emaciated travellers, and was disappointed that I only lost 25lb. So I went trekking, hoping to lose 40lb. I was never satisfied with how my face and body looked, and had this vision of being tall, thin and blonde, with dimples. Every time I was frustrated I would eat chocolate, and a lot more food than I should. So the monkey was still on my back. But his grip was loosening a little.

When I left India I went to England to house-sit for my friend Sarah. In her room there were dozens of pictures of Baba, and as I entered they all turned golden. Then I slept for two days. When I woke I knew that I wanted to be his devotee. I *knew* that he was my *Sadguru (*the one who can take you to enlightenment.*)*

Eventually I had to go home to America, to my apartment on Long Island. Little did I know the hard times ahead for me. When I got back, my daughter begged to live with me, so she moved in. It was like a horror show, as she was using drugs and alcohol. She was only sixteen and skipping school a lot. I couldn't cope with it. I had thought that it was the ultimate that I could be with my daughter again, and that everything would be fine. It wasn't. I was confused, and went back to OA, to the ashram and to Baba meetings to try and get help. But things got worse, and when she started hallucinating I had to put her in hospital. Every time I went to see her in hospital I came home frustrated and distraught. I never saw a place like it. She was behind locked doors. It was a private hospital as my ex-husband had medical insurance, but it was horrible and she was so strange. After every visit I would go home and binge, and got bigger and bigger. When she came out she decided to return to her father. I was devastated and got into a black depression. So I turned heavily to my comfort drug food once again.

Sai Baba had promised me someone in my life, and I started having dreams that a man was coming. I was at a big conference, and that's when Hans came into my life. My dreams had told me what he would look like, and how he would act. When I met him his first words were, "You remember?" Hans was embarrassed, and didn't know *why* he had said that. But I knew. It was an instant heart connection, and he invited me to go to Russia with him. By now my daughter had run away from her father, was living with her boyfriend, and was pregnant. So I couldn't go to Russia as I had her wedding. But later I went to see him in Germany. I knew that he was the one Baba had been talking about. When my daughter had her baby, we both returned to America to see them. We were married within six months.

I went to live with him in Germany. This was challenging in itself for a Jewish woman. I still had the monkey on my back, but with Hans it got easier. Being together nearly all the time I didn't get a chance to binge. Sometimes I did when he went away, but not much. Occasionally I'd throw up and tell him, and he wouldn't react. He'd say, "It's going to fall away." He knew all about it and loved me anyway. I always felt guilty when I gorged on sugar or bread, as I'd been told it was like alcoholism . . . you mustn't take that first drink. I mostly didn't eat those addictive things anymore, but when the desire came Hans used to say, "Just have a little." And I could. I gave myself permission. When we had met I was really fat, but he said that he never saw it. He loved *me,* the soul, not just this physical vehicle, and it was a meeting in the heart rather than an intense physical attraction. It was easy, comfortable, and very healing for me to be accepted the way I am. But *I* still couldn't accept the way I was.

Being in Germany, I noticed that the women looked normal. Nobody was too thin or really obese. They were eating cake and ice cream, and didn't seem to care so much about their bodies, unlike in America where people are so body conscious. They just ate their breakfast, lunch and dinner and had their discipline. I never sat round a table where anyone was really stuffing themselves. Here I never felt threatened because they were just ordinary working people. In America the culture was of great beauties, models, and stars on TV and in the media . . . and many obese people in ordinary life. I still wanted to be thinner, but it wasn't so much on my mind now. My weight gradually got less because I had Hans' love and Swami's gigantic love. I started to accept myself more as I was, and to feel comfortable in my body. I see now it was a step by step process.

Hans and I were involved in a play that some children from Munich were going to perform for Baba, and we went with them to India. We rehearsed every day in the Poornachandra Hall in the ashram. I was playing the voice of Freddie the butterfly, the main role. It was a play about the transformation of the caterpillar to a lovely butterfly. The children spoke in German, and we adults said the words in English to the audience. There was one line I had, "*What is life all about? Just eating and eating and getting bigger and bigger?*" That was my life story! Baba lived upstairs from where we rehearsed, and sometimes he would show up during rehearsals. One day, suddenly there he was standing in front of me as I was speaking that line. He was looking right at me. Only a year later did I realise the irony of what I'd had to say, and that since then I had been at peace with food. I was free from the obsession with overeating, transformed from a fat caterpillar to a butterfly that could fly freely. He took my burden away, the monkey who'd been on my back since I was a little girl.

From the time I set foot in the ashram the fire started, and it's still like that. There have been many problems in our life, and financially we've been hit and put on zero. I've been through much pain over my daughter's mental illness, but Swami has given us so many gifts that I believe one day she will be healed. I'm happy to be free of my compulsive behaviour. Now I eat everything, including sugar and candy, but I watch it. I can have one piece now, whereas before if I had a chocolate or cake I couldn't stop. I no longer have the cravings or the starving feeling I used to experience. The Grace descended on the problem, and I'm immensely grateful to Swami for that.

In 1998 I had an interview with Baba. He asked me, "*What do you want?*"

"I want God." I replied.

"*You want God?*" He said. "*You think too much about your body. Don't think about your body. The body is a water bubble, the mind is a demon. Follow your conscience, follow your heart. You are God.*"

"I try Swami." I said.

"*Don't try, do. You are God. You are the Master,*" He said.

Then I put my head on his feet and kept it there till he said, *"Don't sleep!"* In other words, wake up!

I want to get away from this body consciousness. Swami has given me many experiences of bliss, and when in that state I don't think about my body. When I truly have the experience that I am God, identification with the body will be gone. It's been a long haul, but eventually the addiction was taken away. I'm over sixty now and am okay with it. I'm a woman and like to look nice, but now I accept my body the way it is. I haven't been on a scale now in twenty years, and don't know how much I weigh. Scales used to make me crazy. For the last eight years I've worn the same size, and if things start to get tight I cut down a little.

I used to think about food all the time and was always hungry . . . for food, love, attention and God. But I didn't realise at the time that those were the things I was truly craving. There is great compassion now for everyone that has addictive behaviour. I think it's a longing for love, nurturing, and caring that we feel deprived of, and haven't known how to give to ourselves. Sai Baba gave me this unbelievable love through Hans, which helped to heal my self-hatred, and then finally stepped in himself to end my dramas with food.

Love heals everything.

Man is not born to go in quest of food. Man is born to go in quest of the soul.

- Sathya Sai Baba

15

"I Need to Decide!"

My mission is to grant you courage and joy, to drive away weakness and fear. Do not condemn yourselves as sinners. Sin is a misnomer for what are really errors. I shall pardon all your errors, provided you repent sincerely and resolve not to follow them again. Pray to the Lord to give you the strength to overcome the habits which enticed you when you were ignorant.

- Sai Baba

Manou was born in Vienna, Austria in 1964. I first noticed her when she had just arrived in the ashram in 2001, looking lost and stressed. She told me her story of recovering from heroin addiction two years later. She is a different person now, confident, attractive, healthy and much happier. She has worked hard on healing her pain, and has come a long way in a short time. It has taken much courage and determination. Could therapy alone have had this result? It is surely due to Divine help.

Manou's story: I can't remember much of my childhood. Three years ago, when I stopped taking drugs, I wanted to work with my inner child, so I asked my mother for an early picture of me. She gave me a photo, and I was shocked to see how much sadness there was in my eyes. I was only two. In my face I saw deep pain and hopelessness.

My parents did the best they could, but there was always an undercurrent of tension. They had met in Canada, having emigrated from Austria and Czechoslovakia. My father's family were refugees, and he was working in the theatre as an actor when I was born. There were many problems between them. My mother adored him, but my father thought it was quite okay to have girlfriends. Then my mother started cheating on him too, and she treated me like a friend not a daughter, and shared her sexual life with me. She talked openly about it when I was only seven years old. I was never able to be a child. There was always lying going on around me, but unlike them I was fanatical about the truth. My parents knew they could always get the true story from me.

When I was thirteen my father found out about my mother's boyfriend, and beat her up. I saw her with a torn lip and a black eye. Two weeks before that he had beaten up my sister, and he did it to me too. He was drinking a lot, and I lived in fear of his moods and rage. I went into shock, and I think my development stopped at that time. The pain was overwhelming, and I didn't want to *feel* anything anymore. I prayed they would get divorced. The lying got worse, and my mother used us kids to lie too, which caused *more* trouble. Finally, when I was sixteen my parents separated, and my mother, brother and I went back to Austria. Another difficult time began for us. We had no money, and went to my grandmother's tiny place with no bathroom. It was hard after our comfortable lifestyle in America.

My mother worked like a maniac, with two jobs to support the family. When I was seventeen she found me a small apartment, and I lived alone. I started to work too, and now I had my own money. My friends smoked and drank, and took cocaine, but I didn't want to try. My parents had always told us that drugs were bad and we shouldn't use them. My idea of drug addicts came from films. I thought it meant living on the street and working as a prostitute. I thought you got hooked the first time you did it, and went downhill fast. So I was against drugs.

One evening after work I was thirsty, and my taxi driver took me to a new bar on the way home. As fate would have it, I met the bar owner Peter, who was to be my future husband. I was nineteen and innocent. I didn't know he was using drugs; he seemed so normal. After two years together I still didn't know about hard drugs, until we went to a famous artist's apartment, and were offered cocaine. We took it for thirty-six hours. It was interesting, and I felt fine the next day.

Soon after that we got married, and before long Peter suggested trying heroin. As the cocaine seemed to have had no ill effects, I agreed. We sniffed it. At first I was sick, then after a couple of hours a really nice effect started working. My stomach calmed down, and I had a strong feeling of warmth from head to toe. I had clear visions, like intense dreaming. The next day I woke and felt fantastic. But we didn't take it for another six months.

My husband decided to give up the bar, as he was a frustrated artist and wanted to paint. Then I met the owner of one of the biggest magazines in Austria, and went to work for him in advertising. I loved my job, and suddenly we had a lot of money. Heroin was expensive then, and at first we only took it at weekends. Then it started every day for two weeks, and we decided to stop so as not to get addicted. He had horrible, bad withdrawals, but I had no problems. I was working at a hip discotheque, with lots of drugs around. One night I was offered cocaine and went to a hotel after work, taking cocaine all night. When I wanted to leave, a man locked the door and raped me. I was in shock, but dared not report it. I couldn't tell my husband, but he knew something was wrong. He didn't trust me after that, and started to drink heavily. I was afraid of him when he was drunk, and we had big fights. He wasn't earning much, so I worked long hours to pay the bills. I was getting exhausted.

We both went back to advertising, and made a lot of money. We began to inject heroin for the first time. It was an unbelievable feeling and rush. After a few months money got short, so we started to drink opium tea which was cheap. I encouraged it, as I couldn't stand Peter's aggression when he used alcohol, but he was mellow with opium. After a year, we decided to do a cold turkey. Again he had terrible withdrawals and I was okay. It was a nightmare being with him.

But as soon as we finished the detox, I wanted some *real* heroin. The price had dropped to one third when the Yugoslavian war started. The heroin was coming in from Serbia and Croatia. It was well known that they sold it to buy weapons and finance the war. As it was so cheap we bought some, and injected it daily for a year. Then I decided to go to The Isle of Elba to do a cold turkey. Exactly three days after we left for Elba, the police arrested everyone who was buying from our dealer friend. When we came home and opened the paper, we saw a picture of our dealer looking out at us. It was a shock, but not enough to make us stop. It went on for another six months. I was now twenty-seven.

For the first time I went to my doctor and admitted I had a problem with heroin. He had no idea how to treat it. I was desperate to change, and also told my mother. She phoned my father and told *him* to do something. So I went to stay with him for three weeks to detox. My husband wanted to stay on the opium tea, and I had no idea that you cannot stay clean when your partner is still on drugs. I thought I was strong enough to resist. But after two weeks back with Peter, I was on the tea again.

At the time I had two jobs, but nobody could tell that I was on drugs. I didn't have signs like matchstick pupils, as I controlled my use. I was *very* disciplined. I had an injection before work, then opium tea at work if I got a little edgy, and then an injection or tea after work. Then I could *really* relax. Most of our friends didn't take drugs, and only one couple knew about our habit. Once someone had nearly died of an overdose in our apartment, so we didn't want anyone else there using heroin. It was too risky, and that experience had scared me badly. Mostly we stuck with opium. My life as an addict was extremely limited; I couldn't go anywhere. If there was a birthday celebration which involved going away for the weekend, it wasn't possible for me. If friends invited me to stay the night I couldn't, as I had to get home to have my tea, or my injection. For seven years it was an everyday thing.

In 1998 I wanted to stop, and went to the doctor. They found that I was a carrier of Hepatitis C. We were always careful, so I was surprised. By now I was completely stressed out, we had lost our apartment, my relationship with my husband was difficult, and I was just focused on paying the bills. I had my drug addiction, but at the same time I was a workaholic. Sometimes I only had two days off work a month. After the Hepatitis shock I did a secret detox, and then I had to go for an operation. There was a big fuss at the hospital about my heroin addiction in relation to the anaesthetic. For the first time it became public, and my guilt and shame was overwhelming. While I was recovering from the operation, all that my husband cared about was that I could no longer support him, and he asked me to get money from my mother.

That was the day I decided to leave my husband. My mother was happy about this. But I had only just stopped drugs, and was in complete depression. I had to go through another operation, and I was in so much pain that I called my husband, crying. He found out about a morphine substitute you can inject, which they give to addicts. For five days I used this Capanol to keep the pain under control. But as a result I got together with my husband again, trying to hide it from my mother. Things got worse, and I stayed on the Capanol for weeks and developed a mental craving for it. Then I got Hepatitis B, and had to go back to hospital. Everything was getting too much. My whole soul was screaming, '*I need to decide!*' So I asked for help again from the psychiatrist I was working with. He sent me for detoxification, and told me that I could *not* go home. I desperately wanted to sneak off for an injection there and then, but he sent me at once to a rehabilitation centre. I was so afraid that my heroin addiction would become public that he agreed to send me to an alcohol de-addiction centre, to help me hide the truth.

For ten days I was shut in. When I was allowed out, the first thing I did was go to Peter. Every seven days I could do this, and they only checked my *alcohol* level. They didn't check my urine, so I was free to use heroin. My mind-set was addicted to getting an injection, so *desperate* for that feeling. But something inside was telling me that if I didn't stop now, I was going to die. So I went back to rehab. There was a girl there, an alcoholic, who had been a heroin addict for fifteen years, and she had been clean for fifteen years. On the 15th September 1999 we were sitting in the garden and she yelled, "Manou, if you don't decide now, consciously, that you will never do it again, go upstairs, pack your stuff, go home and get a nice big amount of heroin, and do it. You don't need to cheat on yourself. *Just decide consciously!*" She was so full on. Then she stood up and walked away. This message was so strong, and my desire to live was strong too. That was the day I decided, '*Never again!*'

After stopping I had a new sensation in my heart, like my heart chakra was opening. Sometimes I was walking on the street and could feel love for everybody and everything. After over twenty years of using drugs, for the first time I felt a heart connection, which was overwhelming. It was difficult, as I could *feel* so much physically and every place I went connected me to the old feelings. I started listening to a meditation CD on a daily basis and this helped me to calm down. In my depressive state, it helped me to see the colours and experience the warmth.

But I felt as though my life had stopped. I was feeling guilty, still loving my husband and feeling responsible for him. I was afraid something bad would happen to him, and knew he could not help himself. But I didn't have the energy to help him anymore. My mother sent me on a vacation, thinking that an 'alcoholic' needs a holiday, and I went to Sri Lanka. While there I started dreaming that maybe I could do something with my life. When I came back I told Peter that I wanted a divorce, and I wanted to leave Austria. My physical memory was too strong there, and the weather too grey and depressing. Within six weeks, someone had offered me a job in Sri Lanka, and I was divorced.

In winter 2000, I left for Sri Lanka which I chose because alcohol is not a great part of the life there, and I was aware that you can easily replace one addiction with another. It was hard. I wanted to take care of myself, but I got deeply depressed. Then I met an English man who suggested I go to Colombo and get a job, and I moved there to be with him, despite an inner voice that was warning me not to do it. But in my vulnerable state, I wanted protection and someone to lean on. I worked in a hotel, and one day I was talking to a guest, a German musician. I told him my story, surprised I was admitting it to a stranger. But he was nice and said, "This is not the right place for you. Why don't you go to India? My guru Sai Baba is there and gives interviews to his followers, and materialises things."

All the time that I was on drugs I was also interested in spiritual stuff, and I always believed in God. I didn't practice, but was reading a lot. One book about a Cypriot healer had given me an idea about the kind of guru that I wanted. Since 1989 I had prayed to find my guru, but when I heard of Sai Baba I was not impressed. I believed materialisation was possible . . . but he did not interest me. I was depressed and dependent on my boyfriend, and wanted to marry him and have children, thinking that this would heal me.

But then I had visa problems, and had to go to India for three days, to Chennai. I was in a terrible state, afraid to leave the hotel room, and completely stressed out. One day I noticed a girl in the guesthouse who had an energy that was so *present*. I was attracted to her energy. I was hungry and didn't dare go out, so I asked this girl where I could find something to eat. She said, "Let's go together. We'll go to a restaurant, and then you can come with me to the travel agent." She kept saying, "*Sai Ram*" She told me she had just come from Sai Baba. She could see the state I was in and said, "Why do you want to go back to Sri Lanka where everything is difficult? Swami is in Bangalore at the moment, why don't you go there and see him? Get some rest and he will help you and sort everything out." I got excited, and thought, 'Yes! I'm going to do it.' But I only had a thousand rupees with me. She said, "Don't worry; he will take care of everything." She said she would help me to change my flight.

That night I had a horrible nightmare about two dogs jumping at my throat, trying to kill me. In the dream I was chanting, *'Sai Ram, Sai Ram'* and that's how I escaped. Then when I woke, I got *more* scared. Why did I say Sai Ram? I had only heard it the day before. I thought, 'I'm not going to this Sai Baba. I just want to go home!' This girl had told me she would pick me up at eight in the morning. I didn't have the self-confidence to tell her I had changed my mind, so we had breakfast and went to the Indian Airline office. In the auto I was praying, *'Dear God, I just want to go home.'*

I didn't realize that 'home' was with Baba. We went to the airline office, and it was empty as it was a holiday. I was relieved, thinking I could go straight back to Colombo. Suddenly a door opened, and a man called us in. I was hesitant about changing the ticket, and said, "Oh, if it's not possible it doesn't matter!" The girl went in confidently and said, "*Sai Ram,*" and he replied with "*Sai Ram.*" Then she said, "This girl is not in a good condition, and is not sure if she wants to see Sai Baba." The man said to me, "Listen, this is now Sai Baba talking to you. "*This devotee has given me his body so I can talk to you. I really want you to come to my ashram. Don't worry about anything, just come!*" I started crying, and from that moment on I cannot recall anything. All the scary things like going by auto to the train station, taking the train, and coming to the ashram, were done in a trance.

Anyway, I arrived safely and went into the ashram. At the accommodation office, the man yelled at me for wearing shoes, and said there was no room. Feeling completely lost and helpless, I was crying outside on the steps, and a sweet girl asked me what was wrong. She helped me and found me a space to sleep. In the afternoon I went to *bhajans*. I only had jeans, t- shirt and a tiny shawl, and was very scared. The Western women were wearing saris and Punjabi suits, and I thought I must be mad sitting there. Then the singing started. The door opened, Swami entered, and he was completely covered in golden light. I was thinking, 'I came all the way here to see a fake! He's a magician.' I was disappointed. I thought they had put spotlights on him. I had never seen an aura before, so I thought that this welcome gift he gave me was a technical effect. What impressed me was how nice the people were. They were so helpful. I thought, 'Even if he *is* a magician, the people are very nice, so I'll give it a couple of days.' It took about four days to realize that the light was not a special effect. I didn't see it again.

Then my inner dialogue started with Swami. I could hear a clear voice, and I knew it was not mine. The message was very strong, "*Stay here. Don't go away.*" Instead of staying one week I stayed four. I had a lot of blissful experiences, but at the same time so much pain came up. The first visit was like having permission for being a drug addict, because I had been hiding it all the time and feeling guilty. I met other people there who had stopped heroin, and yet were on the spiritual path. I found that another life is possible, and that drug addiction is a yearning for God too.

After four weeks back in Colombo, I came back to

Puttaparthi. Again the inner voice was strong, telling me to stay. I stayed a week but still wanted to fix my relationship in Colombo, so I returned. My boyfriend and I didn't take drugs, but drank alcohol. I knew now that I didn't want this. The group I was with only wanted to go out and get drunk at the weekend. I only drank a little, and then I would leave and go home. When my boyfriend had to go to England without me, I decided to go back to India. On the third visit I started to really work on myself; I was opening the lid with the pain. Though I knew that Baba was taking good care of me, and was mirroring things in me, I didn't comprehend what was going on. I was still paralyzed in my depression. A lot of abuse patterns came to the surface, Pandora's Box was opened, and it was overwhelming. One part of me wanted to stay and heal, but another part was desperate *not* to deal with it.

So again I went back to Sri Lanka, knowing full well it was not the right choice. Then I lost my job, my boyfriend and my home. I said, "Okay Swami, if you want me to come to India, then you will have to help me." Three days later I had a ticket, and money came from all directions. I had nothing to lose and knew I couldn't go back to Austria. The pain was too strong, and I was afraid I would do something stupid. I didn't want to drink or take drugs again. It was clear that I had to deal with my emotional pain another way. For three weeks, before leaving for India, I cried a lot. But as soon as I entered the plane it all dropped, and I accepted that I was going. On 16th September 2001, I moved to the ashram.

Immediately Swami sent me helpers, and I started doing intense inner work with Cutting the Ties. I cut ties with my mother, father, drugs, and much more. Then I did the Byron Katie work intensely for many weeks. I learned a lot about myself, my patterns and where I had to be careful. I had blissful experiences in meditation, but I was always leaving my body. I never wanted to be here; I still wanted to die. I couldn't cope with the pain, nor could I commit suicide, as then I believed I would have to come back and deal with it again. But I wouldn't have minded if an accident happened. I didn't want to be here and feel the pain.

On the surface I had always been the nice girl, and the good girl. Now a lot of anger came up. For six months *everything* made me angry. One day I was sitting alone in a hotel room, crying my heart out, saying, 'Swami please, I cannot live like this anymore, with so much anger. I don't want to be here. I want to die. Oh, please help me.' That day a clear vision came to me. I was screaming at Swami and my guardian angels, '*If you are there, tell me what to do!*' Suddenly a voice started talking to me, 'You are an old soul. This incarnation is like the blink of an eye. You have decided to come here. You don't need to do anything, just let everything happen. It's like a second in your soul age.' This knowledge has helped me to continue many times. But I was mad at my soul. Why did I choose these experiences? How could I choose drug addiction? I did not value the things I was going through.

One day Swami refused my offered letter, and said, "*Keep it.*" I didn't know what he meant, but I had so many thoughts like, 'I'm not good enough, I'm like a parasite,' and I was disappointed that these patterns were still coming up. I realised that I don't need to fight these thoughts, and I don't need to identify with them either. I got the idea that it's okay to have these thoughts, and I don't need to resist anything. When the sadness comes it's there, and if I accept the feeling it passes a lot quicker. I know that everything I experience with Swami is for my healing. I love Swami; he is my love.

For the last year, I have been working with the methods in Eckhart Tolle's **The Power of Now.** In meditation I was escaping. I saw that I had to stop this, as it was replacing the addiction. I had visions, Jesus and Mary came to me and I saw past lives, but I always left my body. I could not stay in my body. Even when I tried to stay in my heart, I would go to the third eye and I was gone. So for the past year I don't meditate, and try to keep my focus in my body. This is my work. I have to get out of my monkey mind, and go back time and again to *feelings* in my body. Since I started working with Eckhart Tolle I'm giving myself permission to feel. If I feel that I want to die, then I *feel* it. I try not to go into my mind. If I'm depressed, I *feel* depressed. I allow it to be there. It's all going faster now. Before, depression would last weeks or months. Now it lasts hours, or half a day.

The biggest change has happened in the last six months. My self-love has grown. I used to write pages of affirmations saying, 'I love myself.' One day I looked into the mirror and thought, 'Yes, nice!' Sometimes now when I look in the mirror, I really like this person. It's not me anymore. My face has changed, and my eyes have changed . . . everything. It's like a stranger, but at the same time it's a nice stranger. This is beautiful. I feel I've done a good job, and am proud of myself.

One day I was in a group, and asked Swami for an interview. He did not respond and I felt rejected. He was in the middle of the carpet and I had a letter in my hand, asking him what I should do with my life. I was devastated and dejected, looking down. Suddenly I saw his hand coming towards my letter. I looked up and he gave me a big smile, took my letter and asked, "*Where did you come from?*" He asked how many were in the group, then said, "*Very happy.*" It was the first time he had ever spoken to me.

At that time I was expected to go back to Europe for my sister's wedding, and I was scared about going back to Vienna. I was wondering, 'Am I strong enough? What will happen? Will I get addicted again?' So I had prayed to Swami, 'If you think I am strong enough to do this, please talk to me. If you talk to me I will take it to be a clear sign that I am strong enough.' But I had forgotten about this prayer. When Swami walked away from me that day I remembered it, then knew I could go back and face everything. I stayed in Vienna for three months and was very open, and sensitive to other people's pain. But I did not slip back. I cleared that hurdle and came back again to India.

In Austria I had seen my doctor who wanted me to do Interferon therapy for the Hepatitis 'C'. It is expensive, takes a year and has side effects, including depression. I didn't know whether I should do it, so I wrote Swami a letter and asked him to take it if I had his blessing to do this therapy. As I was sitting in the mandir I started to cry, as there was so much fear. My soul was screaming, '*Don't do it.*' But in my mind I had been determined to do it. I was crying so much people were looking at me. Swami came and looked at the letter, and electricity went through me. Then he looked long into my eyes, turned away and didn't take it. This shocked me. As a result I decided that I would not have interferon therapy.

My mother and sister came to the ashram too. So much healing took place between us, and it shifted a great deal. It was a gift. I love my mother very much. I love my father too, but no longer need his approval. Now I can love him the way he is. I was yearning so much for his love, but now I have found *my* love. Swami is my Divine father and mother, and I have found love for myself. It's in the kindergarten, but compared to before, it's huge. If you are an addict you need to have a close look at your personality and your patterns. You cannot do this alone. You need a good therapist, but one who knows about spiritual stuff too, otherwise it's useless. Until I came to Swami, therapy did not help.

It has become difficult with my financial situation, and I don't want to ask my family to send money again. It's time to take care of myself. The biggest part of my recovery work is done and I have learnt so much about myself. I know my weak points, and my strong points. I have asked myself, 'How much has Swami taught you? He gave you so many tools. Now you need to use them. Your strongest tool is your mind. Was I a good pupil? Can I focus, centre and concentrate?' I have to surrender to Swami completely, then he helps me in every aspect of life; I just need to call on him. Three weeks after this questioning a job materialised in the UK, and I have the feeling it's meant to be. Everything has fallen into place. I am at the point of walking again. I have been scared in the process of deciding to leave the ashram, but now it feels good and I know Swami will not dump me on the streets. It's a challenge, an adventure, something positive. I will be working for a spiritual friend. It's time to go back into the world.

When I look back now, I see that Swami was with me and protecting me all my life.

Come just one step forward and I shall come a hundred towards you. Shed just one tear and I shall wipe a hundred from your eyes.

- Sathya Sai Baba

Update from Manou, January 2013

Manou has remained free from heroin, and is now fourteen years sober. She has the occasional fleeting thought about it, but is not tempted. She also gave up cigarettes on 19th April 2010 (typical of addiction that we remember the exact date of quitting!) She gave up through hypnotherapy, but kept half a carton handy in case she couldn't do it. The next day her mind was crazy for cigarettes and she was desperate. She prayed, "Please Swami, I have spent 350 Euro on treatment, and I'm still obsessed! I can't do this. Please help me!" She sensed a reply saying, "*Go and buy nicotine chewing gum.*"

She did this, and soon learned that she had underestimated the withdrawal symptoms. From then on, she managed to handle it. For a year there was an intense craving to smoke at least once a day; and at least ten times a day she felt grateful that she didn't give in to it. At first she put on weight, but now that's also going. Manou has successfully run her own business for seven years in Austria, and now feels drawn to retreat to India and write. Her creativity is bubbling up.

16

Dream On

I am happiest when a person carrying a heavy load of misery comes to me, for he is most in need of what I have to give.

- – Sai Baba

Jim was born in Canada in 1960. He lives in a remote part of British Columbia working as a mechanic at a wilderness centre. I met him at the Whitefield ashram near Bangalore, and we got talking during a long wait for a bus. He had been in India for a month and it was his first trip. I found him open and friendly, though clearly having a lot on his mind. Later we kept running into each other and I told him I was collecting stories about addiction. He looked me in the eye and said, "I have a story." I would never have guessed. Jim and I went on to have some deep conversations and a lot of laughs. He's a sweet man. His addiction was still fairly recent, so he was still going through the ups and downs of recovery. His spiritual zeal is carrying him through.

Jim's story: My first experience of addiction was with alcohol. I started drinking heavily at the age of fifteen. As it progressed, sometimes I'd be drunk for days in a row. It was always whisky. I never thought I'd quit and didn't want to. It seemed normal and I never saw myself as an alcoholic. I hated feeling sick, being hung over, or getting depressed, but I had fun and was outgoing when I drank, and would get pretty wild. It was the only way I knew to unwind.

Even though I drank, I always worked hard and supported my family. I loved my wife and we had three beautiful children. But I know now that my drinking was responsible for the break-up of my marriage. It was a reflection of my upbringing. My Dad drank and the family I came from was violent and abusive. My little sister has been a suicide case all her life, and my other sister is a walking disaster from the abuse. My mother beat me like a dog over and over. I thought it never bothered me, but the rage and resentment I bottled up caused a lot of problems in my life. In retrospect I see that I drank to vent my anger. If I didn't go out and get hammered up at least a couple of nights a week, I could literally destroy the house. I never beat my wife or kids, but I'd break things and rant and scream. Sometimes I'd go out and dump on someone and get into a fight, or just go wild. I'd feel alright for a few days and then have to do it all over again. I thought it was normal; I thought everybody gets mad, everybody drinks. I always blamed it on others, but it was me. I was the biggest loser on the face of the earth, but I couldn't see it.

I'm sorry I neglected so much of my kid's childhood. I missed the camping trips and school concerts because I was too stoned. Those things hurt. My wife told me later that she was always scared of me, so she couldn't open up. I was shocked. I didn't know she was terrified of me. I thought we got on well. In 1995 I had two premonitions that I was going to break up with my wife. Within six months she had left me.

Soon I got involved with a lady, and thought I was in love with her. She was a heavy drinker and abusive when she was drunk, and it ended after eight months. The family was gone, and I'd lost my job right out of the blue. Everything was falling apart and there was no meaning to life anymore. Christmas time came and I was alone, and I felt like giving up on life.

A year later when I was thirty-six, I started getting into cocaine. I had tried it a few times and always enjoyed it as a party thing. Now I decided to try and sell it. I thought I would do some of it and sell the rest, make a few dollars and have some fun. I did just that; made some money, had a great time and forgot all my troubles. Then it escalated and I kept on doing it. By some fluke, I met someone in a bar who came back to my house and showed me how to make crack. And I liked it. It was no big deal, but it was a different way to do cocaine so I started making crack and smoking it. After a week or so I was making up a hit every couple of hours. A few days later I noticed something was wrong. It would be six in the morning, getting light outside, and I was still up. I'd been up all night doing crack. You go through this thing where you just want one more hit, and then you want another. I kept this up, and after a month I couldn't stop. I knew I was addicted.

When crack came along it was hard to eat or drink much, so I quit alcohol because I liked crack better. I'd get totally absorbed in it. Smoking crack was an escape, an altered state of consciousness, an experience that no words can describe. I had already used LSD, speed and hash, and tried heroin. If there had been heroin around maybe I would have got into that. But crack had my name written all over it. One day I mentioned to a friend that I couldn't stop and was going to check myself into a drug rehabilitation clinic. His advice was the worst I've ever had. He said, "Don't do that. Then everyone will know. Just quit on your own." I took his advice . . . but I *couldn't* quit.

So I stayed in my house. I bought four more ounces and kept smoking. I'd go for days without quitting, taking one hit after the other. I got high for five minutes then started to crash, prepared another rock and did it again. I got exhausted, and hated the drugs and myself. I was addicted badly, and it seemed that I couldn't run out of crack. That was spring of 1996. By the time the summer came I was in serious financial problems because of the cocaine. I owned two and a half acres next to my house that was serviced and had a landscaped drive-way, and I gave it away for $9000 . . . for drugs. In the course of the next year I smoked that, and then sold my beautiful boat. I had so much stuff and had to keep selling it so that I could smoke it up. I just couldn't stop. Sometimes I would close my curtains and sit in the house for several days straight, taking one hit after the other, *wishing* the drugs would be gone so that I could sleep. After a few days binge I would sleep. Then when I woke up, I would immediately try to sell something.

I never stole because I had assets. In the end I ran out of things to sell, so I took out another mortgage on my house and smoked that up. Finally I made an effort and got a job as a mechanic, but even with that I couldn't pay the bills. The phone got cut off, and I maxed out all my credit cards and lost them. The Mortgage Company was after me, and the bank foreclosed on my house. I was working all day and smoking all night. It was hell, but I couldn't quit. I even sold my vehicle and managed to borrow one to get to work. The only things I didn't sell were my tools; I wanted my sons to have them.

My boss knew I had a cocaine problem, but I was still doing my job so he didn't care. One day I was sitting in the lunchroom looking in the Vancouver paper and saw a job vacancy on Vancouver Island for a mechanic. I went downstairs, and fifteen minutes later the boss came to me and said, "Jim, it's really slow, I'm gonna have to lay you off. And I'm doing it for my sanity as well as yours." I was late for work every day and it drove him nuts. It was strange because I'd just seen that job in the paper. So I faxed a resume to the place, and got a friend to hook up the phone in my house in their name.

The one thing I never wanted to part with was my beautiful house. It was *mine*, and I loved it. I'd been trying to sell it and not one single person came to look at it. This was strange as other houses were selling and I was virtually giving it away. I had plans of walking away with something and smoking myself to death. By 1998 I had overdosed on crack a few times just to get it over with, but it didn't happen. I just hit the floor, got up and did another hit.

Now I had no money, no vehicle and one night I got into a big fight with a girl I was seeing. She left really mad and I knew it was over. She had thrown a plant against the wall, leaving a dent and dirt all over the carpet. As I cleaned it up, it was going over and over in my head, '*Lost my house, my family, no money, no car, it's all over.*' I wanted drugs but was in debt to the drug dealer and without a car I couldn't get into town in the dark to scrounge any money. Everything was gone. It hit me like a wall. There were lots of lights in the house, and I walked around and switched them on to get rid of the dark. And with all the lights on it was *still* dark. I said, "The lights don't have any light. It's dark in here." I would have killed myself but I didn't want to use a knife, it was too gross, and I'd sold all my guns for drugs. I didn't pray because I thought God wasn't for me. I thought it was the end, and cried like you wouldn't believe until I went to sleep.

In the morning the phone woke me up. It was the place on Vancouver Island. They asked me to come and see them about the job. But I had no money or vehicle to get there. A few minutes later a woman I had done drugs with called, and I told her about the job. She reached into her pocket and gave me $200. This lady had stolen so much for drugs, and ripped me off; so for her to do this was unbelievable. I phoned Jill, the lady I'd had a fight with the night before, and told her I had to get to Vancouver Island for this job. She knew a guy with an old station wagon he would give me. Then she borrowed $70 from her mother, who hated me. We found the car covered in snow. I pulled it out with a tractor and it started right up. It was a great car. So now we had a car and $270 and everything was beginning to click. I didn't know anyone on the island, but Jill had a friend who said we could stay there for free. So we got there, and I worked for ten days. During this time I had an offer on my house, so they faxed me the papers and I signed. Everything was coming together. I knew I was going to take this job, but had *no* intention of quitting drugs.

They gave me a week off to get back and wrap up the house deal. I wanted to get some crack, but I was so busy there wasn't time, and when I *had* time I couldn't get any. I could feel that I was being swept along, with all the synchronicity. At the end of the week I was waiting for my employment cheque to come, so that I'd have money to get back to the island. It didn't come. So I decided to ask my mother if she would lend me $500. We didn't get on at all well. She had only been to my house once in the eight years I was there. We were so distant I had to look her up in the phone book. I was just about to put my hand on the phone when it rang. It was my Mom! She said, "I know you're leaving town and I was wondering if you have enough money." It was unbelievable. She actually loaned me some money. I was sad about leaving the house. In another way I wanted to leave behind all the bad things that had happened there — the pain, the hurt and the drugs. I assumed that I would start doing drugs again, but that it would be a fresh start and I would be able to manage them. Very funny.

When I got back to the island things didn't go right. I planned to work hard, save and buy a house. But I soon found a place to buy drugs and started again. Though I was working fourteen hours a day, six days a week, I wasn't making any money. My ex-girlfriend Jill moved in, then my sister and her boyfriend. It was hard for me, as I was the only guy working and I was supporting them all. I got more and more stressed out. Then one day at the shop I lost it and got into a rage. I threw my tools against the wall and started shouting, "*What's the meaning of life? What's going on? Why am I here? Who speaks to me?*" The bunch of guys who saw this thought I'd lost my mind. They were all standing back watching me. I said to my boss, "I have to take a day off." He replied, "*Hey, no problem!*"

Before this I'd had many premonitions, with some voice in my head telling me what was going to happen. I felt powerless and at the mercy of some THING that was destroying my life. It wasn't just the drugs; it was an unknown factor working against me, and I felt that *something* was out to get me. I was angry that if God existed, then why was He doing this to me?

I'm a pretty private person, and don't talk to people about my problems. The next day I went to Victoria, for a walk to Ogden Point. I was thinking about deep things, and decided that if I couldn't figure out what was going on, and how to be happy, I would kill myself. Deep in my thoughts, I found myself standing on the beach looking down at some kids playing with a crab at the edge of the ocean. A lady came and stood behind me, calling out to them, "Don't fall in the water, you'll get wet."

Without looking at her I said, "Are they your children?"

"Two are mine." She replied.

"It's the best time of your life." I said, "Do you live here?"

"Yes" she replied.

"It's a beautiful city. I just came here to think about things," I said.

Then she shocked me. She said, "I can tell you the meaning of life."

As it turned out, Pamela was a highly spiritual person, a psychic, and a devotee of Sathya Sai Baba. She told me that there was a God and He was within *me*. This was directly opposed to my fundamentalist Jehovah Witness upbringing. She told me about deep spiritual things like rebirth, *vasanas* (deep-rooted tendencies from past lives) and karma. I didn't know what she was talking about, but I could feel a strong energy over us. I'd never felt anything like this before. I turned to her and almost shouted, "*How do I know this isn't another big lie?* I've been looking for Truth and it's all been a big lie!" She was much smaller than me, and she poked me hard in the chest with her finger, saying over and over, "*I know, I know!*" I could see something in her, and that she *did* know. It seemed that I had met somebody who knew about the thing I had been searching for. This lady had been walking on the beach every day for two years and had never before spoken to a single person. She does her mantra and meditates. At the time I had long hair and a beard and looked like a Satan worshipper from hell, yet she spoke to me and gave me her phone number. To this day she wonders why she did it.

Actually, I did believe in God. My mother was a Jehovah Witness, and through those beliefs I saw God as a hateful, vengeful being and was afraid of Him. Because I had refused to become a Jehovah Witness I had been told I was doomed, and that God was not for me. I was scared to die, because I thought there was no hope of an after-life, and I would be snuffed out. I didn't want to live either. There seemed no way out. So Pamela gave me something to cling to.

That was 1999. I ran into her five times in Victoria after that and we became friends. She told me about Sai Baba and the great teachings he had given. Pam became my spiritual mentor, and at that point my life began to change. I still didn't quit drugs, but when I was smoking, she knew. One time I was visiting with her and having a nice talk about spiritual things. Earlier that day I had made an arrangement to pick up some cocaine when I left her house. All of a sudden she got up from our conversation, walked away from me to the kitchen, and started yelling at me, "*Will the real Jim please stand up! Will the real Jim please stand up?*" I was thinking, 'Oh my God, how does she know?' She would occasionally do that sort of thing. A couple of years later I plucked up courage to ask her how she knew I was going to get drugs. She said that she didn't know, and wondered why she was saying that.

When I'd talk with her, a strange energy like an electrical

charge fell over us. The rest of the world seemed to disappear. I could hear it and see it, but all I could focus on was her. There was a ringing in my ears, and her voice became very loud, and there was just us. We would sit on the beach while she talked for an hour or more, with this strange energy. Then some voice deep within me always came and said, *"It's over."* She would suddenly look at her watch and say, "I have to be going to pick up my kids." I could feel the energy leaving when she had gone. It was the most amazing thing, and I have no doubt it was Sai Baba with us. I have been at her house, talking about God, and could feel the energy when it came. It didn't just creep up; all of a sudden it was *there*. I looked at her at those times and she was different. Her eyes would change, and she looked like the Ancient of Days.

Then I moved some distance from Pamela and didn't see her so much. One day I finally listened to the tape of a psychic reading she had given me. The same day I watched the Sai Baba video she lent me . . . twice. I cried watching it. There was so much love coming from Baba, and the look on the faces of the people as he walked by was incredible. I could see how affected they were by his presence. That night I had my first major experience. It was the first of a series of intense dreams, where Baba came to me.

I was in the dark, in blackness. I was on the ocean on a ship, and heard a voice without a body coming up behind me. The voice was crystal clear, like a bell ringing. It said to me, "Jim, you can't get away, not tonight, not tomorrow, never." At the same time this great energy was getting closer and closer, and suddenly it rushed up and hit me with all the force of the Universe. It was terrifying and I woke up doing convulsions on the bed from this energy entering me.

What was this? I'd never felt like this! After I calmed

down I wondered what the hell was going on. Who was this Pamela? I started to think she was possessed by the devil. When I went back to sleep I had almost the identical dream. The next day I was in awe. I wanted an explanation of what was going on. Soon I had another dream.

I was fighting with Baba. He held me down by the shoulders, and as he was pinning me down, I could feel his entire soul blowing into my soul like a hurricane. It was terrific. Somehow, by great will of effort I woke myself up to get away from him.

It was too powerful. I wanted to ask how he got into my dreams and what he was doing to me. Now I know he was fighting the addiction and darkness in me. Before I went to India there were two more important dreams. This seemed to be the way he could reach me on a deep level.

I was walking by a river and I saw a big old house. I went in, and all of a sudden I had to find Baba, though I didn't even believe in him. I ran through every room in a panic to find him. There were many rooms, many floors, and each room was exactly the same with a bunch of doors. I was running and running, then stopped at one of the side doors. I opened it and he was standing looking at me, smiling. It felt so good. Then I woke up

I thought, 'Well, I had another dream about this guy Sai Baba. Strange.' At that time I wasn't quite finished with the drugs. My life was in the process of turning the page. Next night I had the most amazing dream I'll probably ever have.

I was at the house where I lived with my wife, and that I did all the drugs in; the house I fought so hard to keep. I was with my Dad, who had died some time before. There was a flash of light. My father looked at me and said, "You'd better go inside and see what that was." I walked into the house and looked around. It was intense. I saw three tornadoes coming at me. I thought, 'Strange, we don't have tornadoes here, but here they are; they're coming right at me.' I ran under my sundeck and was lying there hiding. I looked out and one of the tornadoes was coming right for me. I thought it was going to rip me to shreds and kill me. I got into the ditch and lay there for cover. I saw the tornado coming between me and the house. By now it was really dark, the wind was howling and it was terrifying. It seemed to be an entity of some sort, demonic and frightening. It stopped in front of me. It didn't have eyes, but I knew it was looking at me, and then it slowly moved on. It missed me and I knew it couldn't come back. I looked up in the sky and it was pitch black. There were three more tornadoes there, black on black. I looked around to run and there was nowhere to go. I thought I was dead and started to cry. Suddenly the three tornadoes were breaking up into black clouds, and abruptly the sky split open from left to right revealing a huge full moon shining on me. I felt a rush of relief. The black clouds and tornadoes were still swirling around at the sides. In the moonlit sky there formed a giant vaporous bull. It had big horns and a hump, and was made out of swirling vapours. It was violent. I wasn't scared of it, but I knew it was a very negative type of energy. He turned round and started walking up the road, away from the house. As I was watching, the vapours were swirling around inside him and the whole thing transformed into a luminous light calf, glowing in the night. He kicked up his heels, running and playing.

At this time I was still using crack a little, and did it twice more after that. Drugs open you up to dark energies, and I was being cleaned out. The last time I did drugs was in late 2000 when I went back home to visit my kids. I had some money, and as soon as I got back all the old triggers were still there. I went to the dealer's place and got an 8-ball, three and a half ounces of cocaine, enough to keep me going for six hours. Then I rented a room at a hotel. I happened to look in the cupboard, and to my amazement, sitting there was a bottle of the chemical I needed to make the crack. I told myself that *something* knew I was going to take drugs, and had put me in this room, so it was okay to go ahead and do it. I did drugs all night and beat myself up so hard about it. I literally tortured myself. The next night Baba came in a dream. We fought, and I was scared. I believe he was fighting the rest of the addiction out of me. I haven't done any drugs since.

But I got depressed after that because I was lonely. I'd quit drugs and was happier, but still wasn't where I wanted to be. I'd been fighting the desire for drugs for a couple of weeks, and felt like I'd given up everything trying to find God. It would come into my mind, and I'd think, "To heck with it, I'll go and buy some." Then I'd say, "No, I can't go back there." This battle was going on in my mind, and after a couple of weeks I decided to do it. Three seconds later the phone rang. It was Pamela. She yelled, "Yeah, some people never get their mind out of the gutter, do they? God doesn't care. He's not going anywhere. It's up to you." I knew it was really over this time. I'd been beating myself up too hard, and couldn't go through that again.

My life did change. Despite all I've done, I get on great with my kids and they love me and seem to have no bad feelings. My relationship with my ex-wife has improved and we are friends. She's an excellent mother and a blessing to the children. Now I find I need to be alone. In Canada I go for days in solitude, because I want 'The peace that passeth all understanding.' Living out in the bush, I've isolated myself from contact with people, and bills and responsibilities. I have a certain amount of peace, but it's not real. As soon as

I'm back with people, it's gone. But it's my way. I feel so connected with God when I'm out there, looking over this beautiful country by myself. I get unspeakably lonely, but I believe that if you put the Kingdom first, all other things will be added to you. So I have less to do with people, but the relationships I do have are beautiful and meaningful.

Jill and I patched up our differences and had a beautiful platonic relationship, one of the closest I've ever had. One day I phoned her as I was depressed, and asked if I could visit. I went to her house intending to stay a couple of days. I had the best visit ever and stayed two weeks. She was not well, and I didn't want to leave. On the ferry home I got really down. I didn't want to go back to work. I only wanted to go to India. When I got off the ferry I started crying and praying, *"I don't want to go back, I don't like winter, and I don't like my life."* I arrived in Whistler and sat in Starbucks crying over my coffee. I was trying hard to lead a spiritual life and be as good as I could be, and I still wasn't happy. Again I was asking, *"What is the meaning of life?"* I wanted to go to India and see Sai Baba and find out why I'm not happy. I felt like killing myself again, because being spiritual still wasn't enough. Unknown to me, my brother was in Whistler at the same time looking for me. He knew about my wish to go to India and was searching everywhere. When we finally ran into each other, he told me he wanted to give me the money to make the trip.

So I worked for three weeks, sold my van and came in January 2002. Part of the reason for the timing of this trip was that Jill died just after Christmas. It was unexpected, and my grief was unbearable. This trip came a few weeks later and gave me something to cling to. Finding God within is now my whole focus of existence. When you've lost everything . . .

family, friends, home, and self-respect, there is nothing to replace it in external life. This yearning for God, this Divine discontent, what the Buddhists call *Dukkha*, keeps me going. It's the driving force.

Life's not always easy, but now I know there is a God and I know He was involved in me quitting the drugs. I'd hurt myself enough, and was about to die . . . and God stepped in, no question. I wish there had been another way, but the addiction was necessary to bring me to where I am now. Baba has said that sometimes God has to break your heart to enter it. And I believe, knot-head that I am, that I had to be brought to my knees and be broken. It was an inevitable part of my process. Sai Baba has affected my life in many positive ways. There are little miracles to keep me going, and he's proved that he is taking care of me. Materially I still have nothing, but I always have enough. Even when I didn't want to work and wasn't looking, some great jobs with terrific money have come my way. I have given money to people who need it, and people have given me money. It's unbelievable. But it's not about money; it's proof that something unknown is going on. The synchronicity in my life since I heard about Baba is almost a cosmic joke.

Since being in India I have been in an intense process. I have had little attention from Baba on the outside, but much has been happening on inner levels. My anger has subsided a lot, I'm a totally different person, but it's still there occasionally. Recently someone stole my shoes after *darshan* . . . and whoa, it was right there again. I was furious! It was the first time I'd felt so angry for a long time, and it was hard to control myself. I thought I didn't have that garbage in me anymore and was deeply disappointed. Then I got angry at the Seva Dals, the ashram volunteers who keep discipline in the large crowds. I saw queue jumping and got ripped off in the shops, and I was mad about it. When I went to bed one night I prayed to my Father and asked if I'd made a big mistake coming here. It didn't feel spiritual, and I wanted an answer.

Again Baba came in a dream:

Sai Baba was walking around giving darshan and I was standing next to a Seva Dal. I looked at this guy and he was bugging me. I kicked him, and pushed him in the face with the flat of my hand, really hard. I hated this guy, and Baba saw me do it. I thought, 'Oh, he's going to kick me out of the ashram' and felt really sorry. He walked towards me and I was sure he was going to kick me out. As soon as he got close to me, there was an overwhelming gush of love. He held out a plate of food and let me know that I was welcome. Then he said, "Why were you writing like this last night?" He wiggled his finger in the air, like he was writing. I said, "I don't know, I can't remember." He said, "Why did you leave that room in such a mess?" Then he reached down and kissed me on the lips like a father, and pressed his hand on the base of my spine, the seat of Kundalini. My consciousness exploded and I was gone. The ferocity of this power was scary, and I fought with all my strength to get back into my body. By a supreme effort I came back and woke up.

The feelings gradually subsided, but I could still feel his hand on my back. Then I remembered that I *had* left the room in a real mess, as I'd been complaining to the guys in the room about the Seva Dals, and pretty soon everyone else was complaining. In my journal, the night before, I had written in big spidery letters, **"Very crabby!"**

Baba's love is driving the anger away. While here I have been crabby a lot, and I'm sure I'm being cleansed of the anger bottled up since my childhood. Baba says, *'Why worry when God, in order to make a lovely jewel of you, heats and melts, cuts and carves, and removes your dross in the crucible of suffering.'*

I spend my time now in deep introspection, and read Baba's writings and other spiritual texts. Here at the ashram I meet other spiritual aspirants and enjoy that. I've met some terrific people. I try to meditate but not consistently yet. I pray all the time, talking to God. On rare occasions He speaks back to me. It comes from some deep place within, and tells me what is going to happen. How I long to hear that voice. Sometimes I have problems relating to the physical form of Baba, because I know that God is within everyone.

After this trip I want a new life, a new Jim. I want to completely step away from the old into the new. From the age of fifteen I've used various substances to deal with my problems. Now, at forty-two, I'm learning a new way to live, facing everything and growing up. I'm not doing it alone. I know God is taking care of me, and I feel blessed.

Swami appearing in dreams is very auspicious. Swami appears in dreams only when he wills it, not when you want. Dreams which are willed by me are very clear, and give no room for confusion or doubt. I come to you and convey what I want in the most direct manner.

- Sai Baba

17

Beam me up

You may think that progress is possible only through my Grace, but though my heart is soft as butter, it melts only when there is some warmth in your prayer. Unless you make some disciplined effort, Grace cannot descend on you. The yearning, the agony of unfulfilled aim: that is the warmth that melts my heart. That is the anguish that wins Grace.

- Sathya Sai Baba

Jenny was born in London, England in 1947. I first met her at Findhorn in 1993, where she was working in the Community Apothecary. She was a shy and private person. When she sang her soft sweetness would come forth, and you could feel her tenderness and vulnerability. She was always someone with much inner wisdom and compassion. She was instrumental in encouraging me to come to Baba where I have been living ever since. Shivani 2003

Jenny's story: Most of my life I lived with secrets. As a child I was terrified of my parent's disapproval and criticism, deciding early on that they would never understand or accept me, so I would hide my feelings and thoughts. I was so scared of their reaction that they didn't even know I smoked cigarettes later in life. I kept my spiritual life to myself too, for fear of ridicule. I felt they never knew me. They had their secrets too. I didn't find out my father was an alcoholic till just before his death, which was alcohol related. It was me who cleared out dozens of king-sized empty whisky bottles hidden all over the house.

It's hard to expose myself. It's easy to share stories with those with the same tendencies; in fact it creates a link of camaraderie. But the burden of hiding things from family, work associates, even the police, meant never being able to relax and be myself. I went to great lengths not to reveal my addictions to tobacco, marijuana and men, living with fear, shame and self-loathing for many years. It is said that we are only as sick as our secrets, and it's wonderful to be free from years of toxic shame. I tried finding freedom through drugs and it eventually brought misery.

I was a baby boomer, born soon after the Second World War. My father had been a tank driver, in the midst of action for six years, and my mother had endured years of bombing in London. They married at the beginning of the war, and didn't see each other till the end. Their first baby was stillborn. They must have been traumatised after the war, and of course that affected me. I was the second child. On the surface all was fine in my childhood, with plenty to eat, and a nice home, I wasn't abused and had all the comforts. But I was starved emotionally . . . there were few hugs or cuddles, hardly any touching or terms of endearment, only the occasional peck on the cheek. I hardly touched anyone throughout childhood and adolescence. There was plenty of quarrelling and criticism, and laughter too, but love was rarely expressed, though it was there. But the word love was taboo in our family. I craved affection, and felt unloved, though actually that wasn't true. I wasn't a happy child, timid and painfully shy. A deep loneliness took root, which would pursue me for a long time, and land me in lots of trouble.

I was lucky to have freedom to roam the countryside, spending hours alone in nature. I remember one day, lying in the long grass gazing at the vastness of the sky, thinking of my insignificance in the infinity of space. That thought freed me from the cage of my own importance, and for a liberating moment I felt at one with the Cosmos. As a child I went to church and loved Jesus, but found the sermons and dogma incomprehensible. At the age of thirteen, I refused to be confirmed in the Church, as so much didn't make sense to me. By sixteen, I had rejected it altogether, and wasn't sure about God.

As an adolescent I was kept on tight rein and studied hard. When I left home and went to University I met stimulating young people, and started to enjoy myself. I had a few boyfriends, then a happy relationship for two years. But I wasn't interested in commitment. Like many of my generation, I rejected my parent's conservative, strict values. The pendulum swung to the other extreme, and I was caught up in the new collective consciousness of the young, believing in free love, drugs, sex and rock and roll. I smoked cigarettes like most students, and got drunk at parties, but I never set eyes on drugs in the sixties. Someone must have been looking after me.

On leaving University with a good degree, I moved to London in 1970 to teach. I met a man who introduced me to hashish and a hedonistic crowd. I found it exciting and fun, and a way to get the attention and affection I had always craved. I was burning the candle at both ends, having a wild time at night, and working hard as a respectable teacher by day. My double life was beginning. Smoking marijuana was illegal, and if caught I would have lost my job. So I played the pure sweet teacher at work, and hid the other life which was taking hold. For the next twenty years, my life was a tug of war between decadence and purity.

Later that year I met Bill, who was to become my husband. He was only twenty and I was twenty-three. He was unemployed, using drugs and had spent some time in mental hospital. But he was charismatic, intelligent, and handsome and swept me off my feet, and I chose to ignore those things. Smoking hash affected my judgement, and capacity for common sense. I lived in an unreal world of romantic fantasy, and we were soon living together. I thought I would change him, but it was me that changed.

He persuaded me to try LSD. I was wary, but agreed to try it. Fortunately I had the sense to realise the power of this chemical, and was cautious in setting up a secure environment. I had a beautiful experience and felt free and blissful. But I questioned the reality of it afterwards, and it became an occasional sacrament rather than a habit. It seemed like a profoundly spiritual experience, where the veils were lifted to reveal reality in its shining glory. It was indescribable . . . but it felt like cheating. However, that glimpse gave me a taste for finding heaven again.

Within a year I became pregnant. My parents were horrified and begged me to have an abortion, as Bill was half-African. They were racially prejudiced and had never met a black person. Of course I was upset, and refused. I had no idea about the realities of motherhood, and happily, romantically anticipated the joys ahead. I decided to give up LSD, as I would have responsibilities now. But I loved hash and smoked it throughout my pregnancy, and in the fourth month we married. My parents did not come to the wedding. I'm sorry I caused them so much pain.

However, when our son was born they fell in love with their first grandchild, and persuaded us to live near them. It was a disaster. I was torn between them and my husband. They didn't get on, to put it mildly. I became more and more depressed and finding it harder to hide my smoking, as they could call in at any time. We decided to move to a remote area in Cornwall, found a job, and set off with ideas of self-sufficiency and country living.

For a few years I was fairly happy, living in a beautiful place, growing vegetables and marijuana, keeping chickens, baking bread, living the simple, domestic life. We made friends with a community of hippies, and raised our kids together. In the sixties and seventies, many of us were looking to open the gates of bliss, and we thought that drugs were a short cut. It seemed a pleasurable way to escape from what we saw as our repressive upbringing. It brought people closer, gave us a tribe, and enabled us to lay aside barriers and inhibitions, not realizing that inhibitions can be there for our protection. I was fairly moderate and didn't smoke all the time. I didn't use LSD again, but was partial to magic mushrooms, which grew locally. They gave me the feelings of bliss and oneness I yearned for.

Before we had left London, something led me to try a Yoga class. While we got into the postures, the teacher talked on Indian scriptures, and the words resonated strongly with me. At the first class we finished by lying on the floor, lights out, in the corpse posture. He talked us into a relaxed state, and I lay there in peace. Suddenly, unexpectedly, out of the silence came the OM from this man's lips. Instantly I was in another state, floating without a body. Maybe I levitated! After the class I was so energized that I walked home instead of getting the bus. I never forgot that. All the way through life, God was giving me little reminders, not letting me get *too* far away.

By 1976 we had two beautiful sons. By this time the marriage was going downhill, and I was living in fear of Bill's temper. He was insecure and jealous, always suspecting me of being unfaithful, which wasn't true. He spent more and more time at the pub, and less with his family. I was alone a lot with the kids, and dreaded him coming home drunk, often waking me to pick a fight. I felt so sorry for the boys, having to hear all this in our small cottage, but I couldn't stop it. As the years went on his verbal abuse and occasional physical violence towards me increased. Sometimes I was afraid he would kill me. I lived in fear, and was blamed for everything. I knew nothing about alcoholism, addiction or mental illness, and felt I was being destroyed. So I turned more to smoking dope and drinking to escape from the pain and confusion. It only weakened me. I felt helpless.

I ran away four times after violent incidents. He always found me and was contrite, swearing it would never happen again. Then all would be calm for a while, and I was treated like an angel. When reading a book on mental illness, the penny dropped and I figured he was manic-depressive. It was a perfect description of his behaviour. Though he went berserk when I told him this, I managed to get him to the doctor. He was given the wrong drug, which induced a massive manic episode. (I only discovered this years later.) All my friends were worried about my safety, and I knew that this time I *had* to get away. I believed in marriage, and had tried hard to make it work, so I felt a failure. I didn't want the kids to lose their father, but I knew I had to do it.

I took the children to the one place my husband would not dare go . . . my parents. I was skinny, a nervous wreck, couldn't sleep, and living in fear of his threats to kill me. He was manic and scary at this time. They were glad to take us in, and were protective, but I was desperate for my own home. I was in so much mental pain; I just wanted to get oblivious with dope or drink. I couldn't do that there. It was my big secret. A kind Indian doctor suggested I go and see him, but I refused tranquilizers; my emotional crutch was marijuana.

The stress of living with my parents was too much, so I looked for another place to hide. After a distressing time in a Refuge for Battered Women, which the kids and I all hated, I found a home in Bristol, and we started a new life. At the same time I was divorced after twelve years of marriage. I was thirty-five, my sons were ten and six, and we were all traumatised. Now I *really* turned to smoking to dull the pain and help me escape from reality. I didn't realize that not facing it would only prolong the agony. I mostly restricted it to evenings when I could fall apart, and kept the days for responsibilities and study. I was training to be a Medical Herbalist and paying for it out of the State Benefit I had as a single parent. So I had to be frugal, and the bills were a constant worry. I felt guilty at spending money on my habit, as the children had little in the way of clothes and toys. My ex-husband didn't contribute till years later, and they rarely saw him.

I was acutely lonely at first, as I knew nobody in this city. After a year I started to go out and meet men. I hoped to find a partner again, but I was too disturbed and living in chaos. Desperate for love and affection, I began a series of brief relationships, trying to hide it from my sons. All these men smoked marijuana and drank, and they would share it with me. My discrimination and defences were being destroyed by the dope, and my standards got lower and lower. In my youth I wouldn't have looked twice at these men, but now I didn't care. I had several relationships with drug dealers, but only got involved with a deal once. My current boyfriend persuaded me to carry a kilo of hash through the streets of the roughest neighbourhood. The whole time I was terrified, and swore I would never do it again. I wasn't going to risk losing my children or going to prison. He dropped me.

I see now that I was addicted to the intensity and emotional excitement of forming new relationships, as I was depressed. I needed the drug of drama to make me feel alive, and craved love and affection. I always gave away my power and lost myself in relationship with a man, putting him first in my life and dropping everything else. Later I discovered that this behaviour had a name, Co-Dependency, and that it is an addiction, and a hard one to cure.

The more obvious addiction was to cannabis, and sometimes the hunger for a joint was so strong that I would go out scouring the city for it, leaving my sons at home. I went to some dangerous and filthy places at times if that was the only way I could get my small lump of dope. If I couldn't get any, I resorted to cheap booze. I was losing respect for myself, and started to feel like one of the dregs of society. Sometimes I was too stoned to cook, and could only manage a sandwich. I enjoyed getting stoned alone as I could listen to music, go into a fantasy world and forget my struggle. When I had one joint I couldn't stop, till I was virtually unable to move. Many times I wished I could be beamed up to bed. By now I felt that I wasn't using the drug; it was using me. I hated myself for the neglect, and regularly had times of straightening myself out, and getting my life more organized.

There were periods of purity when I did Tai Chi or Yoga, and gave up smoking and men (they went together) for weeks or months; but I couldn't keep it up. One time I was riding home from a Tai Chi class, when I had an accident on my moped, and woke up in hospital with amnesia. A nurse was leaning over me saying, "Not to worry, the police are at home looking after your children." That gave me a *lot* to worry about, as I had three marijuana plants four feet high in my bedroom, and imagined a policeman sleeping in my bed, waiting to arrest me when I got home. I was relieved to find that my ex-husband, not the police was there. Many times I had driven stoned and drunk, yet this happened when I was sober and balanced!

I tried hypnotherapy, acupuncture and counselling to give up, but they weren't lasting cures. All my friends were in denial about being addicted, and said they could give up tomorrow if they wanted to. They never did. However I *knew* I had a problem. Then I tried Narcotics Anonymous, but the mind of the addict is clever, and convinced me that compared to the others in the group I was a mild case, and didn't need it. There were heroin addicts, a murderer, and ex-convicts at the meetings. Even so I could relate to most of the stories I heard, and I found the bright, happy faces of the old-timers hopeful. Yet it was hard for me to be around people like that, as I felt so unclean. I never worked the 12-steps, and couldn't accept the rule that one should forgo relationships for the first year of being clean. *That* I did not like. I was certainly in denial about my addiction to relationships, and didn't see how it was connected to the dope.

In 1986 I qualified as a Medical Herbalist and started to

work from home. It was a real calling, and I was good at it. But I had to be careful that no client could smell smoke, as I wanted to come over as healthy and professional. So I cut down on smoking and went for periods of weeks without it. But as soon as there was any stress, I would be out hunting for it again. The swings continued, but now that I was trying to help others I knew that I had to heal myself. I could see my life was going down the tubes, and that I could no longer get away with my habit. I was coughing up scary black stuff, looked terrible when stoned, and not getting any younger. The worst thing was that I couldn't handle my children. Being stoned and naturally gentle, I couldn't discipline them, and being strong willed characters they were getting increasingly out of hand. There was no support from anyone and I was bringing them up alone, apart from occasional respite when they went to my parents. Constantly I felt bad about myself as a mother, loving my children more than anything. Of course they played on my guilt, and manipulated me. Life was *full* of stress.

However, the pendulum was gradually teetering more to the side of purity, and I was searching for something spiritual. I went to a few meetings with well-known gurus, but didn't trust any of them. I wasn't a guru type, and looked down on people who were. But when I read Yogananda's **Autobiography of a Yogi**, it opened me to the possibility that there *might* be genuine Masters out there.

All my life I was a prolific reader, and came across a book on a woman's experiences of meditation in a Thai Buddhist monastery. I was fascinated and wanted to try it. So I went to a talk on meditation by followers of Sri Chinmoy, a guru from New York. I found it gave great relief to my stressed mind and body, and went to meetings for three months, and learned meditation techniques. Then they announced that if you wanted to continue, you had to be celibate. History repeated itself, and I left hurriedly. I still didn't get it.

Then one day I had a revelation while meditating. My mind was quiet, and out of the blue came words from the Bible, *'Be still and know that I am God.'* I *experienced* the meaning of those words. For the first time since childhood I believed there was a God, and knew profound peace and a quiet mind.

Soon I met Iris, a healer who never charged a penny, and she took me under her wing and became my spiritual Mum. She was a great support, and I meditated with her every Monday and learned about spiritual healing. I was smoking less hash now, apart from occasional binges, but the cigarettes were always there. One day, sitting out in the country with my dog, I was reading a book that mentioned, *"Great Beings like Jesus, Buddha, Mohammed and Sai Baba."* I was intrigued, wondering who Sai Baba could be. The next day I asked Iris if she had heard this name. She pointed to a small photo of a man in an orange robe, and said, "Two thousand years ago there was Jesus Christ. Now there is Sai Baba." Immediately I felt as though I had been struck by lightning and my head was tingling, always a confirmation of truth for me. I had always wondered if someone like Jesus could come again. So I borrowed a book, **The Holy Man and the Psychiatrist** by Samuel Sandweiss, and couldn't put it down. Being critical, I tried to find something in Baba's teachings to disagree with, but I couldn't. It *all* seemed like truth and I loved every word. I intuitively believed that he was indeed an Avatar.

I tracked down a Sai Baba group, and as soon as I walked in I was home. One evening at a meeting a man asked if I would like to join his group to stay at Swami's ashram for three weeks. I laughed and said, "That's impossible! I've got no money, two children, a business to run and a dog. I don't go *anywhere*." He suggested I put my name down and see what happens, saying I could pay later if I got the money. I didn't sleep that night and was on the phone first thing in the morning, saying, "*Put my name down.*"

That act of faith got me there. Everything fell into place, and in October 1990 I was to go with a group of ninety people to India. Since knowing about Baba, my life had changed. Early every morning I meditated and prayed to Swami, mostly in tears, to be able to give up smoking. I wanted that more than anything, feeling it was the cause of all my other problems. For most of that year, before seeing Swami in the flesh, I managed not to smoke apart from the occasional relapse. Life got better and clearer, and I had a loving support system in the Sai family, who accepted me with all my weaknesses. A week before I was due to leave for India, the test came when I met an old boyfriend. He was a dealer, to feed his dope addiction, but I was fond of him. He persuaded me to smoke a joint, one led to another, and I spent the night with him. He was against gurus, and tried to talk me out of going to Baba. I felt terrible about my relapse, and knew that Baba would know exactly what I'd been doing. I was so ashamed, and went to India with some trepidation.

I was now forty-two, and had my last cigarette on the bus to the airport, deciding that at least while I was on this pilgrimage I would not smoke. But I had given up any hope of quitting permanently. Arriving in Bangalore, I was exhausted and excited. At our group meeting that evening, we all prayed for what we wanted. My prayer was to be free of the addiction to smoking cannabis and tobacco.

Finally we entered the Prashanti Nilayam ashram, and I felt the peace as soon as I walked through the gates. We were put in a 'shed', basic accommodation with Indian toilets, which were badly in need of cleaning. Some in the group were horrified, and wanted to leave straight away, but I had read enough about gurus to understand that there would be tests, and I was determined to accept all of it. I was so excited about seeing Baba, who to me was Divine, that my heart was racing. For the first *darshan* I had a headache, and was disappointed at first. He was just a little man. But Swami threw sweets to the crowd and one landed in my lap. I felt that was auspicious.

On Saturday our group of thirty was called for an interview. As we sat outside Baba's room waiting for him to come, my mind almost stopped, and I felt at peace. I was surprised, as I had been feeling ashamed and expected to be scared of him. On entering the room I sat right at the back, thinking in awe, 'I'm in God's house! *Me! in God's house!*' I didn't feel worthy. Swami entered and was sweetness itself, making us feel at ease. He materialized *vibhuti* for the women, but when he came to me it ran out. Oh no, I didn't get any, reflecting and emphasizing my unworthiness. The tears came later. For now, I was in bliss. Being close to Swami was indescribable, like having warm love poured into every cell in my body. Never in my life had I felt like this. We were in that room for an hour and a quarter, the best time of my life so far. He materialised rings and lockets under our noses, and talked to us. Miracles and materialisations hadn't attracted me to him, but to see it *was* awe-inspiring. He said nothing to me, but answered all my questions through others and telepathically. An Indian woman gave him a bunch of roses and he threw them to us. I caught an orange rose, and then a white rose landed in my lap. My first thought was, 'Celibacy! Purity!'

Walking away from that room, I was floating. Back in the shed I reflected on it and basked in the energy. One of the things Swami had said was, *"Don't follow your body, don't follow your mind, follow your conscience."* I prayed for forgiveness for all the things I had done against morality and my body, not always in ignorance, but against the prompting of my conscience. I prayed for the strength to follow it in future. There were many tears of repentance.

A few days later I had a dream:

I was in the shed, sitting on my mattress, when Swami came in and walked down the aisle between the sleeping women. He came and sat next to my bed. There was a packet of cigarettes lying there, with one left. I picked it up and to my horror lit it and smoked it, while Swami talked to me. I couldn't stop myself. I was asking myself how I could do this, blowing smoke into God's face! He sat and talked till I finished the cigarette. I didn't remember a single word that was said.

After this dream, the desire for a cigarette or joint simply vanished. Swami, the Supreme Hypnotherapist, took it from me. It wasn't difficult to give up for one second; I didn't even think about it anymore. In fact I found the smell disgusting, and could hardly believe that I had inhaled that stuff deeply into my lungs. I was so grateful that my prayers had been answered. When I got home and told my sons that I had given up smoking, they laughed. They had heard it so many times. This time it was true.

Soon after my return, a man friend invited me out to dinner. I liked him, but didn't want any more casual affairs, and asked Baba for guidance. Walking along the street, I was thinking about this man and wondering what to do. When I looked up, in front of me was a big bush *full of white roses . . .* just like the one Baba had thrown in my lap. It was a freezing December day, and I was amazed to see this. I quickly realized what it meant, and turned the offer down. We remained friends, and I saw how unsuitable it would have been to take it any further. Definitely I was being protected. Similar incidents with white roses happened, and I remained without a partner for the next three years.

But I had plenty to keep me busy. When I had come back from India, I thought it meant all my troubles were over. Some were only just beginning. The spiritual path is not all roses. There are thorns too. My karmas were coming to get me. I wrote in my journal: *'Although things are tough with the boys, I don't feel the pain as usual. I'm feeling Baba's presence so much, and can feel my heart growing and expanding. I accept that I have to go through these struggles, but I no longer have to worry. It's all a game. I must simply play my part and offer it all to Baba. Friends are helping me so much. My friendships are undergoing a revolution.'*

I rarely saw my dope-smoking friends anymore, but now my sons were getting into drugs. They were lying to me and desperate for money, and the youngest was becoming aggressive. He started to behave more and more like his father had towards me, refused to go to school, and was demanding and stealing money from me. Though I was stronger than when stoned, those years had set precedents of indiscipline, and now I had to suffer for it. Because of his refusal to go to school, social workers got involved, but they had no influence over him either. He was clever enough to run rings round them. So I went to Families Anonymous for support, and they were fantastic. By the time he was sixteen, it had become so bad that I knew the only thing was 'Tough Love', and I had to throw him out. It was the hardest thing I have ever done. I could no longer accept being abused. He was angry with me for years, and I was sad and depressed about it. It has taken years to slowly heal our relationship, but now we get on better, and love and respect each other. That took much inner work and prayer, and without the love and support of my Sai friends, I would not have survived it.

Giving up an addiction is one thing. Then we have to deal with the consequences. Every action has a result, and to be irresponsible as a mother created a lot of karma for me. Swami gave me the strength to go through it, and I believe he protected my sons too. Although they still have similar addictions to mine, (as far as I know! Why should I think they would be more open with their mother than I was)? They didn't get into heroin, and that is a miracle. They were surrounded by those drugs in the city. One son even lived with heroin addicts, and despite depression, poverty and unemployment, he didn't succumb. I admire him for that. I'm sure Swami had a lot to do with it too. For years I blamed myself for my sons' problems and addiction to smoking, and so did they *and* my ex-husband.

But ultimately we are each responsible for our behaviour, and no one can be blamed. I used to blame *my* parents too. That's just a cop-out. One thing is for sure; we cannot get away with *anything* that causes harm to anyone. One day we have to face the consequences, and now I live each day doing my best to live a *dharmic* life of right action. I don't want any unfinished business, and by the Grace of God there has been gradual healing of deep family wounds. The only attachments I have are my sons, and they are independent now. I see their lives improving too. When one person comes to Swami, he helps and protects the whole family.

Every year I went back to India and Swami charged my batteries, cleansed me and filled me with energy. On two occasions at Christmas, he gave me a white sari, emphasizing the importance of purity in my life. In 1994 I had another interview and Swami asked me, *"What is the way to God?"* I gave my answer, "Devotion and service." Then Swami said, *"Love all, serve all; that is the way to God."* I had heard this a thousand times, but now it truly came home to me, and I realised that he had given me the key to *my* route to God. Gradually things got easier and I got happier. I found that as long as I kept up a spiritual practice, things went smoothly. If I neglected it, everything started to go wrong. It was not easy for me to be disciplined all the time, but it was obvious that it was beneficial. God tailors the course perfectly for each individual. The way is different for us all, but the destination is the same.

In 1993 I was still lonely, and met a man who was also a Sai devotee. I thought it would be different now that I was living a clean life, and I wanted a husband. After two years of trying to make the relationship work, despite warnings from Swami in an interview, he left me and married someone else. I was devastated, and decided to stay away from men, and wondered again what Swami meant with the white rose. Was I destined to be alone? In some ways I liked it, as I had freedom and life was easier without the emotional turmoil that relationships always seemed to bring. But the loneliness I had suffered from childhood was still there, and I wanted to fill that gap. I didn't know yet that it was Divine Discontent.

Several years later I had another brief attempt at a relationship, with similar results. However this time I saw clearly that my addiction to men was still there. Just because I had avoided entanglements, I had assumed it was gone. But it was lying dormant. Instead of thinking about Swami, which brings me peace and happiness, I was thinking more about the potential partner. It only brought anxiety and misery. It distanced me from God. Again Swami had given me a subtle warning, but the addiction was strong and I ignored it. The result was more pain. This time though, I learned the lesson. I have understood that I am never alone, and will never be alone. It's been a blessing to have so much solitude in my life. It made me go within and brought me to Swami. I don't often feel lonely anymore, and don't need anyone else to make me feel good. Looking outside for satisfaction never worked. Now I find it within, where there is a deep well of peace and happiness, which is there for every one of us to tap into.

Many Westerners take Indian spiritual names, and I had always judged it pretentious. I was surprised when it happened to me, on a bus journey from Puttaparthi to Whitefield. It's a four hour ride, and I was meditating to pass the time. Suddenly an inner voice clearly said, '*Jyothi*'. It felt like it was my spiritual name, but I wanted to be sure. So I wrote Swami a letter, asking him if it really was my spiritual name. At the first *darshan* it became apparent that he was going to sit in the chair up on the dais and not come physically close. So in my mind I asked for a sign. The instant I had that thought the auditorium filled with an intense golden light, radiating from Baba. I could clearly see his orange robe and black hair, but the light blotted out everything else, and all the thousands of people. It lasted throughout the *bhajans*, and I was in a higher state of consciousness for a while.

The Sanskrit word '*Jyothi*' means light. This response to my request for a sign blew me away. I didn't feel worthy of such a name, but saw it as something to work towards, as in the prayer, 'Lead me from darkness to Light.' It happened during my last menstruation, though I did not know that at the time . . . surely symbolic of a rebirth.

I believe that Swami saved my life, literally. In 1994 I had an interview, where he blessed me with long, happy and healthy life, with his hand on my head. Soon after that, a palm reader told me I had been given a life extension. Then later that year I had a dream:

Swami came along a road towards me, and gave me an injection. He said that I should have died from kidney problems.

I feel he has given me another chance, so that I may become this Light which is my true Self. Words cannot express enough gratitude for all I have been given.

Baba says that *every single thing* that happens to us is for our good. The past was what had to happen for my evolution, because I had to realise that indulgence in the pleasures of the world only led to emptiness and suffering. Fulfilling the desires of the senses gives fleeting satisfaction, then more craving. Only when this was realised, by his grace, did I turn to God. Then I started to come out of the darkness of ignorance, and learn that only the Divine can give lasting satisfaction.

Being with Swami is like being in a washing machine, turbulent at times as he cleans and pounds, but with beautiful periods of rest, and each time becoming a little purer, and more at peace. I wouldn't change it for the world.

Purity, love and truth alone can open the gates of bliss

- Sai Baba

Update from Jenny, January 2013

I have not had a puff of any substance for twenty-two years now, and rarely touch alcohol. Giving up smoking was one of the best things I ever did. It all seems like another life, another person. My once wayward son came to stay with me for over a year in India, which was healing for us both. I am involved with home and school for neglected children in India, **The Children's Project,** about whom I have written two books, **Begging for Change** (2007) and **The Power of Love . . . Changes Everything** (2012). Now I practice Cutting the Ties and Emotional Freedom Technique (EFT) and give workshops on Herbal Medicine as well as writing. My life is fulfilling, and the inner growth continues with plenty of challenges along the way. That's life. Going through all those tough times gives a depth and understanding, and compassion for others. But first one has to learn compassion for oneself, and for me that's the hardest part.

18

Rock Bottom?

Man is born with a great thirst and deep hunger for bliss. He has faint memories of being heir to the Kingdom of Bliss, but he does not know how to establish his claim on this heritage. Something in him revolts when he is condemned to die, to suffer and to hate. His inner voice whispers to him that he is the child of Immortality, of Bliss, of Love. But man ignores these promptings, and like one who exchanges diamonds for trash, runs in search of mean pleasures and sordid comforts.

- Sathya Sai Baba

Vikram was born in 1984 in San Francisco. Synchronicity caused us to meet in Puttaparthi in 2004, when he had just read this book. I was struck by his intelligence and leadership qualities. He has much to offer when he uses his abilities in a positive way. Through most of his adolescence they were used in harmful ways, to manipulate, steal and con the system. It is still early days in his recovery, but he is highly motivated to finish with his addiction to meth amphetamine (crystal). May God bless him, and give him the strength to continue.

Vikram's story: My parents emigrated from India to the US when they were married, and I grew up in a stable, loving family. My Mom has been a devotee of Sai Baba for thirteen years, and from the age of six I went to spiritual education classes (*Bal Vikas*). I learnt about good values, mantras and prayers, so had a thorough moral and spiritual education. Although family life was good, I endured a lot of racism as a child. I did well at school until adolescence, and then everything changed.

First I experimented with cigarettes and pot when I was twelve. By the time I was fourteen, I got to smoke so much weed (marijuana) that I would stay at home instead of going to school. I smoked ¼ oz. of weed every day, and was selling it. Also I was experimenting with magic mushrooms, acid, (LSD) coke, and speed, but mainly pot. My Mom could see the pattern, and knew what was going on.

Early one morning, on July 3rd 2000, I was woken up by two huge Tongan guys. My parents had secretly arranged for them to take me to Utah for a Wilderness Camp. At first I thought I was being kidnapped, and I was in shock. I never thought my parents would do that to me; they knew I wouldn't have gone voluntarily. They said I was going to do a two-month program for severe drug addiction and behavioural problems. I said, "There's no way I'll do that for more than a month!" The minimum time was three weeks, but I ended up there for twelve weeks, and that was the longest they'd kept anyone in twenty years. Because I just didn't get it.

It was a nightmare. We hiked fifteen miles a day carrying 90lb packs. I was vegetarian through all this, and hardly ate anything. Naively I thought it was the only programme I was going to do. Nowhere in my mind did I think my parents were going to send me to another place. So I thought I might as well be myself. Had I known it was an assessment centre, just to *start* my rehabilitation, I would've conned the whole thing and been out within four weeks. But I had no idea.

Being myself got me into a lockdown in Maryland, on the East Coast. It was like hell . . . ten months of not being able to do anything. It hardened me. But I conned the system, and got out of that programme so fast I broke all the records. I soon got my crest, which you needed to go home for visits, and got my senior crest before they even allow you to, and terminated in ten months. The minimum is twelve.

Then they sent me to a therapeutic boarding school in Utah. I knew I had to act to get out quicker. The staff had a tough job, and some didn't have any idea how to deal with the kids. At first I gave them a hard time to the point where they wanted to quit, but when I got myself together I made sure everyone else did, and the staff respected me and treated me more like one of them. I pretty much had that whole place under the reins, and was leader in the group of thirty-five people. I had a fake ID sent through the mail, and cigarettes, alcohol and drugs were going through me. I kept all the guys in check, and the senior counsellors knew that. So when we got drug tested my tests were overlooked. If I smoked cigarettes they turned away. This was amazing for me, because if you fail you have to go back to wilderness, and that's two weeks of hell. They knew that if I left, the place would fall apart. People were acting out, and if they back talked staff or anything unacceptable to me, I would stop it. I had my own rules.

I never got caught smoking weed. It was a good situation for me, and I had a lot of leeway. But in the end I was using my powers as a leader in a good way for the staff, and in a negative way for myself. I got what I wanted, and started to think I could get away with *anything* and developed a giant ego. I always smoked weed in Utah, and was taking speed too. I got through it for six months, till the senior counsellor overseeing my drug tests was caught. He was fired, and I was caught too. They found twenty-six of my drug tests, and all but two were positive. They sent me back to wilderness camp.

After a month, I went back to the Utah school and graduated. Then I went to India for three weeks with my parents and brother, and stayed with the family. It was a transition time for me before going home again. I came back home on Mom's birthday, and within two days I got my license and a car, and was offered a job with my Dad's friend making good money as a loan processor. I was in Community College full-time and working fifty hours a week. Within two months I met my girlfriend. I was seventeen. It was way too much for me to handle.

I was taking the usual weed and mushrooms, but was changing the drug every week, as I wasn't addicted to any of them. But I didn't keep it that way. Once I found something I really liked I stayed with that. At that time it was coke. Cocaine for me was the white devil. I couldn't stop; I had no control over it. It wasn't a social thing for me anymore. I had a 'cold' for six months, as coke makes you sniff all the time. My Mom asked me one day, "What's going on?" In Indian families it's not acceptable to be doing drugs, and my Mom's not one to overlook it. A lot of my friends' parents turned a blind eye, and blamed other people for the problem . . . but not my parents. They addressed it without shame and took it on. Of course I denied it, but they soon got to know that I had a serious addiction to cocaine.

I soon stopped going to school, but kept my job for eight

more months. I was earning a lot of money and buying up to an 8-ball of coke every day, then it worked up to 5g a day. That's a lot of coke for one person. I did it by myself, which I knew was a problem. I would do it before I went to work, in breaks, and then after work I'd buy more. Then I wouldn't stop from five in the evening till nine in the morning. I couldn't eat or sleep, so I lost about forty-five pounds, which was a huge sign for my parents, plus I couldn't breathe through my nose. At times I had to eat the coke as my nose was too stuffed to snort it.

Also I was broke, and ran up all my credit cards. I quit my job, and went through a period of living on my own. My girlfriend helped me out, and I had a good apartment, but I blew it after a month. The woman who rented me a room couldn't live with me because of my habits. I wasn't noisy. The paranoia you get with cocaine and meth is so high that you don't make any noise. I would just sit there and get stoned, paranoid all day to see if the other person was awake. It's a horrible feeling, trying to be a closet user, as I was. At home I would be afraid to sniff in case Mom heard me, and that had a terrible mental effect on me.

The only time I could be free using drugs was at a friend's house, where everybody was doing it. It was not acceptable to most of my friends and I couldn't hang out with them anymore. It was too depressing for them. I had to carry a bag of tissues with me because my nose would bleed all day, and I was close to having a deviated septum in my nose. Then coke wasn't enough anymore and I went towards meth amphetamine (crystal) which was almost $100 a gram. It gets you higher for less, and my problems with a stuffy nose were gone because it's anti-histamine. I dramatically lost even more weight. I'd be up for a week at a time. It kept me up longer than coke, with barely any hangover. That went on for almost a year.

It wasn't just the drugs. I was addicted to excitement, a quick fix and the adrenaline rush. I could never tolerate being bored, and always needed stimulation and instant gratification. So I got into petty crime and cars, not because I needed the money but as methods to preoccupy my mind when I was depressed or sad. One night, I was driving home at 4am and fell asleep at the wheel. I'd had no sleep for five days, and was coming down off my high. I was doing 45mph on cruise control when I hit a tree, and took the light pole out. When I woke up I thought, 'I don't want my body to be all mangled' and started saying the Gayatri Mantra, which I'd learned as a kid. Before I could finish the mantra, it was all over. The car rolled six times and stopped upside down, completely mangled. I broke my window and crawled out without a scratch.

I knew Swami had protected me. I have always repeated the Gayatri Mantra when I was in trouble. Now I also say it when I'm *not* in trouble. At this time I was going back and forth to the family home, and went to India twice to sober up. I saw that my life was going from having a car, job, college, and beautiful girlfriend to having nothing. I *wanted* to be sober and thought the addiction was over.

But it wasn't over. When you're doped out you have a criminal mentality. I got into trouble with the law for attempted car theft, credit card fraud, and petty theft, and got locked up for a couple of days. My parents bailed me out. Till now, I'd been able to con myself out of situations and beat the system. This was different. I was taken in a second time for seventy-two hours. That wasn't enough for me. My parents considered it rock bottom. I didn't consider it anything, just three days of my life. They put me on house arrest. I was allowed to go out, work, and live a normal life, but not take drugs. It didn't stop me. A friend returned a favour, and called round to the house every day with drugs for free. My family welcomed him, and had no idea what was going on.

Then I failed house arrest by getting a dirty drug test. My girlfriend came for lunch with my family on my twentieth birthday. So I had to tell them there had been a call for me to go back to jail for two months. My Mom started crying. It was my first birthday at home for five years, as I'd always been in rehab before. This time there was no option to get bailed. Later, on the phone from County Jail, I told Mom there was nothing she could do to get me out. I'd been smoking all night, depressed because I was still high, and coming down. I was crying, but I asked Mom to stop as she was crying really hard, and I needed her support. So I asked her to pray for me. She taught me the Sai Gayatri over the payphone, and I told her to leave it to Swami, and that I would recite the mantra. I remember telling her, "I need external help from Swami now, or I won't be able to get through this."

They transferred me to three different correction facilities inside. I was in a really cushy one at first. The minimum security was easy. You had free time all day, could go outside, had TV, and it was more like summer camp. There were a lot of drugs there. But I was only there three days. When I asked for a vegetarian diet, which is my right, they transferred me to maximum-security jail. Usually you have to get caught using drugs or get into a fight, but not me. I knew Swami was doing that so I didn't have it easy. I went into a twenty-three hours a day lockdown to do time. They were all murderers and attempted murderers there. I thought, 'What the hell am I doing here? I come from a good family.' It forced me to reflect, because I had not been reflecting at all. I was with Spanish speaking cellmates who spoke no English. You are in the cell twenty three hours a day, and that's a real sense of jail. That's what woke me up.

I spent two weeks there before they sent me to medium security. Reading was the only form of entertainment, and I started reading a lot of literature on Swami. My Mom would send letters every day, with photocopied pages of books. That's when I got two chapters of The Ultimate High, which Mom found on the internet. It affected me a lot. I found that other people had the same problems or worse, and they got help with Swami. I realised that there is hope, and surrendered everything to Swami.

Also I was dealing with my girlfriend. She took no drugs herself, and had tried to make it work with me. We were going to get married. For an Indian girl that's a huge thing, and she was my life when I wasn't on drugs. She stuck with me through everything, till this last time. She had told me that if I screwed up again, we wouldn't be together anymore. But I didn't listen. She was writing me a lot of letters in jail at first, and then they stopped. The phone calls were fewer, and she stopped picking up my letters. I knew something was wrong. When I came out she told me she'd cheated on me. I was crushed, and felt like using again. But I didn't.

I got out of jail on Oct 8th 2004, and came to the ashram on Oct 17th. Those nine days in between were crucial. It was vital to not use. My friends supported me and it wasn't that hard. And I found strength from Swami, because I had been saying the Sai Gayatri mantra in jail all day long, and putting everything in his hands. I thought I wouldn't be able to deal with losing my girlfriend, as she'd been such a good part of my life for two and a half years and I screwed it all up. Normally I can't deal with abandonment, but Swami took a lot of that pain away. If he hadn't helped me with that, I don't know what I'd be doing now.

I have faith, but it's not as strong as some people's. I haven't had much attention from Swami and sometimes feel down about that, but I do think he has made it easier. The ashram is the best place for me to be right now. I've not been a good luck charm for my parents; this whole story has not been easy. I've seen some of the darker side that I never wanted to see in my entire life. I've seen women abused, prostitution going on, and people stabbed. I've had guns drawn on me and put to my head. I've seen a lot of violence over drugs, yet I was just out there to get high. I didn't want to see any of that garbage. I've tried everything from heroin to pharmaceutical drugs, and there's *nothing* that is worth it. I don't get the high I do from being sober.

I don't get the Divine high either, though I've heard a lot about it. I'm not at that level yet, but trying to reach it. I'd rather be there and have it be sustained, than through a substance which is a fake reality. I first saw Swami when I was eight, then again at eighteen, but I never got any attention, and drugs distanced me from him. It is hard to believe in anything when you are using so hard. I wasn't one of those who use drugs for spirituality. I just used it to get high. I took drugs because I wanted to feel better than I was already feeling.

As a child I dealt with a lot of racism, and held a grudge for a long time. That's where my ego comes in, and I'm very defensive. I used drugs to suppress my insecurities. My brother did too, and when I went into rehab, he took my addiction. He asked to buy weed from me, and I gave in. We're very close and he's had a rough time too, but he's doing well now and doesn't smoke cigarettes, drink or use drugs. He's very involved with Swami. My uncle also came to believe in Swami. He was so atheist that if you mentioned God he would laugh. Now he's been to Puttaparthi four times in a year, and sits for every *darshan*. My grandmother was also an atheist, and alcoholic. She had her four drinks every night, and wouldn't go anywhere if she couldn't drink. She quit smoking cigarettes after fifty years, and quit drinking *with no effort* after seeing Swami for the first time. She died eight years later of lung cancer, but there was no suffering and she was at peace.

There has been so much drug use that I would expect my body to be tangled or scarred, and I'd be brain dead, but my mind is as sharp as it was when I wasn't using. Through God's Grace I caught it in the nick of time. I know some people with severe mental retardation from taking drugs. I think damage was done, but a lot of it has been reversed. To go back to the US and stay sober will be a big test, and I'm up for it. I'm still on probation, so if I do it again I'll go back to jail for a long time.

I've been sober three months now, and I don't have any desire to use. The physical addiction is long gone, but I know if I started smoking crystal again it would get intense right away. I don't think about drugs much, but still think about my girlfriend a lot. I've taken precautions to stay away from the old crowd, and I'm moving to Southern California because I don't want to be around them, and they don't want to be around me. It's no fun for them being with someone who is sober. But I still call them once in a while to tell them I love them, and hope they get away from using.

I know I need to find something to fill the gap. I plan to go to Alcoholics Anonymous, and do ninety meetings in ninety days, to keep me on track. I want to go back to school, and my parents are supporting me one last time. It's my final chance. I know a lot of transformation happens when you leave Baba's presence, but I don't expect it to be easy. I know it is early days, and I'll be four months clean by the time I get home. Hopefully it will go well. I have a lot of faith that it will.

If only you surrender your wish and will, your fancies and fantasies to God, He will lead you aright and give you peace and joy. You must not run after diverse ends and fleeting pleasures. Leave everything to God; accept whatever happens as His will.

- Sai Baba

Update from Vikram, February 2013

I've been sober now for over seven years, and have a family with three daughters under four years old. I'm happily married to my wife of four years. I own and operate a successful staffing agency, and I am also a food consultant. Since my release from jail in 2007 I have bought two homes, and am looking to start another business soon. All is well. I'm not a practicing devotee any longer . . . I believe in God, but nothing specific. You have no idea what I went through to have to hit rock bottom, and then go through a long and hard road to be where I am today . . . but it was definitely worth it.

Epilogue

The Road to Recovery

People think that they enjoy sense objects. But in fact, objects enjoy them. Indulging in pleasures of the senses turns people into weaklings. They get diseases and grow old earlier by such indulgence. Worldly enjoyments are not permanent. You may have worldly enjoyments, but you should always have God as your aim and goal of life.

- Sathya Sai Baba

Dramatic, unstable, painful lives . . . it is clear from these stories that addicts do not know how to take care of and nurture themselves, physically, emotionally and spiritually. Abuse of any substance is self-destructive. *After* giving up a substance or habit it is necessary to face the consequences, *relearn how to live life*, and to heal the emotional wounds which may have caused the person to be prone to addiction. The emotional scars resulting from the lifestyle of the addict need healing too. The body is often ravaged, toxic and malnourished after substance abuse, so extra care needs to be taken at the physical level too for a return to health. The road to recovery can be bumpy and full of pot-holes and bends at times, but sometimes has great scenery and lots of laughs. And the destination is well worth the journey.

Long term recovery rates from addiction are not impressive. So I have been pleased to hear that almost all in this book that I traced have managed to keep turning the pages to recovery without relapse. There are many methods and supports for recovery. Family intervention, well planned with expert support, forcing addicts into rehab is common practice in the US (see Vikram's story) and claims to have a 50% long-term success rate. In the UK it is only just beginning to be used, but only the well-off have access to it. Twelve Step programmes probably have the next highest success rate. The National Health Service in the UK is free, but does not have a good record with addiction, more so as funding is being cut back more and more. The main treatment of heroin addiction is replacement therapy with methadone, through which only 2-5% achieve abstinence. It may be cheap in the short-term, but in the long-term?

"Ask and it will be given to you. Seek and you will find. Knock and the door will be opened to you."

- New Testament, Luke 11.9.

One thing that most of these stories have in common is that the person, though not religious, reached the pits of despair and called out for help. They may not have had any concept of God or belief, but instinctively prayed in the desperate hope for succour; and the response came in different guises. Help may come in a conversation, a book, from another person, or a dream . . . in an infinite number of ways. The Higher Power knows exactly what is needed for each individual. Our limited selves don't know the way out when we are in the prison of addiction, but there is a consciousness that does know, and has the key. You just have to ask. It will present the escape route in a way that you will understand, and that is perfect for you.

Even if you do not believe in this, what have you got to lose by trying it and being open to the possibility of a miracle in your life? Scientific research has come up with evidence that prayer works. Why not do your own research and find out if anyone out there is listening? Nobody else can tell you what to do. You have to find your own way to be the best you can be. But you *can* ask for help. Our ego will be telling us that we can do this alone . . . but that's the part you would be wise *not* to listen to. That's the part that wants us to keep suffering.

We often start to use drugs in our teens, when peer group pressure is strong. This is the danger time and it takes great strength of character to resist. The temptations of belonging to a group are irresistible to one who is alienated and lonely. The bond created by taking drugs together, however unreal, is powerful. Experience shows that one of the first things a recovering addict must do is break away from that group, and access to the drug. Then you find who your true friends are. This can mean going through a time of loneliness, as one has to form a completely new group of friends, which can take time. It's hard. This is one of the values of the Twelve-Step and other support groups, as one has instant access to people in the same boat, and many who have been clean for years. They understand, and do not judge.

Giving up anything leaves a vacuum that nature wants to fill. Sai Baba said the following to a New Yorker in an interview: *"As regards those habits that have gripped you, there are two methods by which you can discard them. The first: deprivation, denial. This can yield only temporary success. When pressure relaxes, the habit re-asserts itself and it becomes difficult to resist. The second: become so absorbed in something far more pleasing that the habit falls off by itself."* So find what you like doing, and that has no harmful consequences for you or anyone else. Here are some ideas.

Meditation and Relaxation. These are beneficial on many levels. They reduce stress, improve memory and mental clarity, calm the mind and can benefit many physical problems as the body is intimately associated with the mind. Spiritually, we become purified and closer to our real Selves. For meditation to be effective and to make progress in stilling the mind, regular practice is helpful. In the beginning this requires self-discipline, but soon it becomes a joy, and if missed one notices the difference that day. It is best to find a regular time and place, even if it is only five minutes, and practice daily. It's advisable to find a competent teacher or join a group, to learn techniques.

Exercise. You could try sport, lifting weights, dance, Yoga, Tai Chi, and Martial Arts, the list is endless. Physical activity is great for addicts as they are often out of touch with the body and unfit, and exercise stimulates endorphins, the anti-stress hormones, making the person feel good on a natural high.

Yoga. This is good for mind, body and spirit. Swami Satyananda Saraswati, founder of the **Bihar School of Yoga**, tells a story of how he retired to a cave to meditate and smoke *ganja*, (marijuana) which he thought would heighten the experience for him. He did that for three months. When he went into this practice he had a photographic memory. When he came out after three months he had lost it, though he still had a good memory. He says that this world is an illusion, and when we smoke *ganja* we're adding a delusion to an illusion, which is an obstacle to reaching the goal of Yoga . . . union with our true nature. He said it definitely gives you a different consciousness, but *not* a higher consciousness.

He went into a prison to give Yoga lessons, but nobody would listen to him. They smoked in front of him, and offered him cigarettes. They were disrespectful and rude. He has a practice of *yoga nidra*, which is a deep relaxation that takes you right to the point of meditation. He started to give them this, and they lay on the floor and followed it. He was surprised when they asked him to come back the next day. They didn't want to do any yoga postures; they just wanted *yoga nidra*. They loved it.

Here is the experience of a yoga teacher in the UK, who teaches in prisons: she says, "I don't usually know if the yoga is having any effect, as students are moved often. But sometimes they stay in touch through the Prison Phoenix Trust, which supports prisoners, and encourages them to turn their cells into a place of spiritual retreat, rather than simply a place where they are 'doing time'. And changes do happen.

Henry was in my yoga class. This is an extract from his letter: 'I was born in Scotland and had a terrible childhood. This is my fourteenth sentence. For years I was a violent, angry, hateful person, bigoted and prejudiced. I was abused as a child, and one day when I was sitting in meditation, in my mind I saw my father, his father and my own son, and I realised how easy it could be to repeat what my father had done to me and to my own son. I had tried all drugs. Once I stayed awake for fourteen days on drugs just to see what it was like. The start of my sentence saw me having lost my family, my children, my home and my business. I was in a lot of pain, and someone told me there was a yoga class where they did relaxation. When I told my teacher that I was a drug addict, she suggested I should stop punishing myself. Twelve months later I realised she was right. At last I am doing something for myself.

I moved to Maidstone prison next, where there were stabbings, burnings, beatings and drugs. It was a great temptation to slip back. There was no place to practice yoga, apart from my cell, and no class. So I emptied out my cell apart from the bed, and kept it just for yoga. Then the officers started to notice, and the lads did too. A couple got interested and I started to teach them what I knew. It made me feel better.

Many people have helped since I started on the path. It seems to me that whenever I have really needed something, it comes along.

The first thing I came to understand is that people have to want to change. They think when the sentence comes to an end, the pain is all over. Meditation helped me to understand that isn't so, perhaps because I was in enough pain to see it. I meditate every morning and evening. If I had to say what yoga has done for me, I guess it has made me happy.'

This yoga teacher continues, "I receive many letters from prisoners, saying what yoga has done for them. All of us who teach in prisons see how it works. Just sitting on the floor with your shoes off, with everybody starting at ground level, has benefits. Many are lacking in self-respect and self-worth. Through yoga, students begin to recognize that we are all coming from the same place, and that is healing. They start to stand straighter, and feel better about themselves. Some who come aren't really in their bodies, as they've done so many drugs as an escape from the pain. Yoga is helpful because you are asking people to embody themselves, to feel where their feet are on the ground, to feel the parts of the body in contact with the floor, and to feel the energy moving through.

When some first come to class, they don't want to be embodied — it is too painful. But through yoga it gradually comes to feel safe. *Yoga nidra* practice was especially popular. There is so much stress in prisons (and outside!) and this is a wonderful way to release it. You begin to clear emotional blocks, and to slow down the brainwaves to alpha and even theta, a meditative state. Peace of mind. The *yoga nidra* tape was also in demand with many prisoners who were not in the class.

To practice yoga you only need an area your own length. You will find yoga classes everywhere in the community. Yoga people are generally not judgmental; you've got an opportunity to meet new friends, so you don't have to go back into the same environment. There's an opening to go into a different mode. Yoga is far more than postures, and breathing exercises. It affects the mind and the life force (*prana*) itself. Addiction starts in the mind, so it must be addressed at this level. Yoga calms, heals and restores balance at a deep level. It is a complete philosophy, and provides guidance in good values and right ways of living, which if practiced will bring happiness and peace. So many are lost in the wilderness of negative thinking and behaviour, and have not been taught ways of living which are positive. Yoga can provide this."

Service to Others. There is nothing like helping others to take the emphasis off oneself and one's problems. The

Twelve Step Programme recommends helping others as a therapeutic approach, and in giving one receives back far more. For recovering addicts, gardening and conservation work is grounding, and a powerful way to connect deeply with nature, *and* feel one is being productive. Look out for voluntary conservation work in your area if that appeals to you. It is healing to breathe deeply, listen to the sounds nature, and feast your eyes on the beauty all around.

Care for the body. When we start to care for ourselves, a new experience for most addicts, we automatically want to nurture our bodies. Old eating habits need to be broken if one has eaten haphazardly and survived on junk food. It is important to think carefully about food, and to make up for any deficiencies caused by abuse and neglect of the body. If there is liver damage or any specific problem, it is advisable to find professional help. There are many natural remedies and therapies for detoxification and stress that can speed up a return to health.

As the worldwide problem of addiction increases, so also spirituality and awareness is growing. But there is still denial about the extent of drug use, and the amount of damage caused even amongst our children. It needs a change in consciousness to turn this around. Maybe there needs to be a critical mass of people who do not use mind-altering substances, who want to see a world free of this danger for our children. When large numbers of people take a stand, it can make a difference. When non-smokers started to make a fuss about passive smoking, and litigation against the tobacco companies increased, almost overnight there was a global change of public attitude about smoking. When a group called Mothers against Drunken Driving (**MADD**) formed and got publicity, the drink/driving laws in the US got stricter. Is there anything you can do? There *is* something; you can pray for all those suffering, for divine intervention to cleanse the planet of this epidemic of addiction, causing so much misery. If a mass of people were to do this, it would make a difference. Let's not *judge* the addict on the street, or in the office or home. Let us send them love and try to understand.

My prayer is that these glimpses into the lives of ordinary people, who were able to overcome their addictions and change their lives, will give hope and inspiration to those who are still caught; also to their loved ones who often suffer as much, feeling helpless watching them spiral downhill. I hope the stories will lessen judgements towards addicts, and give more understanding and compassion. Know that it is possible to change and to lead a happy, healthy life . . . if that's what you *really* want.

Addiction is just one part of the divine drama; everything is a stage we have to go through in our journey back to our true being. And part of that journey is to start to forgive yourself for everything, and be the best that you can be. I wish you well.

"Though a man may be soiled with the sins of a lifetime,
Let him but love Me, rightly resolved, in utter devotion:
I see no sinner, that man is holy.
Holiness soon shall refashion his nature
To Peace Eternal."

- Krishna, Bhagavad Gita

A saint is a sinner who never gave up
Every saint has a past
Every sinner has a future

Useful Contacts

Alcoholics Anonymous
www.alcoholics-anonymous.org

National Council on Alcoholism and Drug Dependence
www.ncadd.org

International Sai Organization
www.sathyasai.org

Cutting the Ties That Bind
www.phylliskrystal.com

Byron Katie
www.thework.com

About the Author

Jenny Gaze was born in London in 1947. She graduated with BA in Social Studies from The University of East Anglia, and did a Post Graduate Certificate in Education. After teaching in the East End of London, she married and retired to the country to bring up two sons in the hippy seventies. She had a practice as Medical Herbalist for over twenty years.

In India she is involved with a home and school for street children, and was inspired to write Begging for Change about them in 2007. In 2012 a sequel The Power of Love . . . Changes Everything was published.

Jenny is a proud mother and grandmother, and spends summers in England and winters in India.

www.jennygaze.com

Acknowledgements

To the friends who supported me and sounded me out, encouraged me and kept me going . . . you know who you are. Thank you.

To Matt Maguire at Candescent Press, thanks for your patience, promptness and thoroughness with the cover and book design, and the many smiley faces!

To Kim Wedell, a wonderful artist friend, for the cover painting.

Made in the USA
Charleston, SC
13 October 2013